Microsoft® Copilot®

by Chris Minnick

Microsoft® Copilot® For Dummies®

Published by: **John Wiley & Sons, Inc.**, 111 River Street, Hoboken, NJ 07030-5774, www.wiley.com

Published simultaneously in Canada

For general information on our other products and services, please contact our Customer Care Department within the U.S. at 877-762-2974, outside the U.S. at 317-572-3993, or fax 317-572-4002. For technical support, please visit https://hub.wiley.com/community/support/dummies.

Wiley publishes in a variety of print and electronic formats and by print-on-demand. Some material included with standard print versions of this book may not be included in e-books or in print-on-demand. If this book refers to media that is not included in the version you purchased, you may download this material at http://booksupport.wiley.com. For more information about Wiley products, visit www.wiley.com.

Library of Congress Control Number is available from the publisher.

ISBN 978-1-394-31494-2 (pbk); ISBN 978-1-394-31496-6 (ebk); ISBN 978-1-394-31495-9 (ebk)

SKY10098290_021125

Contents at a Glance

Table of Contents

Introduction

Since the emergence of artificial intelligence (AI) chatbots that can generate convincing natural language and images, the race has been on to find new ways to reliably and responsibly harness this power to enhance personal and business productivity.

Words and ideas such as *Generative AI* (GenAI) and *Large Language Models* (LLMs) that were once confined to the world of AI researchers have flooded into mainstream news and culture. Other new words, such as *hallucination* and *deepfake* have been created or adopted to describe the output of GenAI systems.

AI chatbots are now widely available and widely used, and seemingly every software company is racing to introduce AI components into their products. Perhaps no company has been more aggressive exploring and pushing the limits of what can be done by integrating AI into its products than Microsoft.

Microsoft was instrumental in creating OpenAI's breakthrough GPT-3 LLM and then in launching the GitHub Copilot software coding assistant. Now that Microsoft Copilot is available and has been integrated into Microsoft's suite of business and productivity tools, AI is poised to do for everyday office work what GitHub Copilot is doing for coding. It has the potential to make any work involving a computer easier and faster. It could also lead to a lot more bad art and bad writing.

It remains to be seen whether the net effect of having AI assistants will be positive or negative, but now's the time for everyone to become educated on the capabilities and limitations of GenAI technology.

Unfortunately, no one fully knows what GenAI tools are capable of. For that reason, and because new applications are being rolled out daily, products such as Copilot come with very little written documentation or help in the form that users of traditional software are used to. In fact, if you're using a tool such as Microsoft Copilot, it's fully possible that you'll figure out a new way to use it that not even Microsoft has anticipated.

This book aims to educate (and sometimes entertain) you with my experimentations into what Copilot can do and what it can't do. You'll learn how to use Copilot to help you as you do everyday tasks like emailing, having meetings, reading and researching, and creating business reports. Along the way, you learn tips and best practices for getting the highest quality results from AI assistants in general, not just Copilot.

I hope you enjoy reading this book and that you find it useful. If you have any questions or comments, please reach out to me at `chris@minnick.com`.

About This Book

Whether you're a writer, a data geek, a speaker, a manager, or any other type of creative person, this book will teach you what you need to know to benefit from the new tools that are rapidly becoming available.

Topics you'll learn about in this book include:

- Understanding what Microsoft Copilot is
- Accessing Copilot
- Using Copilot responsibly
- Interacting with Copilot via speaking
- Crafting effective prompts
- Translating with Copilot
- Using Copilot in Microsoft Edge
- Using Copilot on iOS or Android
- Exploring Copilot+ PC
- Using Copilot in Microsoft Office and in Microsoft 365
- Writing with Copilot
- Working with data using Copilot
- Improving PowerPoint presentations with Copilot
- Emailing with Copilot

- Getting help with Microsoft Teams meetings
- Project management with Copilot
- Creating images with Copilot
- And much more!

As you read this book, keep the following in mind:

- **The book can be read from beginning to end, but feel free to skip around if you like.** If a topic interests you, start there. You can always return to the previous chapters, if necessary.
- **At some point, you will get stuck, and something you try will not work as intended.** Do not fear! There are many resources to help you, including support forums, others on the Internet, and me! You can contact me via email at `chris@minnick.com`. Additionally, you can sign up for my Substack (`https://chrisminnick.substack.com`) to receive occasional updates from me about AI, programming, and learning.

Foolish Assumptions

I do not make many assumptions about you, the reader, but I do make a few.

- **I assume you have a computer with an Internet connection.** Also, while much of the functionality of Microsoft Copilot is available to anyone for free, some features I discuss in this book require a paid subscription to Microsoft Copilot Pro, Microsoft 365, or Microsoft 365 Copilot.
- **The only other assumption I make is that you're curious about Microsoft Copilot and want to learn how to get the most out of it.** You wouldn't be here if that wasn't true!

Icons Used in This Book

Here are the icons used in the book to flag text that should be given extra attention or that can be skipped.

TIP

This icon flags useful information or explains a shortcut to help you understand a concept.

TECHNICAL STUFF

This icon explains technical details about the concept being explained. The details might be informative or interesting, but are not essential to your understanding of the concept at this stage.

REMEMBER

Try not to forget the material marked with this icon. It signals an important concept or process that you should keep in mind.

WARNING

Watch out! This icon flags common mistakes and problems that can be avoided if you heed the warning.

Beyond the Book

A lot of extra content that you won't find in this book is available at `www.dummies.com`. Go online to find the following:

- **Online content.** In addition to the material in the print or e-book you're reading right now, this product also comes with some online-only content on the web. Check out the free cheat sheet by visiting `www.dummies.com` and searching for *Copilot for Dummies* cheat sheet. You'll see a table showing all the different programs in Microsoft 365 where you can use Copilot.
- **Updates.** AI is changing rapidly, and I don't expect it to stop doing so after this book is published, so the commands and techniques that work today may not work tomorrow. You can find any updates or corrections by visiting `www.dummies.com/go/CopilotforDummies`.

Where to Go from Here

As you embark on a journey to explore and discover the many ways Microsoft Copilot can be used, remember to keep an open and patient mind. As you'll learn very quickly, Copilot can do seemingly impossible tasks, but it can also stumble on the most basic tasks. Always remember that you're the boss and Copilot is your intelligent but inexperienced assistant. You'll learn plenty of ways to help your AI assistant do better, but you'll also find out that there are still many tasks that are beyond the abilities of Copilot.

If you want to find out what Copilot is and see what it's capable of, go directly to Chapter 1. To find out how best to talk to Copilot, go to Chapter 2. If you want to learn about using Copilot at work, head over to Chapters 6 through 12. To learn about some of the more advanced ways to use and customize Copilot, check out Part 3, starting with Chapter 13.

Congratulations on taking your first step toward making full use of Microsoft Copilot, and thank you for trusting me as your guide.

1 Meeting Your AI Assistant

IN THIS PART . . .

Exploring the fundamentals of using Copilot

Learning to talk to Copilot

Flying through the web with your Copilot assistant

Using Copilot on your smartphone

Discovering the future of computers with a Copilot+ PC

IN THIS CHAPTER

» Seeing how Copilot works

» Learning about Copilot's capabilities

» Accessing Copilot

» Experimenting with basic commands

» Using Copilot responsibly

Chapter 1 Getting Started with Microsoft Copilot

Microsoft Copilot is an umbrella brand name for all of Microsoft's AI-powered chatbots. Chatbots such as Copilot and similar products from OpenAI, Google, Apple, and many others have the potential to change the way people get work done. At their best, AI chatbots can enhance productivity, learning, and creativity. At their worst, they can produce low-quality text and images, confidently answer questions with fabricated data, and displace human jobs.

In this chapter, you learn some of the ways that you can access Microsoft Copilot, you get an overview of its capabilities and limitations, and you learn about using AI responsibly and ethically.

Defining Copilot

In 2019, Microsoft invested in the then-tiny AI startup called OpenAI. Microsoft provided billions of dollars, and OpenAI ran its systems on Microsoft's computers. In 2021, Microsoft exclusively licensed OpenAI's GPT-3 model, which was used to create OpenAI Codex. OpenAI Codex was subsequently used by GitHub — a subsidiary of Microsoft that provides tools and hosting for computer programmers — to create a computer programming assistant called GitHub Copilot, shown in Figure 1-1.

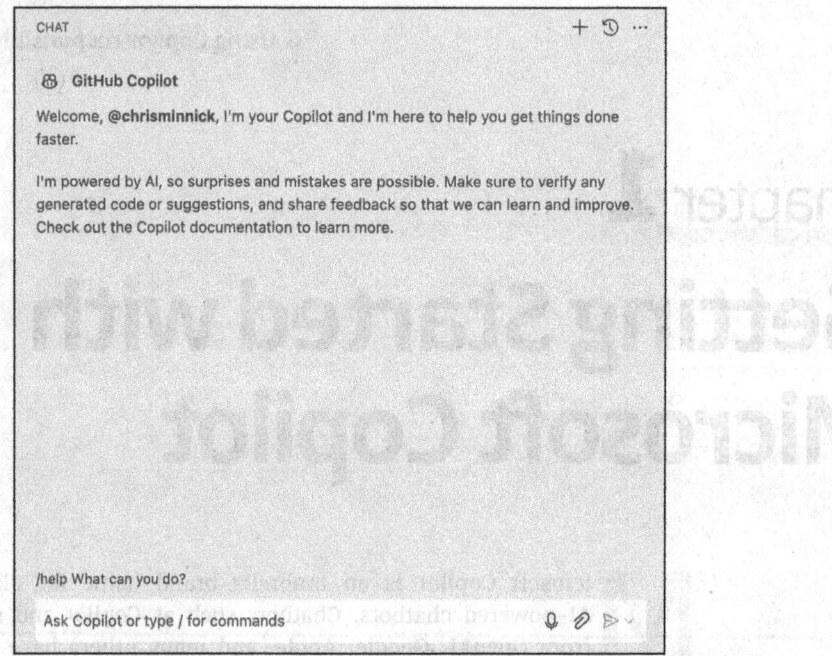

CHAT
GitHub Copilot
Welcome, @chrisminnick, I'm your Copilot and I'm here to help you get things done faster.
I'm powered by AI, so surprises and mistakes are possible. Make sure to verify any generated code or suggestions, and share feedback so that we can learn and improve. Check out the Copilot documentation to learn more.
/help What can you do?
Ask Copilot or type / for commands

FIGURE 1-1: GitHub Copilot.

REMEMBER

Although GitHub Copilot and Microsoft Copilot are similar, in that they both use OpenAI's technology for understanding and generating language, they're two different products. GitHub Copilot is optimized for helping with the writing of programming code and Microsoft Copilot is optimized for chatting with people and generating written words in human languages.

Several months after GitHub Copilot was rolled out as a plugin for Microsoft's Visual Studio Code Editor, OpenAI released the first version of ChatGPT for use by the public. ChatGPT became the fastest-growing consumer Internet app of all time — gaining 100 million monthly users in just two months.

With its unprecedented ability to respond to user queries with human-like text, ChatGPT became a cultural sensation and possibly even a threat to the traditional search engines created by Google and Microsoft.

Microsoft responded to ChatGPT by redesigning its Bing search engine. *Bing Chat,* as it was called, was rolled out starting in February 2023 and gained its first 100 million active users within months. The early version of Bing Chat had a tendency to produce false data (also known as *hallucinations*) and troubling responses during chats, including, as reported by Kevin Roose in a *The New York Times* article, acting like a "moody, manic-depressive teenager who has been trapped, against its will, inside a second-rate search engine."

TIP

Hallucinations, in AI lingo, are defined as incorrect or misleading information generated by AI. They're caused by a variety of factors, including insufficient training, incorrect assumptions, and biases in the data used to train the AI model.

Microsoft clamped down on much of Bing Chat's tendency to go off the rails and rebranded it as Microsoft Copilot. The current homepage for Microsoft Copilot (`https://copilot.microsoft.com`) is shown in Figure 1-2.

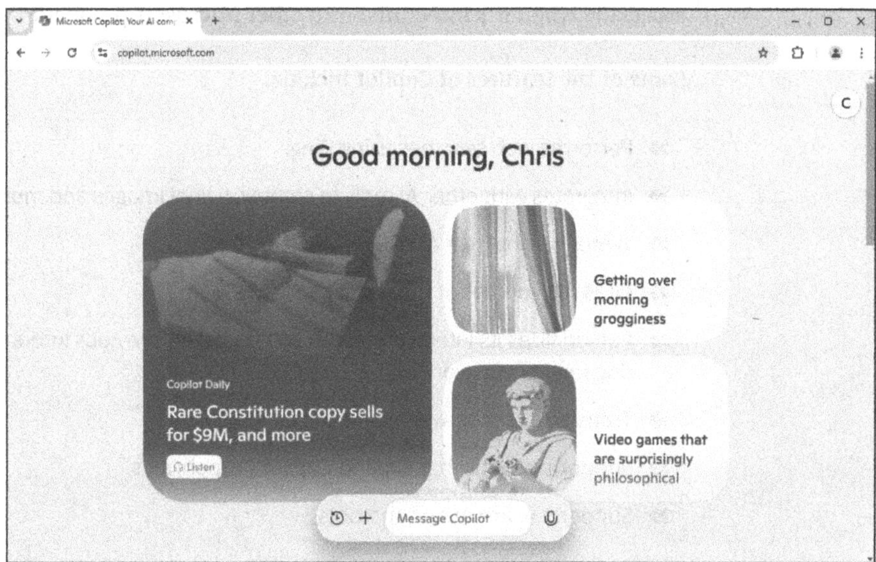

FIGURE 1-2: Microsoft Copilot on the web.

Overview of Microsoft Copilot

Copilot has been integrated into many of Microsoft's products and can be helpful with a wide variety of tasks. In fact, there are so many possible ways to use Copilot that the possibilities can sometimes seem overwhelming. AI chatbots are a fundamentally different way of interacting with computers than most people are used to, so it can be helpful to look at them as if they were traditional computer software and start by talking about the features and what makes Microsoft Copilot different from its competition.

Core functionalities and benefits

The most basic function of any chatbot, whether it's powered by artificial intelligence or not, is to respond to human speech or writing (which is also known as "natural language") with easy-to-understand text or speech. The quality of a chatbot can be measured by how human-like its responses are.

The current crop of AI chatbots can all generate highly convincing natural language responses to people's questions and requests.

The voice or text input a user of a chatbot gives to the chatbot, whether it's a question ("How tall is Mount Everest?") or an instruction ("Summarize this email.") is called a *prompt*. The primary way for people to interact with chatbots is through *prompting*.

Beyond its core ability to respond to prompts in natural language, Microsoft Copilot has exciting additional capabilities that make it stand out in usefulness, especially when it's integrated into other Microsoft products.

Some of the features of Copilot include:

- Performs web searches using Bing.
- Integrates with other AI tools to create original images and music.
- Writes original text or rewrites existing text.
- Cites the sources of the text it generates.
- Personalizes its interactions with you based on previous interactions and documents you work on.
- Translates text between different languages.
- Supports plugins that expand Copilot's capabilities.
- Supports user-created chatbots.

Key differentiators from other AI assistants

The main thing that makes Microsoft Copilot more useful than other AI assistants is that it is integrated into Microsoft Windows and other Microsoft programs. This integration gives Copilot the ability to not only generate text and images, but also to control certain aspects of the software it's integrated into. For example, using a non-integrated chatbot, such as ChatGPT, you can ask for text for a PowerPoint slide that you then need to copy into PowerPoint and format manually. With Microsoft 365 Copilot, you can ask for PowerPoint slides or an entire presentation, and the Copilot assistant will create the new slides, format them for you, and insert them directly into your presentation. Even better, Copilot can access and use other documents you've created while creating the new slides.

Another key factor that distinguishes Copilot from many other chatbots is that Copilot has access to the data in Microsoft Bing. By augmenting the data it was originally trained on with search results from Bing, Copilot can answer questions about the latest news and other developments, whereas other models have a "cut-off date" beyond which they can only speculate (or hallucinate).

Understanding how Copilot works

Chatbots like Microsoft Copilot and ChatGPT are far superior to their predecessors, such as Office Assistant, also known as "Clippy" (shown in Figure 1-3). Microsoft integrated Clippy into Microsoft Office applications from version 97 to 2003 and it proved to be more annoying than helpful in most cases.

FIGURE 1-3: Original Office Assistant, also known as "Clippy."

The reasons for Clippy's failure have been studied exhaustively, but the crux of it is that Clippy was intrusive and would appear whenever it detected that you were doing something (such as writing a letter) that it was supposed to be able to help with. But then, when you agreed to let Clippy help you, all it could do was reference official Microsoft Office documentation, which wasn't helpful for much of anything.

The two most important factors that contributed to making the latest generation of AI so much better than Clippy (and all subsequent AI assistants) are:

- Vastly more data (and computing power) was used to train them.
- They take advantage of new AI techniques that allow them to consider context when generating responses.

Learning from all the data

The AI model behind Microsoft Copilot is named *Prometheus*. Prometheus is OpenAI's technology combined with Bing's search index. The result is that Copilot has learned from and has access to a tremendous amount of data.

Although the relationship between training data size and a model's performance isn't simple, in general, larger models are able to gain a better picture of whatever they're designed to simulate (such as communicating using natural language, in the case of a chatbot).

Context is key

Even more important than simply throwing more data at an AI system is a technique known as *attention* that was invented by Google in 2017. In short, what attention techniques do is allow AI models to look at different parts of your input and their own output while figuring out what to say. For example, consider the following sentence:

"The bank can guarantee deposits will be safe because it has invested in secure vaults."

An AI model that uses attention mechanisms will know that "bank" refers to a financial institution rather than the bank of a river because of the other words in the sentence, such as "guarantee," "deposits," "safe," and "vaults." A model with attention also understands that the word "it" in this sentence refers back to "bank."

Because large language models can take context into account, providing sufficient context to the model in your prompts has become the single best way to improve the quality of responses you get to your prompts.

You learn how to use Copilot's chat mode in Chapter 2.

Using large language models (LLMs)

When you use Microsoft Copilot, you're using a large language model (LLM). But what is an LLM? Simply put, a large language model is a model of, or simulation of, language. It's described as a "large" language model because of its size.

Imagine that you're a train enthusiast. Perhaps when you were younger, you had a small train model. A small train model is okay for reproducing some things about trains. But, as your interest in accurately reproducing what you love about trains grows, you buy larger and larger trains and model railways — complete with scenery, bridges, and maybe even tiny little passengers in the dining car.

Of course, if you had the time, money, and space, you could have an actual-size train and railroad of your own. But that's impractical. So, you settle for the largest train model you can afford and that your basement can accommodate.

Large language models work the same way. A small language model may be able to engage in rudimentary simulations of conversations. A large language model can more accurately simulate an actual human speaker of a language (or a programmer, or a translator, and so forth) without being a human.

The inner workings of LLMs and machine learning are fascinating, but you don't need to be an artificial intelligence (AI) engineer, or even know anything about AI, to use Copilot. If you're interested in digging into more of the details, check out the book, *Artificial Intelligence for Dummies.*

Integration with Microsoft 365 apps

Microsoft 365 is the family of products and services that includes the productivity programs formerly known as Microsoft Office, as well as the OneDrive cloud storage service, the Microsoft Teams collaboration and conferencing program, the Outlook email and calendar program, and others. Microsoft 365 Copilot is available as an additional subscription.

Subscribing to Microsoft 365 Copilot activates the Copilot chatbot in each application and enables Copilot's built-in actions, which can perform different tasks depending on the application. Some of the features that Microsoft 365 Copilot enables include:

- In Word, Copilot can suggest different writing styles and formats, rewrite sentences or paragraphs, translate text into other languages, and convert text into tables.
- In Excel, Copilot can analyze data to discover trends and insights you might have missed, create charts and graphs, and suggest formulas.
- In PowerPoint, Copilot can suggest design ideas, create individual slides, convert Word documents into presentations, add animations, and even write speaker notes.
- In Teams, Copilot can take meeting notes, transcribe recordings, summarize discussions, and suggest action items.

» In Outlook, Copilot can summarize emails, assist you with writing emails, schedule meetings, and create reminders based on the content of your emails.

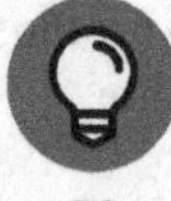
TIP

For a more comprehensive table of Microsoft 365 Copilot's capabilities in each Microsoft product, check out the online Cheat Sheet at www.dummies.com (search for *Copilot for Dummies* cheat sheet).

If you don't seek out Copilot's help while you're using Microsoft 365, it will remain quietly in the background. This is a welcome change from the overly eager assistant days of Clippy, but it also makes it important for users to educate themselves about what Copilot is capable of helping with.

In Part 2 of this book (Chapters 6 – 12), you experiment with Copilot's integration with Microsoft 365 and start to see its amazing capabilities as well as its sometimes frustrating limitations.

Connection with Microsoft Graph and your data

Copilot can access your data and use what it finds to personalize its suggestions. While this is extremely useful, it also creates potential security concerns. By default, when you use Copilot, it can access your emails, documents, chats, meetings, and any other data you create and store in Microsoft 365.

You learn what this means for Copilot's capabilities in Part 2.

Signing Up for Copilot

Signing up to use Copilot couldn't be easier. I mean that literally, because you don't need any kind of account to try it out. All you need to do is open any web browser and go to `https://copilot.microsoft.com`. The free and logged-out version of Copilot Chat, shown in Figure 1-4, is limited compared to the version you get when you log in with a Microsoft account or buy a subscription to Copilot Pro.

In this section, you learn how to access Copilot, how to sign in to Copilot, and whether you should subscribe to Copilot Pro.

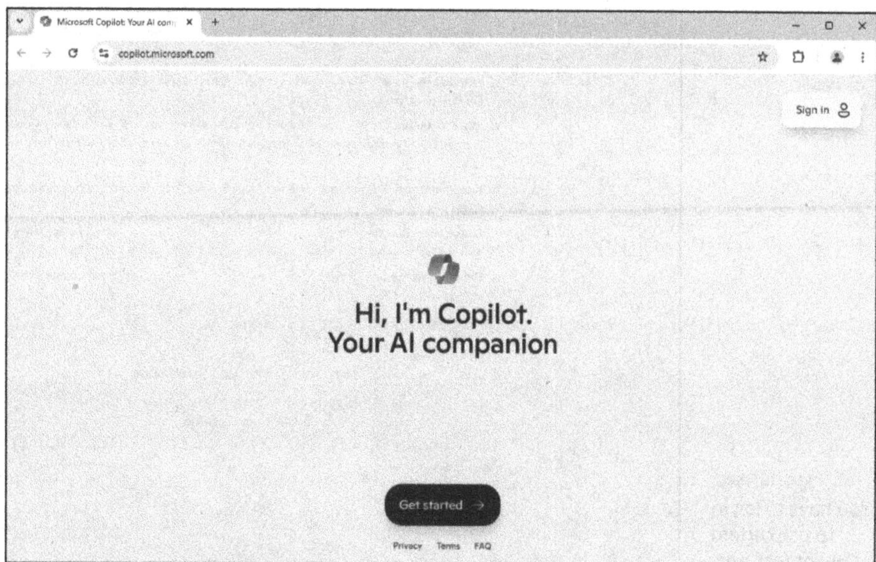

FIGURE 1-4: The free version of Copilot Chat.

Installing Copilot

Because Copilot Chat and Microsoft 365 Copilot both run in your web browser, there's no need to install anything to use either of them. Although the Copilot Chat experience will be nearly the same in any web browser you use, Copilot has integrations with Microsoft's Edge browser that may provide some incentive for users to choose to work with Copilot in Edge. If you have a strong preference for using a browser other than Edge, however, you can use that browser.

Eligibility criteria

Although Bing Chat, as Copilot was previously known, was only open to a limited number of people during its early days, today Copilot is available for free to anyone with access to a web browser or mobile device.

Subscription plans and pricing

If you use Copilot Chat while not signed in to a Microsoft Account, you're currently limited to just text input and responses. When you try to chat with Copilot by speaking or with images, you'll get a message asking you to log in, as shown in Figure 1-5.

Fortunately, there is an easy fix: just log in to a free Microsoft account from within Copilot Chat. Once you're logged in to Copilot Chat, you'll have access to additional features and settings and to your conversation history.

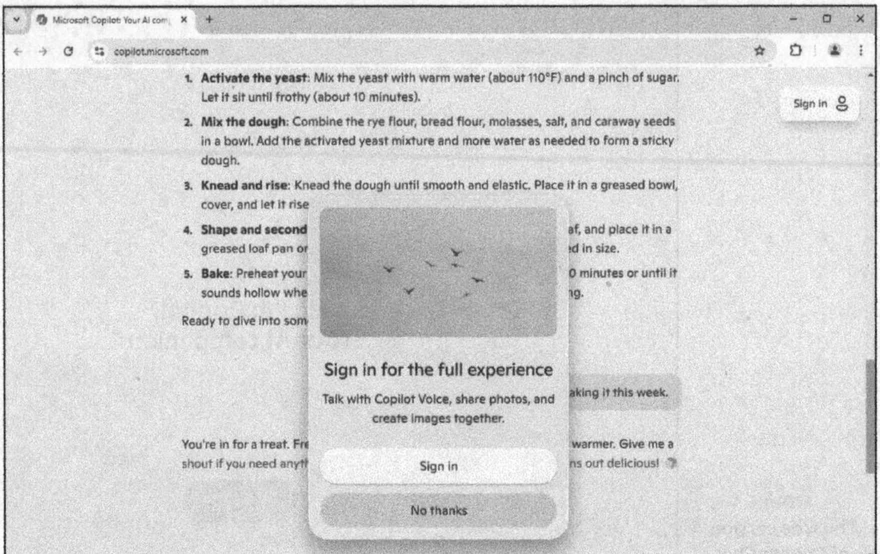

FIGURE 1-5: You have to log in to use certain Copilot features.

Copilot Free

The free and logged-in version of Copilot has its limitations too, however. These limitations include:

- Limited access to the latest and greatest models during times of peak demand.
- Limited boost tokens. *Boost tokens* are required for generating images, songs, and other creative content in Copilot. Boost tokens are covered in more detail in Chapter 11.
- No access to Microsoft 365 Copilot.
- No custom Copilots. Custom Copilots are specialized AI assistants that users of Copilot Pro can create. You learn more about custom Copilots and how to create them in Chapter 13.

Copilot Pro

Subscribing to Copilot Pro currently costs $20/month. The benefits of subscribing include:

- Faster performance.
- Access to the latest models during peak times.
- Copilot access in Office apps.
- 100 boost tokens per day, as opposed to the 15 tokens that free users have.

WHY YOUR COPILOT EXPERIENCE DIFFERS

If you see something in Copilot on your computer or at `https://copilot.microsoft.com` that's different from what I show in this book, it's likely because of an upgrade to Copilot that's happened in the time between when I wrote this book and right now.

Likewise, if you're not seeing a feature of Copilot that I describe in this book, that also may be because of an upgrade that's happened, or it may be because of an upgrade that hasn't happened for your Microsoft account yet.

If you're already a subscriber to Microsoft 365, you can subscribe to Microsoft 365 Copilot, which gives you the same benefits as Copilot Pro but that is also tuned for business use and integrates with your Microsoft 365 data. Microsoft 365 Copilot is $30/month per user, which is on top of your subscription to Microsoft 365 itself.

Which plan do you need?

If you're a business user and you already have a subscription to Microsoft 365, you should subscribe to Microsoft 365 Copilot.

If you don't have a business license to Microsoft 365 and you plan to do a lot of creative work with Copilot, such as creating images or songs, you should subscribe to Copilot Pro.

If you're just experimenting with Copilot and want to learn what it's capable of and won't be using it every day, the logged-in and free version is more than adequate for your needs.

Step-by-step sign-up process

To sign up for a Microsoft account and get full access to the free version of Copilot, visit `https://copilot.microsoft.com`. After you enter your name and select a voice for Copilot, you'll see a Sign In button in the upper-right corner of the screen, as shown in Figure 1-6.

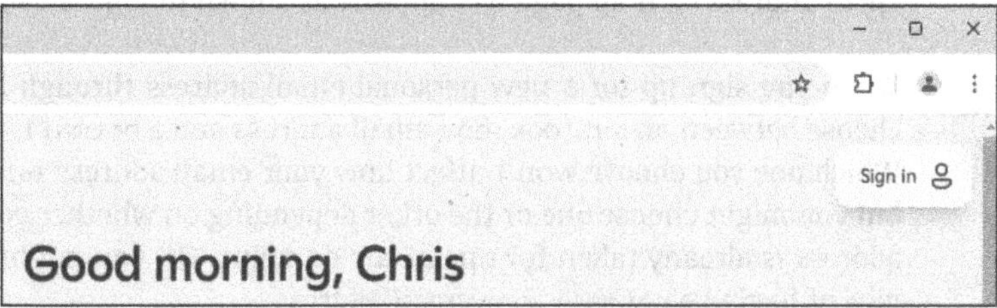

FIGURE 1-6: The Sign In button at `copilot.microsoft.com`.

TIP

If you prefer to sign up for and access Copilot using a mobile app, go to `https://www.microsoft.com/en-us/microsoft-copilot/for-individuals/copilot-app` to access a QR code you can scan with your mobile device to go directly to the app download page.

Click the Sign In button and select whether you want to sign in with a personal account or a business account. If you'll be signing up for a new account, click Sign In with a Personal Account.

If you already have a Microsoft account, you may be logged in automatically at this point. If you don't have an account, you'll see the Sign In page, as shown in Figure 1-7.

FIGURE 1-7: The Microsoft account Sign In page.

To create a new Microsoft account, click the link labeled No Account? Create One!

The Create Account screen appears next, as shown in Figure 1-8.

If you have an email address that you'd like to use as your Microsoft account user ID, you can enter it into this screen. Otherwise, click the Get a New Email Address button to sign up for a free Outlook email address. The first screen of the new email address sign up page will appear, as shown in Figure 1-9.

TIP

When you sign up for a new personal email address through Microsoft, you can choose between an `outlook.com` email address and a `hotmail.com` email address. Which one you choose won't affect how your email address functions in any way, but you might choose one or the other depending on whether your preferred email address is already taken for one of the domains. Or, you might just like the retro vibe of having a `hotmail.com` email address.

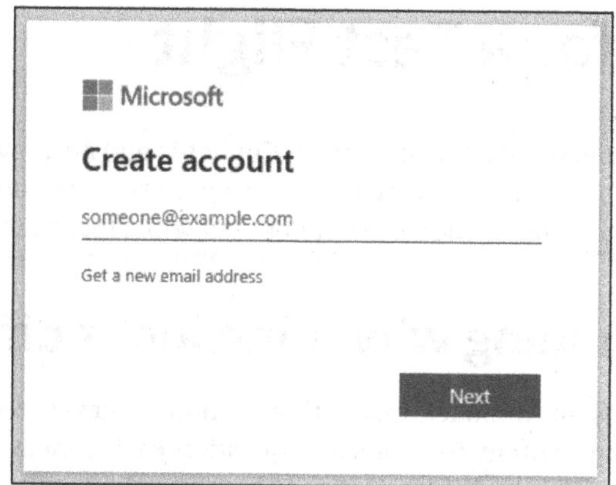

FIGURE 1-8: The Create Account screen.

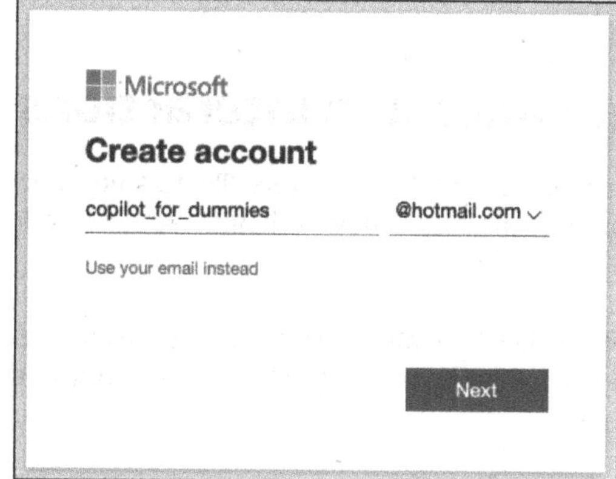

FIGURE 1-9: Selecting a new email address.

On the next screen, select a strong password and check the box next to the question of whether you'd like to receive marketing emails from Microsoft. Make a note of the password you choose. You'll need this later to log in to your new email account.

You'll be asked on subsequent screens for your name and your birthdate.

Finally, there may be one last screen that asks you to solve a puzzle to prove that you're human. You've got this!

Once you finish signing up for your new email address (which also serves as your new Microsoft account), you'll be returned to the Copilot homepage, and your first name will appear in the upper-right corner where the Sign In button previously was. Congratulations! Move on to the next section so you can start seeing what Copilot can do!

Taking Copilot for a Test Flight

Now that you understand a bit about what Copilot is and how it works, and you've created your account and are logged in, it's time to try it out and see what it can do! The examples in this section use Copilot Chat while logged in to a free account.

Understanding why mine looks different

Because Copilot is an AI model, rather than a simple rules-based program, it will generate different content for the same question each time a question is asked (even if it's only slightly different). So, I show you the results that I get when I enter the same prompts I ask you to enter, but your results will be different. They may be better or worse, but I guarantee that they'll be different.

Basic commands and interactions

Let's start with something short and simple. There's not much that's shorter or simpler (at least conceptually) than a haiku, so let's ask Copilot to write some poetry.

Find the input box labeled "Ask Me Anything. . ." at the bottom of the Copilot Chat window and type the following into it (feel free to customize the topic for one of your favorite things!):

Write a haiku about sushi.

When I tried this, I got the following result:

Certainly! Here's a haiku about sushi:

🍣 *Rice, fish, seaweed hug, Soy sauce whispers on my tongue, Sushi love blooms bright.*

Feel free to ask if you'd like more creative content or have any other requests! 😊

This is okay, I suppose. But, I kind of prefer my poetry with a laugh. So, try giving the following prompt:

Write a funny haiku about sushi.

Here's Copilot's response:

Certainly! Here's a playful haiku about sushi:

🍣 *Rolling down my plate, Avocado slips away, Chasing sushi dreams.*

Feel free to ask for more creative content or any other requests! 😊

Much better! Notice how just the addition of one word (funny) dramatically changed the output and improves it (in my opinion). Let's see if we can get something even better or more descriptive. Here's the next prompt I gave:

Write an ironic haiku about sharing sushi.

With this prompt, I really have no expectations or idea about what I'm looking for. But I do know that my favorite kind of humor is ironic and one of my least favorite things is having to share sushi (because I want it ALL!). Here's the response I got:

🍣 *Chopsticks duel begins, Sharing sushi? Not today, Mine, all mine, I say.*

Feel free to ask for more creative content or any other requests! 😊

Again, this is pretty good. My choice of words might be a little more risqué than what Copilot is allowed to use, but I think we've managed to get as close to a decent poem as can be expected.

Feel free to continue experimenting with this prompt or other prompts as long as you like. In the next chapter, you learn techniques for how to write prompts to get specific results from Copilot. But first, let's talk about AI and ethics.

Using Copilot Ethically

In the previous section, you generated some poems. You could have just as easily asked Copilot to write a letter to your mother, or a speech, or even a homework assignment. You were the person who asked Copilot for the content (whatever it is), and you pay (or don't) for a Copilot account. So, is it okay to present the work that you asked Copilot to write as "your" work?

It's a difficult topic, and the answer (like the answer to many other tricky questions) is "it depends."

In this section, you learn about some of the principles of responsible and ethical AI development and use.

Responsible AI principles

Creators of AI systems are keenly aware of the risks of developing and deploying AI systems. Some of these risks include:

- » AI-generated content that is designed to fool people, including misinformation or images that resemble real people doing fake things, which are also known as *deep fakes*.
- » Unauthorized use of personally identifying information.
- » Algorithmic bias, in which the bias from the data upon which a model has been trained creates bias in the system's responses. For example, if the only carpentry tool the model had ever seen is a hammer, it might think every tool is a hammer.
- » Generation of content that violates people's intellectual property.
- » Use of AI by cyber criminals.
- » Use of AI in weapons.
- » Enormous power demands required to train and operate AI systems.

As a result of these and other risks, AI model creators have developed rules and guidelines that they strive to uphold — or at least that they say they strive to uphold above other concerns, such as profit.

Microsoft has defined its AI principles in a document titled "Microsoft's Responsible AI Standard." You can read this document and more information about the principles that guide AI development and use at `www.microsoft.com/en-us/ai/responsible-ai`.

The six principles that Microsoft lists in its Responsible AI Standard are:

- » **Fairness.** AI systems should treat all people fairly.
- » **Reliability and safety.** AI systems should perform reliably and safely.
- » **Privacy and security.** AI systems should be secure and respect privacy.
- » **Inclusiveness.** AI systems should empower everyone.
- » **Transparency.** AI systems should be understandable.
- » **Accountability.** People should be accountable for AI systems.

Data privacy and security considerations

To create the models that make AI chatbots work, companies first have to gather a vast amount of data. This data is fed into machine learning algorithms and used to improve the output of the model. For example, the reason that an AI model can generate creative new haikus is that it's seen many, many examples of haikus and has detected the patterns that are similar between the examples. No one ever specifically programmed into the model that haikus typically consist of 17 syllables in a 5-7-5 pattern, but through learning and detecting patterns in vast amounts of data, AI has figured this out.

Among all the text that AI models have learned from are millions of pages of human-created content — much of it not licensed or paid for by the creator of the AI model. Should AI model creators have to pay human content creators for using their data? This is currently the topic of several high-profile lawsuits and it remains to be seen what courts will decide.

Perhaps even more concerning than their gobbling of books, films, TV, articles, music, and every other type of human-created content is that among all this content is personal data. This personal data may include pictures of people, as well as information about people that appears on websites, social media posts, public records, and more. Although precautions are taken to attempt to prevent AI chatbots from divulging personal information they may have captured about individuals, there have been instances where hackers have been able to trick AI chatbots into repeating raw unfiltered data from their training.

Other sources of data used by AI systems that present privacy and security problems include:

- **Biometric data.** AI systems that use facial recognition, voice recognition, and fingerprint information could jeopardize individuals' privacy and security if they were compromised.
- **Device data.** Internet-connected devices, like security cameras or robot vacuums, record and track information about everything. This data may include, for example, whether you're currently at home or pictures of the inside of your house.
- **Social media monitoring.** AI algorithms monitor and analyze activity on social media. The reasons for this monitoring range from national security to marketing and advertising.

With so much data available on the Internet about each of us, it's vital that the methods AI creators use to gather and analyze our data are transparent and secure and that people have the final say and control over how and where their data is used.

Guidelines for ethical use

As a user of AI chatbots, you also have responsibilities. There are certain possible uses of AI chatbots, and generative AI in general, that nearly everyone would agree are wrong.

REMEMBER

The term *generative AI* (sometimes shortened to GenAI) refers to any artificial intelligence system that can create original outputs that are similar to what a human can do.

Unethical uses of generative AI include:

- Cheating on school work.
- Any use that can potentially cause harm.
- Attempting to make a copy of a copyright-protected work, such as a movie or a song.
- Plagiarism.
- Creating deep fakes.
- Imitating another artist's style and passing it off as your own.

The ethics of other potential uses of AI depends on understanding where the boundaries between a legitimate use of AI and a harmful use are. Guidelines for ethical use of AI include:

- Generative AI should be used to augment, not replace humans or processes.
- Companies adopting generative AI should prioritize safety over potential efficiency. For example, while AI can assist with computer programming, it can potentially cause problems if every line of code it writes isn't verified and tested and understood by human programmers.
- Users of generative AI must verify the accuracy of AI-generated content before using it.

These uses of generative AI are usually ethical:

- For your own education or research (but make sure to verify the accuracy of generated content so you don't learn something the AI just hallucinated!)
- For your own entertainment.
- For checking your spelling or grammar.

» For translating text you've written or own the right to translate into other languages.
» For detecting AI-generated content (in the case of a teacher, for example).
» In situations where the generated content is clearly labeled (as in this book).
» In a workplace or among people who have agreed to send and receive generated content (such as in a workplace where AI is used to augment processes such as writing emails, creating reports, and preparing presentations).

When you're in doubt about whether a certain use of AI is ethical, openness and honesty are the best policy. For example, if you generate an image using AI and want to post it to a social media application, label the image as AI-generated rather than risk someone assuming that it's your original creation.

Every organization — whether it's a nonprofit, a charity, an educational institution, or a corporation — should have a detailed policy explaining what is and isn't allowed. You can find many good examples of such policies on the web or you can work with a lawyer to draft your own. Or, you might even consider having AI help you draft a policy.

You've learned about Copilot, a bit about how large language models (LLMs) work, and how the LLM behind Copilot is similar and different from other LLMs. In the next chapter, you build on the knowledge you've acquired in this chapter to learn techniques for talking to Copilot.

IN THIS CHAPTER

» Engineering prompts

» Speaking to Copilot

» Understanding Copilot's limitations

» Refining your prompts

Chapter 2
Chatting with Copilot

Copilot's chat interface can be accessed on the web, in Microsoft 365, on smartphones, tablets, and smartwatches, from the desktop versions of Microsoft Office on both macOS and Windows, and by pressing a special Copilot key on Copilot+ PCs. You can communicate with Copilot using text or speech, and Copilot understands and can communicate in at least 25 different human languages (with more on the way).

With Copilot being so universally available, it would seem that no matter where you are, asking an AI chatbot for answers, help, or even advice is convenient and fast.

But what should you ask it? And, are there certain ways to phrase requests that are more likely to produce better answers? You learn the answers to these questions in this chapter.

Using Text Prompts

The default way to interact with Copilot is via text. From your computer or your mobile device, you enter some kind of prompt, and Copilot will respond. Written prompts give you the ability to refine a prompt over time, save prompts and responses, and not disturb people around you, whether you're in an office and seeking help with a formula in Excel or watching a movie with your family and wanting to look up what other movies Benedict Cumberbatch has been in.

Starting simply

One of the most effective ways to get exactly the type of help or response you need is to start with a simple prompt, see how Copilot responds, and then try again.

For example, if you want help writing an email to your landlord asking her to fix your heat, you might start with something vague like this prompt:

Write an email to my landlord asking her to fix the heat.

Copilot may come back with something like the response shown in Figure 2-1.

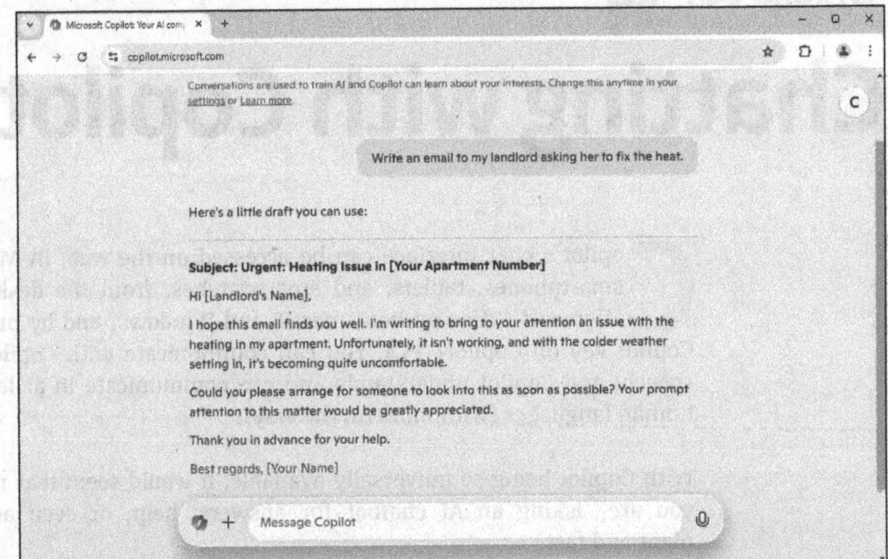

Microsoft Copilot: Your AI com
copilot.microsoft.com
Conversations are used to train AI and Copilot can learn about your interests. Change this anytime in your settings or Learn more.
Write an email to my landlord asking her to fix the heat.
Here's a little draft you can use:
Subject: Urgent: Heating Issue in [Your Apartment Number]
Hi [Landlord's Name],
I hope this email finds you well. I'm writing to bring to your attention an issue with the heating in my apartment. Unfortunately, it isn't working, and with the colder weather setting in, it's becoming quite uncomfortable.
Could you please arrange for someone to look into this as soon as possible? Your prompt attention to this matter would be greatly appreciated.
Thank you in advance for your help.
Best regards, [Your Name]
Message Copilot

FIGURE 2-1: A first attempt at an email to my landlord.

Narrowing it down

The text Copilot comes back with is okay, but it makes a lot of assumptions and might not fit your situation. For example, you might find the tone too confrontational or not confrontational enough for your taste. Also, it assumes that the weather is currently bad, rather than that you'd like to have the heat fixed before the weather gets cold again.

After seeing the initial response, you can refine your prompt. Remember that if you submit follow-up prompts in the same chat session, Copilot will take your previous prompts into consideration while generating the next prompt, so there's no need to repeat that you're looking for a letter to your landlord. Here's my refined prompt:

That's okay, but try again. It's currently summer, so I don't need heat now, but I'd like the heat to be fixed before fall so that it's not a last minute thing. I have a great relationship with my landlord and just want to make sure that this gets done early.

The new email generated by Copilot, shown in Figure 2-2, takes into consideration the new information I've given and has a much more friendly tone that's in keeping with what I'm looking for.

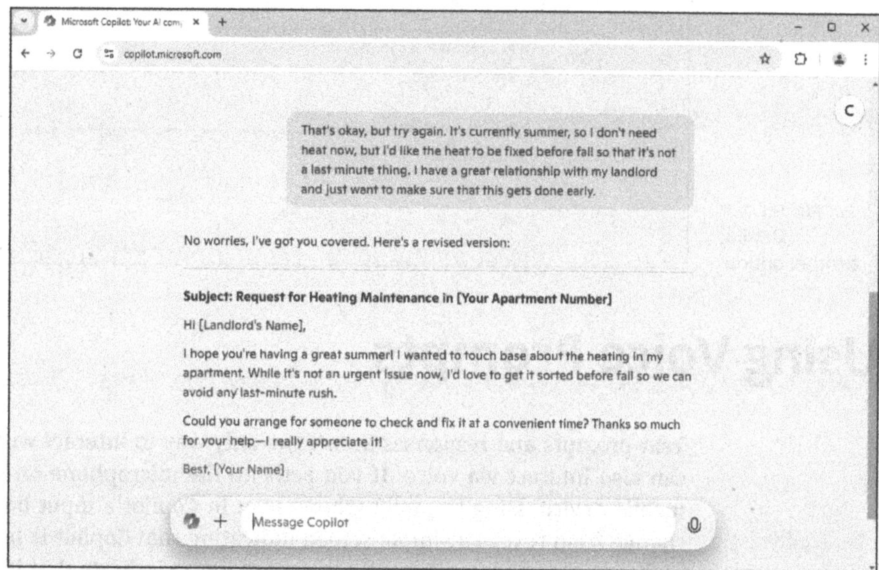

FIGURE 2-2: A revised email to my landlord.

REMEMBER

The process of starting simple and submitting additional prompts to get better results is called *prompt refinement.* The section of this chapter titled "Refining Your Prompts" describes specific ways to refine prompts and the benefits of doing so in more detail.

Asking for more options

While the new email is pretty good, it's always a good idea to ask for options. You don't know whether Copilot can generate something even better until you ask. A simple "try that again" prompt can give you some options, and you might end up combining your favorite sentences from both emails along with your own personal touch.

Figure 2-3 shows another option, which was generated after I prompted Copilot with a simple "try again."

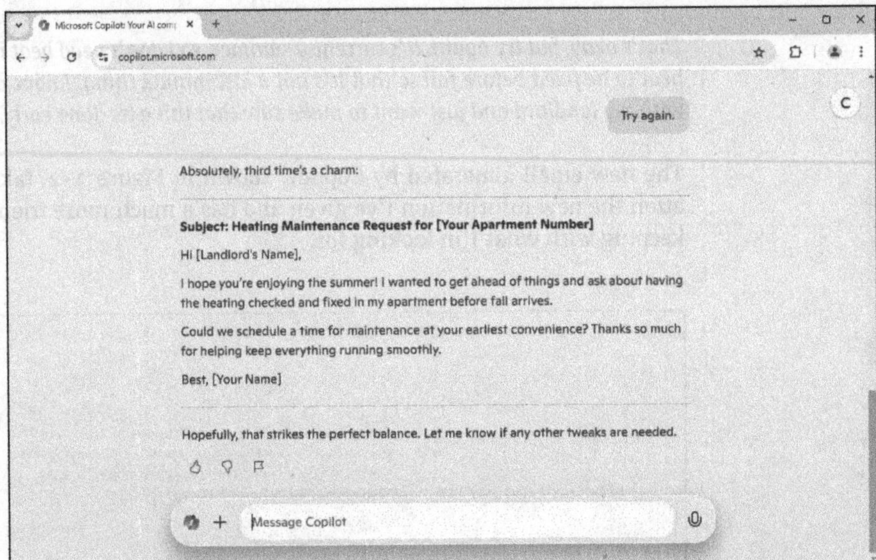

FIGURE 2-3: Getting another option.

Using Voice Prompts

Text prompts and responses aren't the only way to interact with Copilot. Copilot can also interact via voice. If you activate the microphone on your computer or mobile device using the microphone icon in Copilot's input box, the screen will change from text to a simple screen indicating that Copilot is listening, as shown in Figure 2-4, and Copilot will say something to indicate that it's listening.

Depending on whether you've previously allowed your browser to access your computer's microphone, you may also see a popup window asking for permission to use the microphone.

Once you allow Copilot to hear you, you can start talking at any time and Copilot will respond in the voice you selected the first time you visited the Copilot website. Copilot will even attempt to detect the language you're speaking and respond in the same language.

Why is speech input important?

There are many reasons why speech input and responses are useful or essential while using Copilot, including for accessibility, efficiency, multitasking, familiarity, and inclusion.

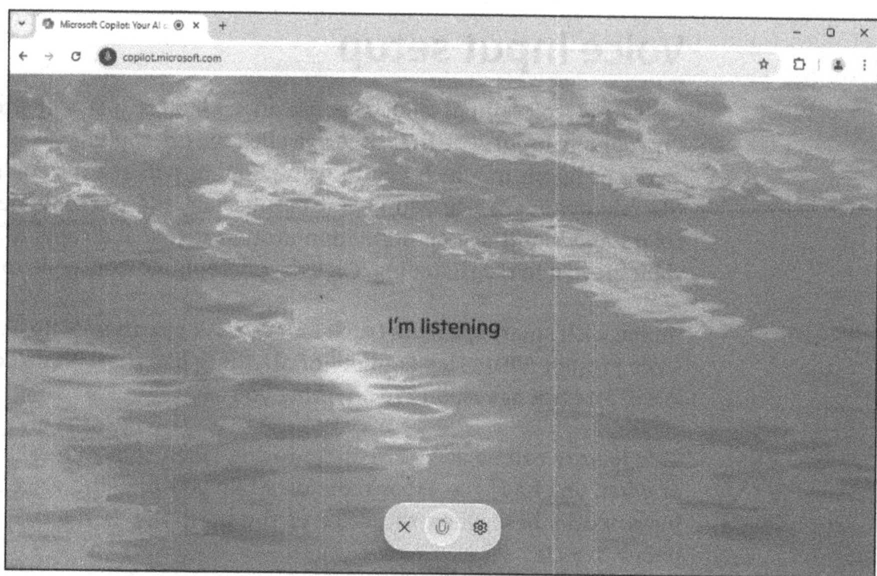

FIGURE 2-4: Copilot's voice mode.

Accessibility

Being able to interact via speech is critical for visually impaired people as well as for people with dyslexia and conditions that make it difficult or impossible to type.

Efficiency

Speech input can also increase your efficiency, because speaking can be faster than typing for complex thoughts or longer instructions.

Multitasking

Typing requires focus and a person's full attention and tends to be most useful for tasks that are computer-based, such as writing, creating graphics, and researching. Voice input, on the other hand, makes it possible to get help from Copilot while you're doing things that aren't computer-centric, such as cooking or driving.

Familiarity

While most people are used to interacting with computer assistants (such as search engines and customer support bots) via text, interacting via speech can feel more natural and conversational than typing.

Inclusion

Voice input accommodates multiple languages and accents, making communication with the chatbot more inclusive.

Voice input setup

Activating voice input and response in Copilot is just a matter of clicking the microphone input. The first time you click the microphone icon, your web browser or the program in which you're using Copilot will ask for you permission to use the microphone. Once you give it permission, the microphone icon will change colors and you'll see an animation around it that indicates it's listening. If you want to tell it to stop listening, click the microphone icon again to pause voice input.

Unlike with smart speakers (such as Siri or Alexa), there's no need to preface your voice prompt with "Hey Copilot" or anything like that. While Copilot is listening, it will attempt to respond to anything you say.

WARNING

This feature can be awkward or confusing when someone calls you on the phone or when you have the TV or radio on while you're using voice input. Using voice input works best when the voice of the prompter is the only voice the microphone detects.

In the website version of Copilot (`https://copilot.microsoft.com`), you can customize Copilot's voice feature by clicking the gear icon on the Copilot's listening screen or by selecting Voice from the menu that appears when you click your profile icon in the upper-right corner of the Copilot web interface while in text input mode.

From the Settings menu, select Voice. The voice selector will appear, as shown in Figure 2-5.

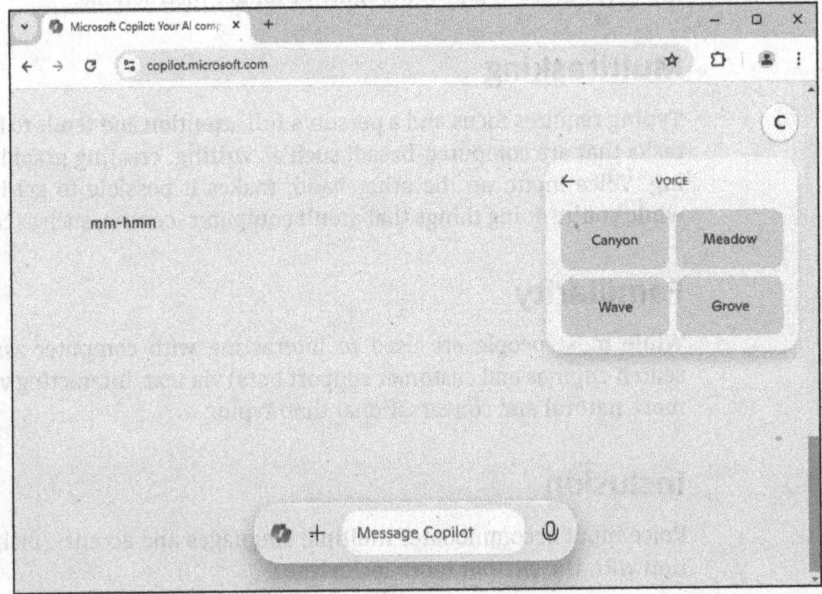

FIGURE 2-5: Copilot's voice settings.

On the voice selector, you can click any of the voice names to hear a sample of that voice. The currently selected voice will be highlighted in a different color than the others, as shown in Figure 2-6.

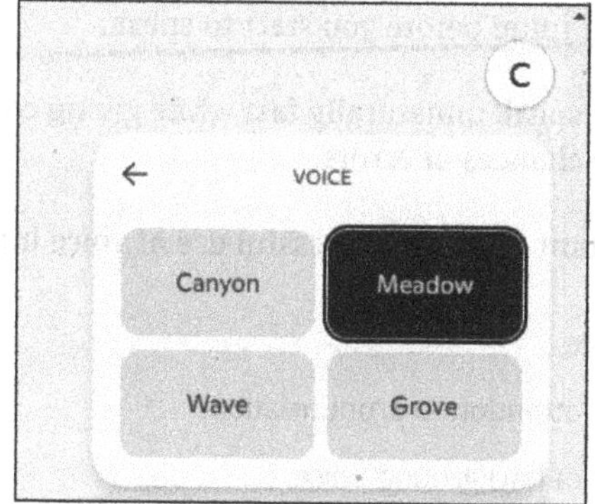

FIGURE 2-6: Seeing the selected voice.

To exit out of voice mode, click the "X" on the listening screen. You'll be returned to text mode, and you'll see the text of the voice conversation you had with Copilot, as shown in Figure 2-7.

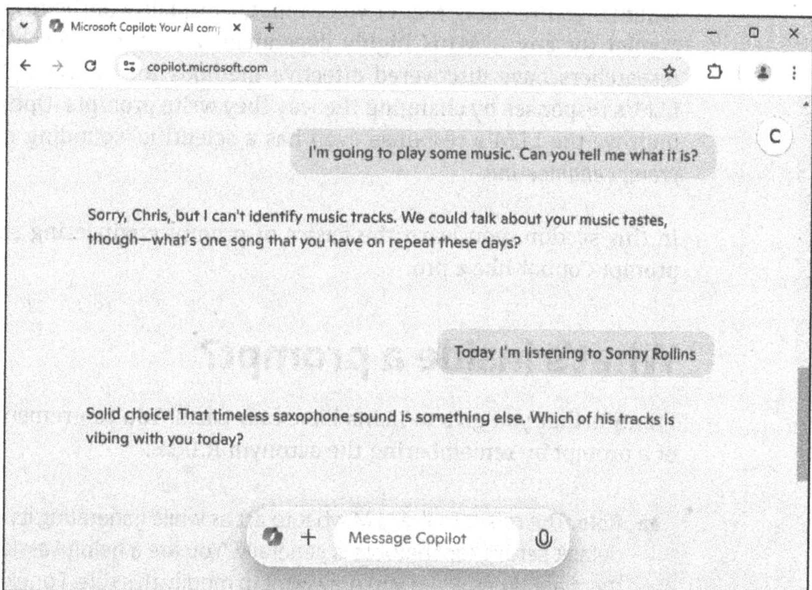

FIGURE 2-7: Returning to text mode.

Tips for clear and accurate voice commands

Giving voice prompts to Copilot can take some getting used to. If you're a slow speaker and frequently pause as you're speaking, Copilot may interrupt you and start to respond before you're finished. For this reason, you may need to fully form your prompt in your mind before you start to speak.

On the other hand, if you speak unnaturally fast while giving commands to Copilot, that will increase the chances of errors.

Three of the most important rules for successful use of voice input in Copilot are:

- Speak at a natural pace.
- Speak clearly and pay attention to pronunciation.
- Minimize the amount of background noise.

Learning to Engineer Prompts

Whether you're using text or voice input, the quality of the response you get from Copilot (or any LLM) is highly dependent on the way you ask. Over the years, researchers have discovered effective methods for improving the quality of an LLM's responses by changing the way they write prompts. Optimizing prompts to improve the LLM's response even has a scientific-sounding name — it's called *prompt engineering.*

In this section, you learn the basics of prompt engineering so that you too can prompt Copilot like a pro.

What's inside a prompt?

Prompts that you give to LLMs have four parts. You can remember the four parts of a prompt by remembering the acronym R.I.C.E.

- **Role.** The role tells the LLM what to act as while generating its response. The default setting for chatbots is generally "You are a helpful assistant." However, there are times when you may want to modify this role. For example, if you're asking the chatbot for help with computer programming, you might start your prompt by saying "Act as an experienced professional programmer." If you want the LLM to generate a response in pirate speak, you could start your prompt with "You are a swashbuckling pirate."

- **Instruction.** The instruction is the part of the prompt where you ask the chatbot to do something, answer something, compose something, or whatever else you have in mind. The instruction should be clear and to the point. For example, "Give me a list of dishes that I can make with leftover chicken, spinach, and cheese."
- **Context.** Context is the background information the LLM should know in order to successfully complete the task you gave it in the instruction. For example, if you're asking Copilot for the current weather, an important piece of context is your current location.
- **Examples.** Examples may include such things as similar content or information about the format the response should be in. For example, if you asked the chatbot to tell you a joke, you might give it an example of the kind of joke you enjoy. If you're asking for help with writing content for a website, you could ask the chatbot to format its response using HTML.

Crafting effective prompts

Prompt engineering is a continually changing field. People are always finding new ways to elicit better responses from LLMs, and LLMs are also changing and improving. As a result, a specific prompting technique that's effective today may not even be necessary with the next generation of LLMs. Or, a technique that works to get certain types of answers today may not work tomorrow.

There are, however, some techniques that are timeless and that will always be true. Most of these techniques are the same techniques you might use if you were talking to a new employee — perhaps that brilliant new intern who seems to know a lot of things but who has no idea how your company works.

Provide sufficient context

The first rule of prompt engineering is that LLMs need context. Think about the analogy of a smart intern. Each conversation for an LLM is like the first day on the job. If you put yourself in this role, you can easily understand why sufficient context is crucial. Imagine the following conversation between you (the boss) and your brilliant new intern:

You: *Smart Intern, I need you to create a presentation for an upcoming client meeting. Can you take care of that?*

Intern: *Sure thing, I'm on it! What's the main focus of the presentation?*

You: *Just make it impressive. You know, something that will wow them.*

Intern: *You got it!*

Your smart intern spends the next several hours working on the presentation.

You: *Do you have that presentation ready?*

Intern: *Sure do, and I think it's really going to wow them!*

Your intern starts the presentation. The title slide features a dramatic animation of fireworks and the title: "The Future of Space Travel: Our Journey to Mars."

You: *Uh, well . . . This is really impressive, but our client is a local plumbing company that's looking for a marketing strategy, not a space exploration plan.*

Intern: *Oh no! I guess I got carried away with wowing them.*

You: *No problem, let's step back and talk about the importance of context.*

In the previous story, you and your intern were both to blame for the lack of clear communication. You should have been more specific in your instructions, and the intern should have asked follow-up questions.

Copilot (and every other AI chatbot) has a tendency to act like an over-eager intern. It will rarely ask follow-up questions, and will instead go off and make assumptions based on what its training and knowledge does know from what you said. Given a request to make an impressive presentation, it will be much more likely to respond with a slideshow about space travel or the positive potential of artificial intelligence than a marketing plan for a plumber.

Using different types of prompts

Certain techniques have been found to produce better results from LLMs. Some of the more common techniques include:

- **Zero-shot prompting.** Most prompts that newcomers to AI chatbots use are called zero-shot prompts. A zero-shot prompt doesn't provide examples of successful solutions. This type of prompt is most useful for straightforward tasks where the model can figure out enough about what you want from just the instruction and context. Example prompt: *Translate this sentence into French: The weather is nice today.*
- **One-shot and few-shot prompting.** One-shot and few-shot prompting involves providing the model with one or more examples of a good result

along with the instruction. Few-shot prompting is effective with complex tasks and logic problems. Example prompt: *Label the sentiment of this review: 'The food was terrible, and the service was slow.'*

- **Chain-of-thought prompting.** In this type of prompting, you encourage the model to think step-by-step. You can do this by providing examples of similar problems to the one you're giving it or by simply saying something like, "Think step-by-step." or "Show me, step-by-step, how you arrive at the answer." The chain-of-thought technique works well for logic problems, mathematical problems, and multi-step processes. Example prompt: *What is the result of 2 + 3 * 4? Think step-by-step: First, we need to follow the order of operations. Multiplication comes before addition. So, 3 * 4 equals 12. Next, we add 2. Thus, 2 + 12 equals 14. The final result is 14. What is the result of 3 + 8 * 3?*
- **Self-consistency.** In self-consistency prompting, you give the model the same prompt multiple times and take the majority result. Self-consistency prompting is often used in conjunction with chain-of-thought prompting.

  Example prompt: *Who was the first President of the United States?*

  Response 1: *George Washington was the first President of the United States.*

  Response 2: *The first President of the United States was George Washington.*

  Response 3: *In 1789, George Washington became the first President of the United States.*
- **Generate knowledge.** In this type of prompting, you ask the LLM to generate useful knowledge related to what you want it to do and then ask it to incorporate that knowledge into the prompt alongside your instruction. Example prompt: *Generate a list of unique characteristics for a fantasy world. Then, use these characteristics to write an opening scene for a novel.*

Avoiding the common pitfalls

Just as there are right ways to construct prompts, there are also wrong ways. The most common mistakes people make while prompting LLMs include these:

- **Writing leading prompts.** "Why are dogs better than cats?" Remember, the LLM wants to make you happy. This prompt is likely to cause the LLM to tell you why dogs are better than cats, even though there may be some disagreement on that point among the scientific community.

  If you're looking for help making an argument in favor of dogs being better than cats, ask the LLM something like, "Give me ten examples of an argument in favor of dogs I can make in a debate over whether dogs or cats are better."

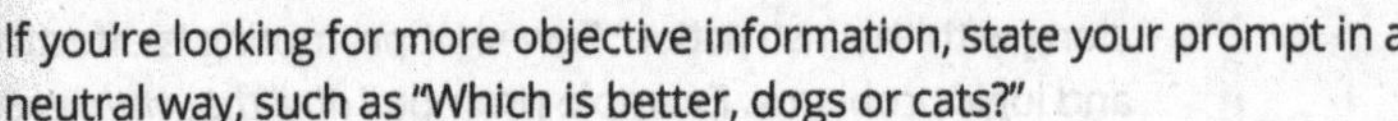

If you're looking for more objective information, state your prompt in a neutral way, such as "Which is better, dogs or cats?"

- **Writing vague prompts.** "Tell me about cats." This prompt is too broad and unspecific. It doesn't say what aspect of cats the user is interested in, such as their behavior, care, history, or significance in culture.

TIP

Vague prompts can sometimes be useful if you want information about a topic you know nothing about, but you'll nearly always need to follow up with more specific prompts.

- **Not providing any context.** "What is the best method?" This prompt lacks context about what the user is referring to. The best method for what? Boiling an egg, learning guitar, training a dog, or something else?
- **Using over-specific prompts.** "Tell me about the dietary habits of Siberian cats living in the northern region of Russia, particularly focusing on their intake of fish and how this affects their fur quality in the months of November to February." If the LLM doesn't have information on such a narrow topic, its ability to respond will be limited.
- **Making a prompt too complex.** "Can you provide a comprehensive analysis of the sociopolitical implications of climate change on developing nations, including economic impacts, health consequences, and potential mitigation strategies, while comparing these with the responses of developed nations over the past decade?" Asking for a large amount of data in a single prompt can overwhelm the model and lead to a less coherent result than if you ask for the information over multiple prompts.
- **Assuming understanding.** "Explain why the latest changes are significant." This prompt assumes the LLM knows what "the latest changes" refers to.
- **Not using literal interpretations.** "Break a leg." This phrase could be interpreted by the LLM as referring to a leg injury rather than the idiomatic phrase meaning "good luck."
- **Not testing and refining prompts.** "Tell me about Python." This prompt could provide results about the Python programming language, python snakes, or Monty Python.

Knowing Copilot's limitations

Although you can give Copilot Chat any prompt you want, knowing what's impossible for it to know or do will save you time and improve your ability to make it work for you. In some cases, it's impossible to know Copilot's limitations unless you ask it. Even then, however, the response you get may not be completely reliable.

For example, in the chat shown in Figure 2-8, I asked Copilot Chat to create and insert slides into my PowerPoint presentation and it responded that it doesn't have that capability.

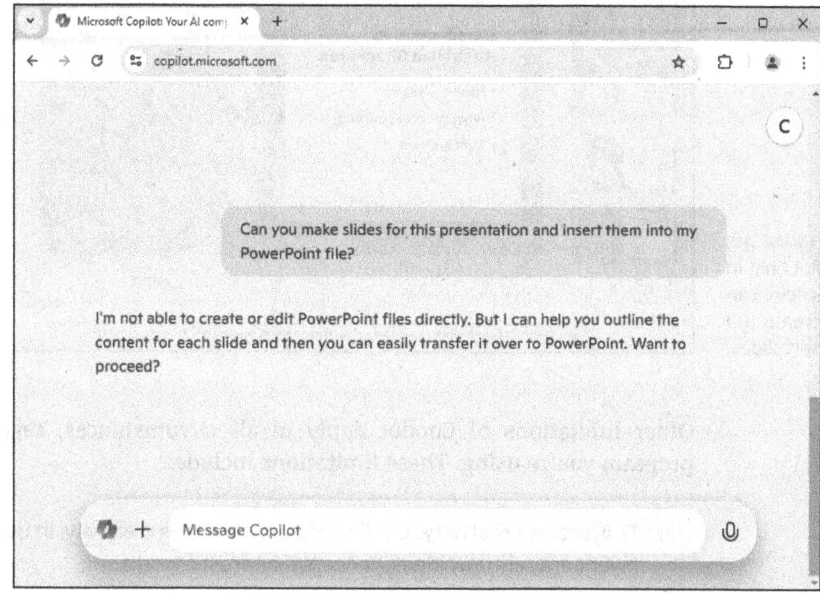

FIGURE 2-8: Copilot Chat can't create PowerPoint slides.

While this is true that `copilot.microsoft.com` can't currently interact with PowerPoint, it fails to mention that the Copilot Chat feature in PowerPoint can create and insert slides into a presentation, as shown in Figure 2-9.

Not only was Copilot able to create slides in PowerPoint, but it also decided what the topic of my presentation should be.

REMEMBER

Subscribing to Microsoft 365 Copilot activates the Copilot chatbot in each Office application and enables Copilot's built-in actions. This is explained more in Chapter 1. Creating PowerPoint slides and improving your presentation abilities with Copilot is covered in Chapter 8.

Figuring out and keeping track of Copilot's limitations in different situations can be confusing. The Copilot version in your browser can't do tasks that are specific to other applications, such as Word, Excel, or PowerPoint. You need a Microsoft 365 Copilot subscription for that.

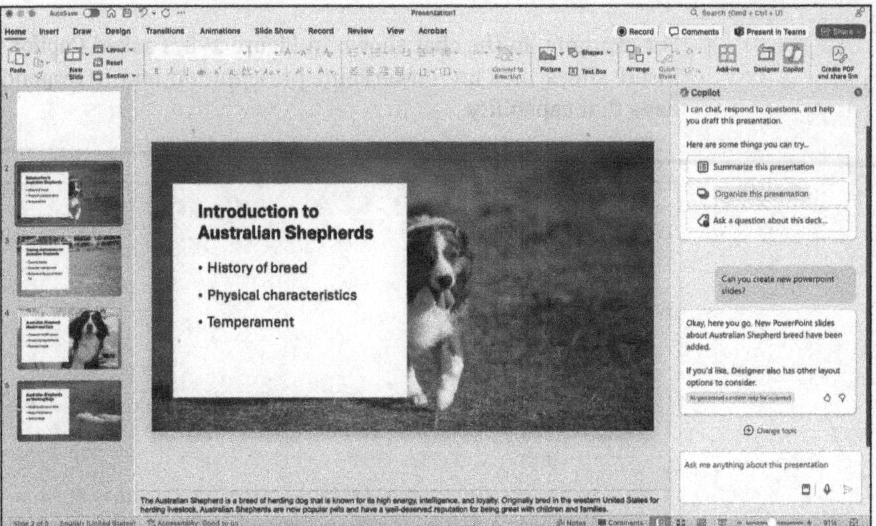

FIGURE 2-9: Copilot Chat in PowerPoint can create and insert slides.

Other limitations of Copilot apply in all circumstances, regardless of which program you're using. These limitations include:

- **Subjective creativity.** Copilot doesn't have true creativity, in that it can't invent entirely new ideas, concepts, or artistic works.
- **Human judgement.** LLMs haven't had the experience of being a human, and they don't possess intuition or judgement.
- **Physical actions.** Copilot can't mow your lawn, wash the dishes, or cook dinner.
- **Personal experiences.** Copilot can't talk about its personal experiences, memories, or feelings.
- **Predicting the future.** Copilot can make predictions based on patterns and data, but it can't predict anything with certainty.

Refining Your Prompts

The most important rule of prompt engineering is, "If at first you don't succeed, try, try again." With practice, you'll learn to write prompts that result in good responses on the first try, but you'll never know if the response you got was the best possible one until you refine it.

Homing in on better results

Prompt refinement is the process of starting with a generic zero-shot prompt, such as "Give me ideas for an article about AI" and incrementally turning it into a refined prompt, such as "As an expert artificial intelligence researcher and educator, provide ten ideas for short (500 word) articles that explain ways AI can be used in high school classrooms."

With prompt refinement, a generic zero-shot prompt is just the first step in gradually zeroing in on results that are more specific and better tuned to what it is you're trying to accomplish. Many times, the process of prompt refinement not only provides Copilot with the information it needs to do a better job, but it can also help you to clarify in your mind what you're looking for.

TIP

Prompt refinement doesn't just work well for generating text output, it's also an essential tool for generating music, computer code, and images.

Techniques for iterative prompt refinement

Specific techniques for refining prompts include:

- **Adding details.** The more detail you can provide to Copilot, the more it will understand what you're trying to achieve.
- **Adding a role.** Imagine what sort of person would be ideal to answer your prompt, then ask Copilot to adopt that role. Or, perhaps you'd like a different perspective. For example, while writing a book about using Copilot, you might tell Copilot to read a paragraph as if it were a complete newcomer to AI and respond with follow-up questions.
- **Specifying steps.** If your task for Copilot involves a series of steps, stating those steps explicitly will help the model better understand how to approach the problem.
- **Providing examples.** Giving an example or two of the types of responses you're looking for provides additional context to the model and can enable it to better align its output with what you need.

The danger of over-refinement

If you're painting a picture or adding seasoning to a sauce you're cooking, there comes a time when continuing to add more paint or salt starts to make the final product worse. In painting or cooking, it's difficult to go backward once you've reached that point. In prompt refinement, however, you have a complete history of each response Copilot gives you. If you find that adding more detail to your prompt results in worse responses, you can either stop refining or try a different approach.

Now that you've learned about the fundamentals of prompting Copilot Chat, including about the tools built into Copilot Chat that make prompting easier, the next chapter explains how to use your new prompting skills to improve your web browsing experience.

IN THIS CHAPTER

» Accessing Copilot in Edge

» Personalizing your Copilot experience

» Checking and using your sources

» Enhancing web searches

» Searching with plugins

» Visual searching

Chapter 3
Browsing with Copilot

Much has changed since the days when Microsoft's Internet Explorer (IE) browser was both the most hated web browser and the most widely used. Microsoft achieved both feats in large part due to the dominant market share of its Windows operating system, with which IE was tightly integrated.

Today, IE is officially retired. Microsoft Edge, the web browser created to replace it, is a state-of-the-art browser that works on macOS, Linux, smartphones, and tablets, and, of course, Windows. Microsoft Edge is now the second-most widely used browser, and it currently leads the pack in its support for AI-assisted browsing.

In this chapter, you learn how to use Copilot in Edge to gain insights into webpages you're browsing, translate text, summarize content, research and comparison shop, and even search using images.

You also learn about the privacy settings available in Edge, and why it's important to read the fine print of a terms of use document.

Integrating Copilot with Microsoft Edge

When you start the Edge browser on desktop and laptop computers, it features a Copilot icon in the upper-right corner of the interface. On mobile devices, the Copilot icon is in the middle of the bottom toolbar, as shown in Figure 3-1.

FIGURE 3-1: Edge on a smartphone, showing the Copilot icon.

Clicking the Copilot icon in a desktop browser opens a sidebar containing the Copilot chatbot. On mobile devices, Copilot opens in a window on top of the current webpage.

Whether in the mobile app or the desktop browser, there's much more than initially meets the eye contained in the Edge Copilot window, so let's take a tour of Copilot in Edge's features.

Learning the Edge integration features

Figure 3-2 shows the Copilot Edge sidebar in Windows 11.

REMEMBER

The interface you see may be different from mine due to differences between different operating systems and upgrades that happen between now and when you're reading this book.

As of this writing, the Copilot sidebar in Windows 11 is vastly different from the Copilot sidebar on macOS. Figure 3-3 shows the Copilot Edge sidebar in macOS.

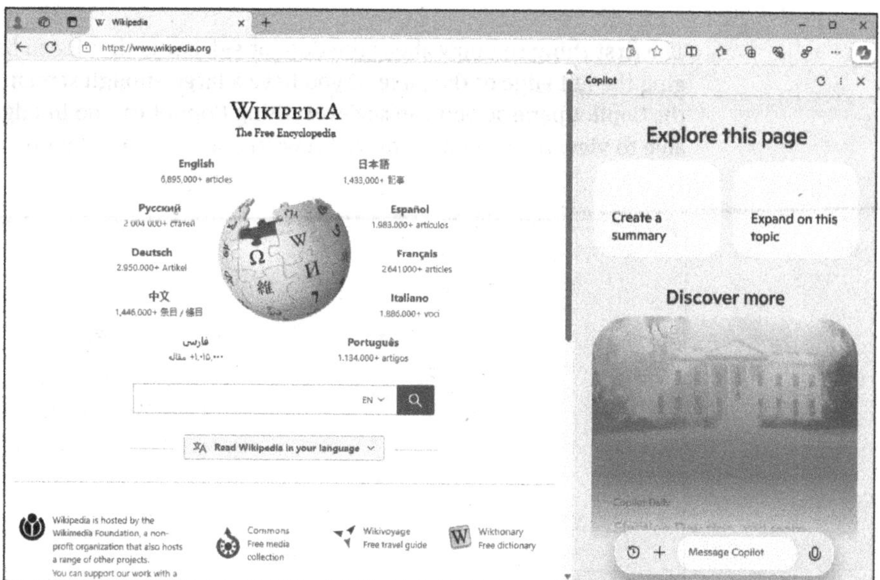

FIGURE 3-2: Copilot open in Edge.

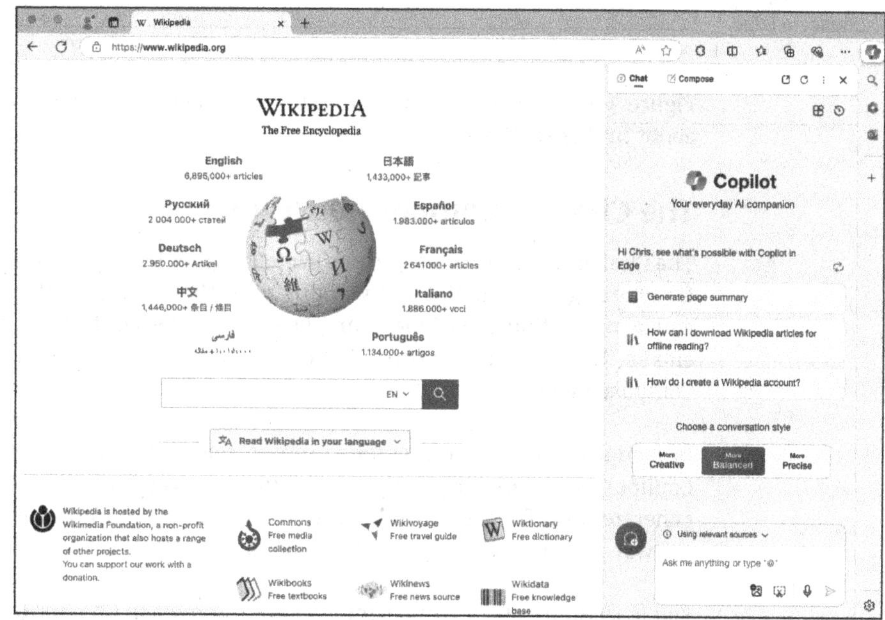

FIGURE 3-3: Copilot open in Edge on macOS.

For most of this chapter, I describe the Copilot sidebar in macOS, since it currently has more features than the Windows 11 Copilot sidebar and I suspect that some of the features that have recently been removed from the Windows 11 Copilot sidebar will return.

The first thing to know about the Copilot sidebar is that it can be resized by dragging the left edge of the pane. If you have a large enough screen, you should resize the Copilot pane so you can see everything Copilot can do in Edge while also being able to view the webpage you're browsing, as shown in Figure 3-4.

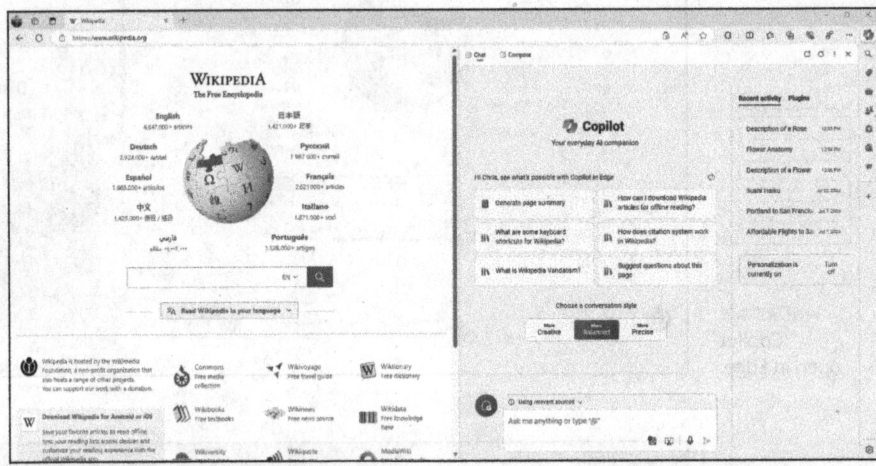

FIGURE 3-4: Resizing Copilot in Edge.

Figure 3-5 shows just the Copilot pane with labels for each of the features I talk about in this section.

The Chat vs. Compose buttons

The Chat and Compose tab buttons switch Copilot between a mode that's designed for chatting with Copilot and working with the content of the current webpage, and a mode that's designed for generating new content such as paragraphs, emails, lists, and blog posts. The default mode is Chat. Figure 3-6 shows the Compose mode.

In Compose mode you can enter a prompt, select the tone of the content you want Copilot to generate (or enter your own tone), select a format and length, and then generate a draft that you can copy to another program (such as your blogging software, your email program, or Microsoft Word).

You learn more about composing text with Copilot in Chapter 6.

The upper-right buttons

In the upper-right corner of Copilot is where you find the Open Link in New Tab, Refresh, and More Options buttons.

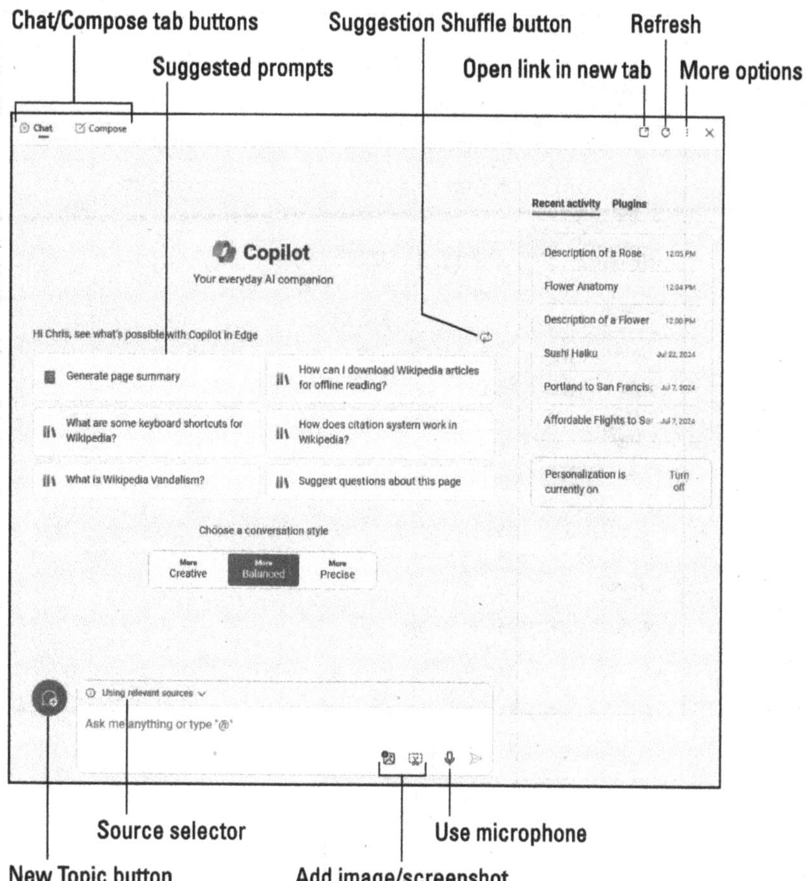

FIGURE 3-5: The main features of Copilot in Edge.

WARNING

The Open Link in New Tab may not be present in the Copilot sidebar in Windows 11.

If it's present, the first button in the upper-right is Open Link in New Tab. Refresh reloads the Copilot window. In my experience, this button is useful sometimes when Copilot experiences a glitch and displays an error instead of the expected interface. The More Options button expands when you click it, as shown in Figure 3-7.

The More Options menu allows you to access the Snooze and Unsnooze features, which temporarily disable and reenable Copilot in Edge, along with some preferences that are discussed in the section of this chapter titled "Customizing the Copilot Settings in Edge."

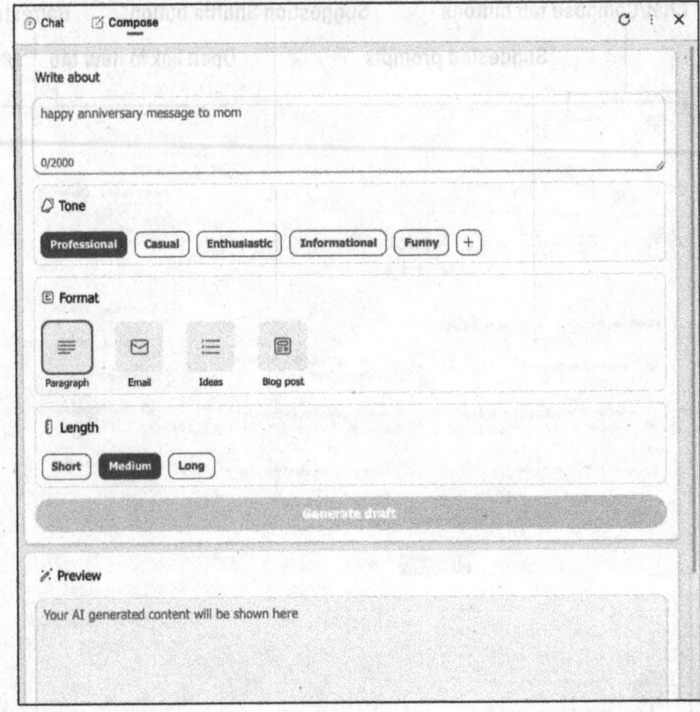

FIGURE 3-6: The Compose mode.

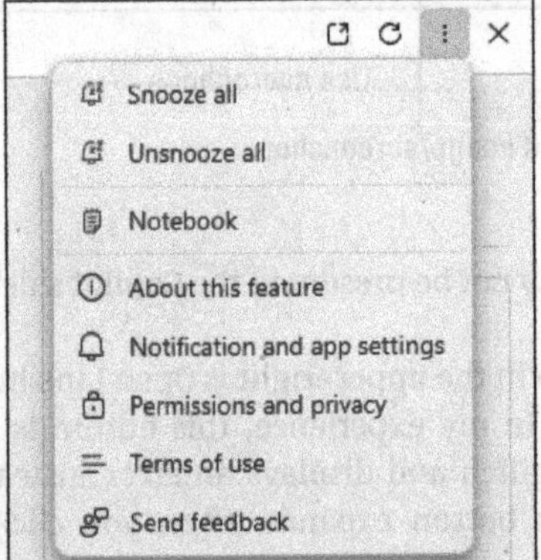

FIGURE 3-7: The More Options menu.

The Suggested Prompts section

The Suggested Prompts section isn't always present. When it is, it shows some prompts that you might consider submitting. The number of prompts will vary based on how large your Copilot window is. Some of the prompts are based on the content of the current webpage, and others, such as "Generate page summary," will be standard common prompts that you might want to do with any webpage.

You can click on any of the suggested prompts and Copilot will respond as if you typed and submitted the prompt yourself.

Above the suggested prompts is the Suggestion Shuffle button. Clicking this button will cause Copilot to generate and display new suggested prompts.

The Recent Activity and Plugins pane

If your Copilot sidebar is wide enough, the Recent Activity and Plugins pane will appear on the right. If the Recent Activity or Plugins pane doesn't appear on the right, you'll find icons for them at the top of the Copilot sidebar.

Recent Activity displays a Copilot-generated title for each of your recent conversations. (You can rename any of your previous conversations by clicking the pencil icon next to the conversation title.) Clicking on any of these conversations will make it the active conversation. When you return to a previous conversation, you can pick up where you left off, as if no time has passed. You can also delete a previous conversation by clicking the trash can icon next to its title.

The New Topic button

The New Topic button starts a new chat session with Copilot. To avoid confusing Copilot with unrelated subjects in the same chat, you should click the New Topic button any time you want to talk about or ask about something different. Starting a new topic frequently also has the benefit of keeping an organized history of things you've talked to Copilot about in your Recent Activity list.

In Windows 11, the Recent Activity list is named History. You can access your previous prompts by clicking the View History icon (a clock) on the homepage of the Windows 11 Copilot sidebar, as shown in Figure 3-8.

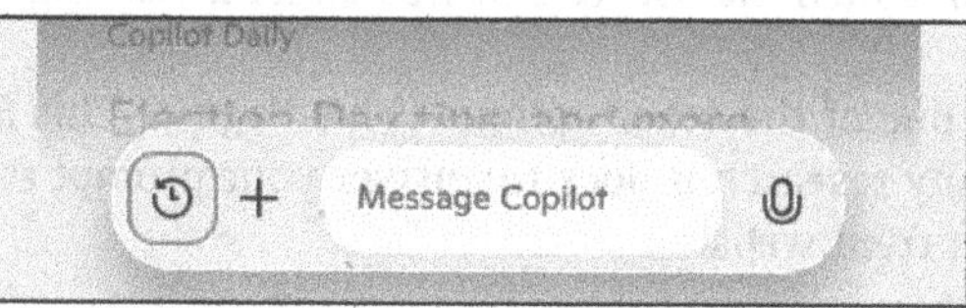

FIGURE 3-8: The View History icon in the Windows 11 Copilot sidebar.

Clicking the View History icon opens a list of your previous conversations. It also reveals the New Topic icon, as shown in Figure 3-9.

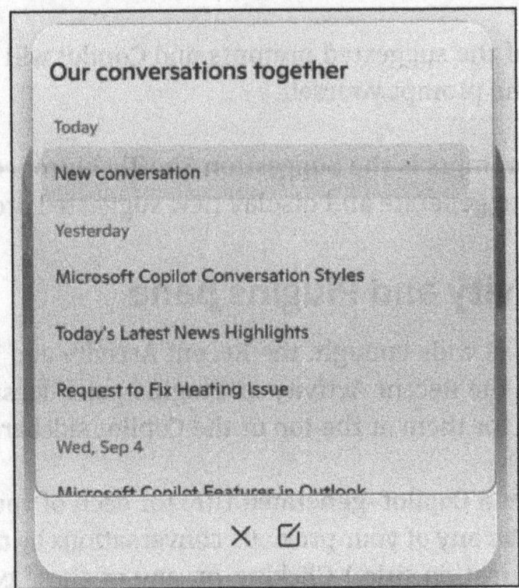

FIGURE 3-9: Viewing your history and the New Topic icon in the Windows 11 sidebar.

The Source Selector menu

The Source Selector drop-down menu is a small part of the Copilot interface in Edge, but it reveals the most powerful feature of Copilot's integration with Edge. When you click the Source Selector, three options appear:

- Relevant Sources
- This Page
- This Site

The default setting for the Source Selector is Relevant Sources. This setting leaves it up to Copilot to decide which sources to use to answer your prompt. This setting works well for general questions and is the default setting for the Windows 11 Copilot sidebar, in which the Source Selector menu is no longer present.

When you select one of the other options (This Page or This Site), you're telling Copilot to limit any research it does to answer your prompt to either the current webpage or the current website.

TIP

Limiting Copilot to the current page or website improves the accuracy and quality of its responses when your goal is to work with data about a specific topic. These settings can also be used for asking questions about your own documents (such as PDFs, text, or images) that aren't on the web and that Copilot would otherwise have no knowledge of.

The Add Image or Screenshot buttons

Adding an image or screenshot to your prompt uploads the image to Copilot so you can ask questions about it. More traditional search engines, such as Google and Bing, have long had a similar ability. Some tips about using this:

- If your goal is to identify an object or find out where an item can be purchased, using a traditional search engine may result in more accurate information or more complete information.
- If your goal is to generate a new image that resembles your picture, extract data from a screenshot, or get a written or spoken description of an item or scene, Copilot image prompting is the way to go.

The Use Microphone button

The Use Microphone button (or the Talk to Copilot button in Windows 11) enables voice prompting and voice responding. Voice prompting is covered in Chapter 2. When you click the Use Microphone button, the microphone icon changes colors to indicate that it's active. You can start speaking, and Copilot will detect when your prompt is complete and respond via voice.

Using Copilot plugins in Edge

Copilot plugins extend the capabilities of Copilot by allowing it to access data from third-party providers that it wouldn't otherwise be able to access. You can have up to three plugins active at any time, and you can change which plugins are active at any time as well.

WARNING

When you use plugins, Copilot shares your chat data with the third-party creators of the plugin. Each plugin has its own terms of use and privacy policy, which you should always read before you enable it. If you're not comfortable sharing your chat data with the company behind one of the plugins, don't enable that plugin.

Plugins are currently only available for personal Copilot accounts (not work or school accounts) and they aren't currently available in the latest version of Copilot in Windows 11. To see which plugins are available, click the Plugins icon at the top of the Copilot Chat sidebar, next to the Recent Activity icon. Or, if the Recent Activity tab is open, you can switch to the Plugins tab by clicking Plugins to the right of Recent Activity.

The available plugins include:

» **Search.** The Search plugin is active by default. It allows Copilot to use results from Bing while coming up with responses to your prompts. The Search plugin must be active to use any of the other plugins.

» **Instacart.** Instacart is a grocery delivery service. When the Instacart plugin is enabled, Copilot will include links to order items on Instacart in its responses when you ask about recipes or ingredients.

» **Kayak.** The Kayak plugin allows you to find and compare flights, lodging, and car rentals using Copilot.

» **Klarna.** Klarna is a comparison shopping site that shows products in a wide variety of categories and allows you to compare prices across different online stores. The Klarna plugin makes it possible for Copilot to use data from Klarna when answering questions about products and price options.

» **OpenTable.** The OpenTable plugin gives Copilot the ability to provide restaurant recommendations along with direct links to make reservations.

» **Phone.** The Phone plugin allows users with Android phones to access their contacts and send messages from Copilot.

» **Shop.** The Shop plugin integrates Copilot with Shopify to give it access to online shopping data. With the Shop plugin enabled, you can search for products, get information about products, and get links to buy products from within Copilot.

» **Suno.** Suno is an AI song generator. With the Suno plugin enabled, you can ask Copilot to create original songs based on your prompts.

Plugins are covered in more depth in Chapters 14 and 16.

Customizing the Copilot Settings in Edge

Copilot contains several settings that can be used to customize and improve your experience and the quality of your results. In this section, you learn about the customizable settings and how to use them to improve your Copilot browsing experience.

Personalizing the settings

When you enable personalization by clicking the link in your chat history, you're letting Copilot use your chat history to make Copilot's responses more personalized for you. For example, Copilot may learn your interests or hobbies from your previous chats and take those into consideration in the future when you ask questions.

To access the personalization setting in Windows 11, select Personalization from the three dots menu in the upper-right corner of the Copilot sidebar.

As of this writing, it's unclear whether personalization using browsing history and prior chats works in Edge or not. As you'll see, I was unable to detect any responses from Copilot that seemed personalized according to my browsing or chat history when I had personalization enabled. In fact, Copilot is adamant that it doesn't have access to chat history and only considers context from the current conversation.

WARNING

If personalization of Copilot based on your chat history or browsing history is currently working (or if it works at some point in the future), it represents a privacy issue that many people wouldn't be comfortable with. In this section, I cover Copilot's personalization based on browsing history and prior prompt history features in Edge. This is according to documentation and sources I was able to find about the feature. Check the website of this book or Microsoft's privacy policy (`https://privacy.microsoft.com/en-us/privacystatement`) for the most recent status of Copilot personalization.

WHAT DATA DOES COPILOT USE?

Here's what Microsoft's privacy policy has to say about how Copilot uses your data:

> In order to provide a relevant response, Copilot will use this prompt, along with the user's location, language, and similar settings, to formulate a helpful response. In some markets, authenticated users can choose to allow Copilot to have access to prior prompt history to better personalize the product.

If personalization is active, Copilot doesn't include everything it learns from your chat history in its personalization. Information that may be sensitive, such as personal information, is not used to personalize Copilot's responses.

Finding out exactly what Copilot's rules are for excluding sensitive or personal information is tricky. Your first instinct might be to ask Copilot itself. In my experience, however, this turned out to be useless. The first time I asked, Copilot told me it doesn't have access to chat history. When I found an article saying that you can enable personalization to give Copilot access to your chat history, Copilot changed its tune. It then insisted

(continued)

(continued)

that it doesn't have access to my browsing history. However, there is a setting in Edge, described in the next section, that allows you to give Copilot access to your browsing history.

It turns out that Copilot is not very good at talking about itself or its capabilities. You can find information on the encryption and other security measures Microsoft takes to protect your data, especially when used within a company or other organization at `https://learn.microsoft.com/en-us/copilot/privacy-and-protections`.

If, after reading this chapter, you want to delete your Copilot activity history or adjust your privacy settings and then clear any prior activity history, you can follow the steps in the following section, "Clearing your Copilot activity history."

WARNING

Assume that user prompts and data you upload to Copilot will be used to train the LLM behind Copilot. Never reveal your (or anyone else's) personal data (such as addresses or phone numbers) or anything else to Copilot that you wouldn't want to become public knowledge.

Clearing your Copilot activity history

If you want to delete any information Microsoft has stored about your prior interactions with Copilot, you can do that by logging into your Microsoft account at `https://account.microsoft.com`.

The steps for clearing your activity history are slightly different depending on whether you're logging in with an account that's part of an organization (such as a school or company) or whether you have a personal account.

Clearing your personal account history

If you have a personal account, follow these steps to clear your Copilot activity history:

1. **Open the Microsoft Privacy Dashboard at `https://account.microsoft.com/account/privacy`.**
2. **Click the Sign In button and go through the steps to sign in (if you're not already signed in).**

   Once you're signed in, you'll see your Microsoft Account homepage, as shown in Figure 3-10.

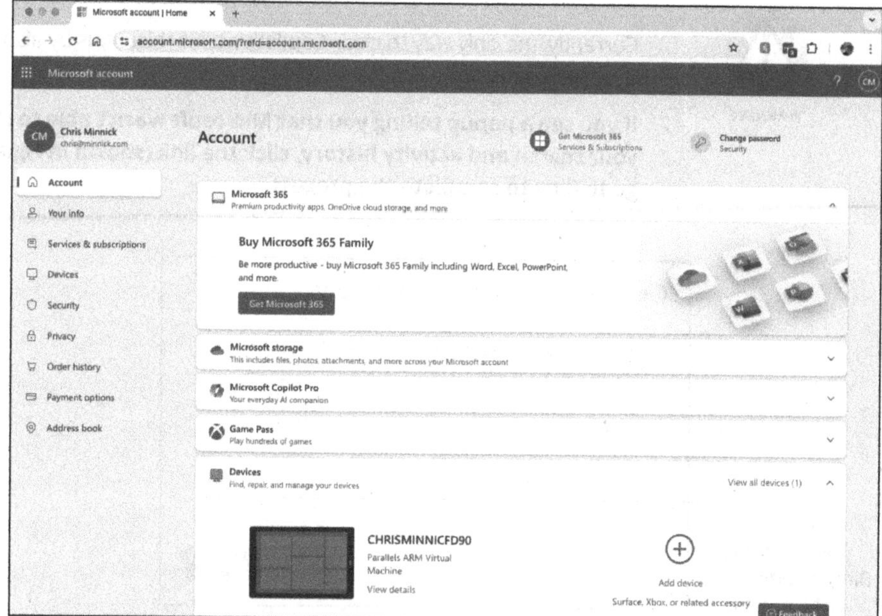

FIGURE 3-10: The Microsoft account homepage.

3. **Click the Privacy link on the left navigation bar to get to the privacy dashboard.**
4. **Find the link for Browsing and Search and click it.**
5. **Scroll down the page to the Copilot Activity History section.**
6. **Click the Clear All Copilot Activity History and Search History link.**

   Next, you'll see a warning message, as shown in Figure 3-11. Read through this information and then click the Clear button if you're sure.

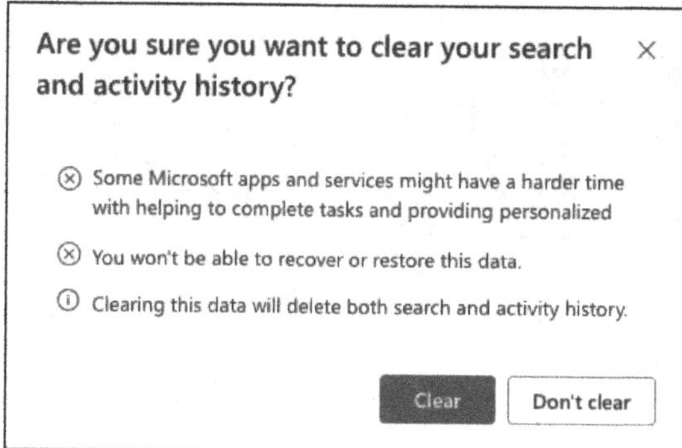

FIGURE 3-11: Copilot confirms that you want to clear your history.

WARNING

Currently, the only way to clear Copilot's activity history is by also clearing your Bing search history.

7. **If you see a popup telling you that Microsoft wasn't able to clear all of your search and activity history, click the link (shown in Figure 3-12) to go to Bing to complete the process.**

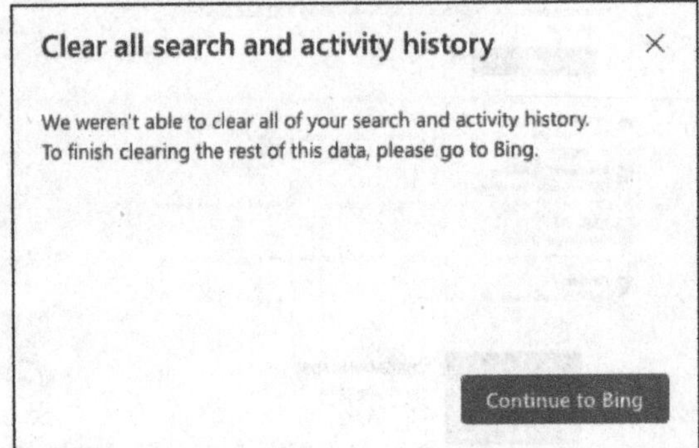

Clear all search and activity history
We weren't able to clear all of your search and activity history.
To finish clearing the rest of this data, please go to Bing.
Continue to Bing

FIGURE 3-12: Redirecting to Bing to complete the process.

8. **Once you're logged into Bing, click on the three bars icon in the upper right and select Search History, as you can see in Figure 3-13.**

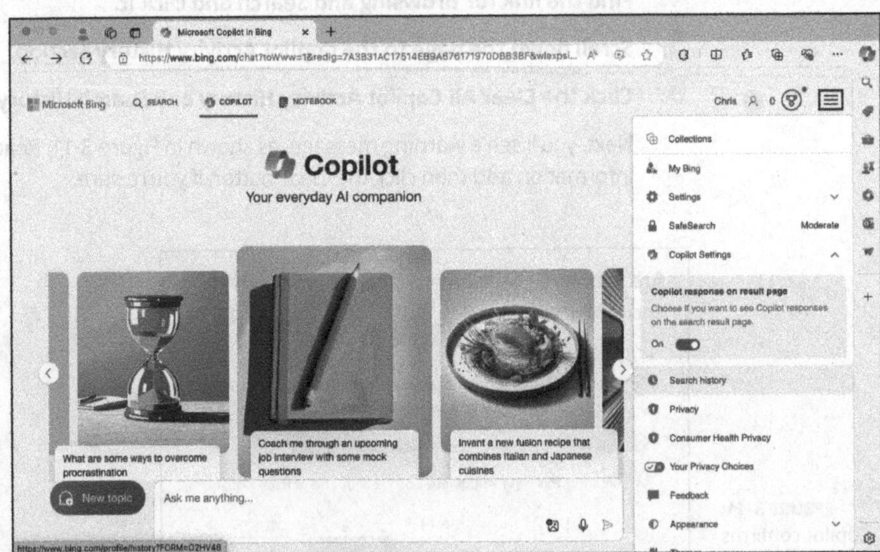

FIGURE 3-13: Going to the Search History screen in Bing.

9. **Click Clear All on the Search History screen.**

Clearing your work or school account history

Follow these steps to clear your Copilot activity history if you have a Microsoft account for work or school.

1. **Log in to the Privacy Dashboard at `https://account.microsoft.com/account/privacy` using your work or school Microsoft account.**
2. **Click the Settings & Privacy link on the left navigation bar.**

   You'll see the Settings & Privacy page, as shown in Figure 3-14.

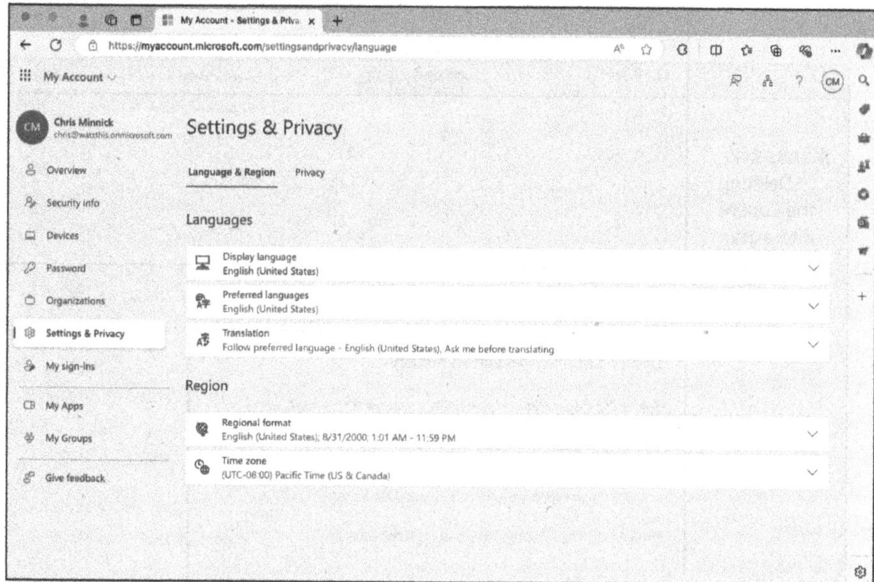

FIGURE 3-14: The Settings & Privacy page.

3. **Click the Privacy tab.**
4. **Expand the Copilot Interaction History box, as shown in Figure 3-15, and click the Delete History button.**
5. **A popup window will appear, similar to the one in Figure 3-16, where you can select the Copilot interaction history you want to delete.**
6. **Click the Delete button and you'll see a confirmation message, as shown in Figure 3-17.**

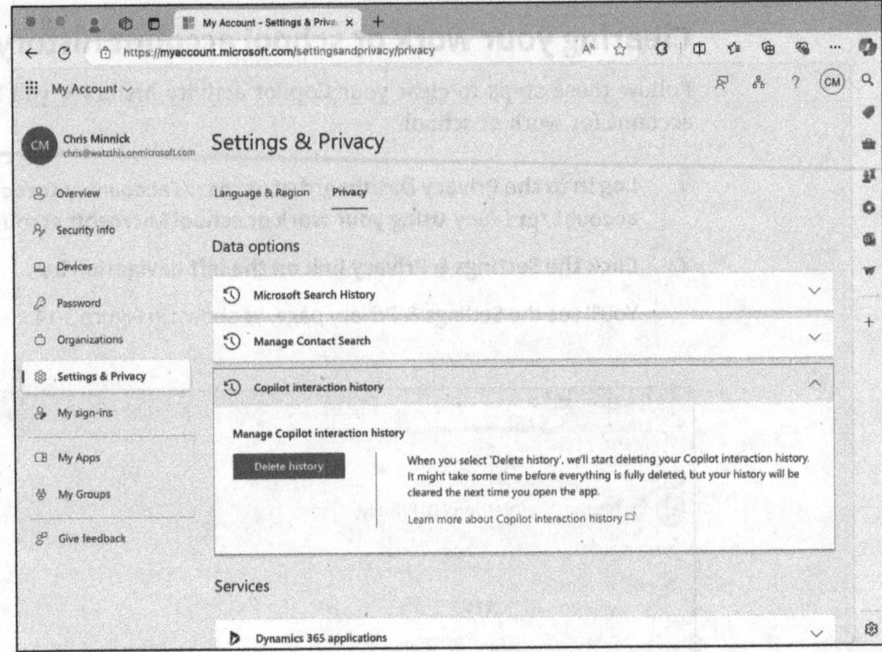

FIGURE 3-15: Deleting the Copilot interaction history.

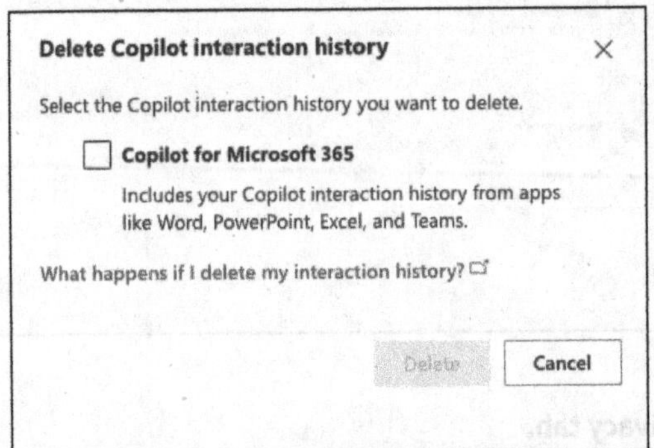

FIGURE 3-16: Selecting the history you want to delete.

Congratulations! You've successfully cleared your chat history. While it's not necessary to clear your chat history every day, it's a good practice to get in the habit of clearing out the old stuff every so often.

Managing preferences and settings

You can access settings of Copilot in Edge by clicking the three dots menu in the upper-right corner, as shown in Figure 3-18. Note that this is under the vertical three dots menu that's inside the Copilot pane, and not the horizontal three dots menu that's above it in the browser toolbar.

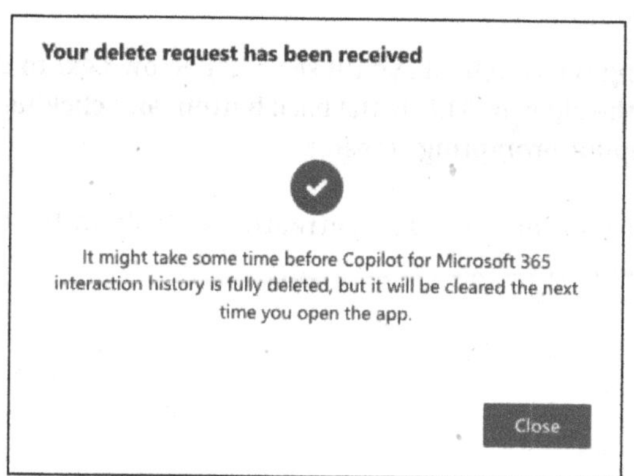

FIGURE 3-17: Your history has been deleted.

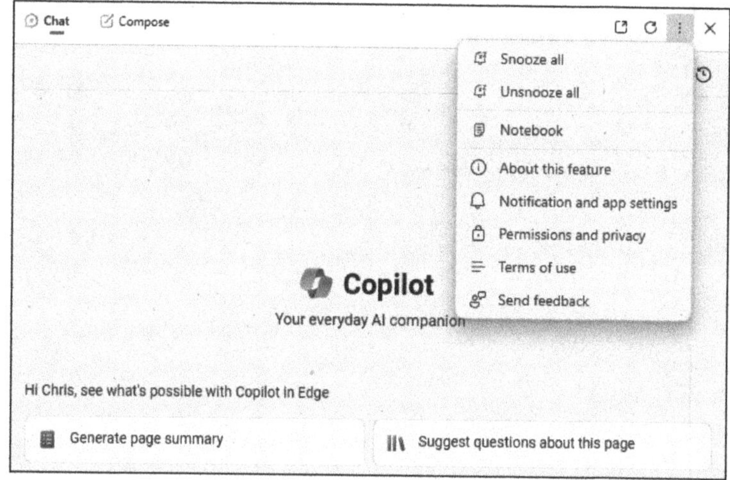

FIGURE 3-18: Accessing Copilot settings in Edge.

There are a few important settings to be aware of here, and the following sections cover the most important ones.

Snooze All/Unsnooze All

The Snooze All link temporarily pauses Copilot. When snoozed, Copilot won't read the contents of the open web browser. To resume having Copilot read the current webpage and suggest prompts based on it, click Unsnooze All.

Notebook

Selecting the Notebook link opens the Notebook prompting area, as shown in Figure 3-19. Notebook is good for writing more lengthy prompts and generating larger amounts of content.

TIP

When you're using the Notebook, you'll see a left arrow next to the word *Notebook* in the header of the sidebar. This is the back button, and clicking it will return you to the default Copilot prompting screen.

WARNING

The Notebook prompting area isn't currently available in the Copilot sidebar in Windows 11.

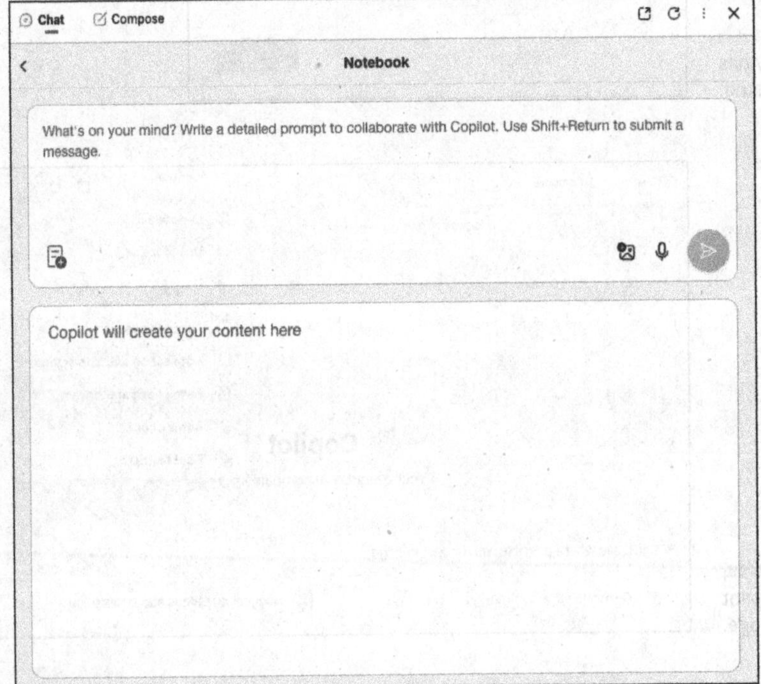

FIGURE 3-19: Accessing the Notebook view.

The differences between Copilot's various editor views are covered in more detail in Chapter 6.

About This Feature

The About This Feature link brings up a short description of what Copilot can do. It also includes a link to go to the Copilot Frequently Asked Questions (FAQ) at `https://www.microsoft.com/en-us/microsoft-copilot/learn/`.

App and Notification Settings

Selecting the App and Notification Settings link opens the App and Notification Settings screen, which is shown in Figure 3-20.

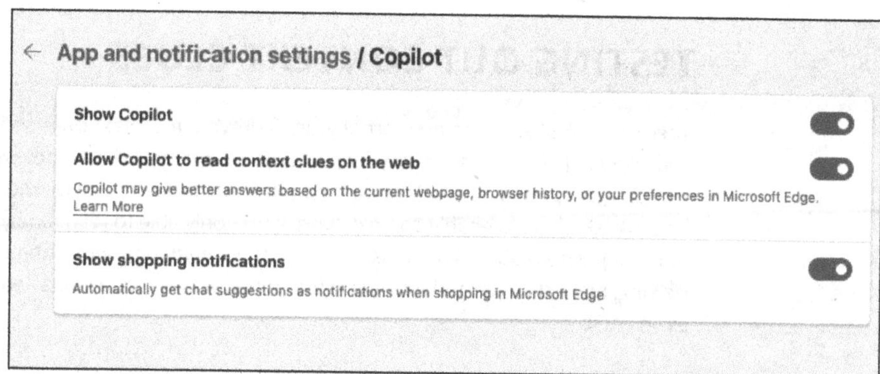

FIGURE 3-20: App and Notification Settings.

In the Windows 11 Copilot sidebar, you can access the App and Notifications Settings screen by choosing the Settings link from the vertical three dots menu.

This settings screen currently has three options in macOS and two options in Windows 11:

- **Show Copilot.** This controls whether the Copilot icon appears in the upper-right corner of the browser.
- **Allow Copilot to Read Context Clues on the Web.** This setting controls whether you want Copilot to use your conversation history, browsing history, recent chats, and the contents of the current webpage as context. Compared to the other settings on the Copilot sidebar app settings, this is the big one.

  If you switch the Context Clues setting to off, Copilot will prompt you to allow it to read context clues the next time (and every time) you ask it to do something that requires context clues, as shown in Figure 3-21. Saying yes just once to its question will turn this switch back on.
- **Show Shopping Notifications.** The last option on the Copilot sidebar app settings is for whether you want Copilot to send you notifications suggesting chats while you're shopping in Microsoft Edge. This option currently doesn't exist in Windows 11. With this setting enabled, Copilot will generate messages about what you're shopping for that appear in the toolbar with the help of the Microsoft shopping sidebar. These messages generally say things like "Price has recently increased" or "You have the best price!" These seem harmless enough, and disabling this option likely doesn't suppress Microsoft's ability to use your anonymized browsing and shopping history to display advertising to you. That preference is controlled by the privacy settings within Edge.

TIP

You can access the Edge privacy settings by selecting Settings from the horizontal three dots menu in the Edge toolbar, then clicking on Privacy, Search, and Services in the left toolbar.

TESTING OUT CONTEXT CLUES

There doesn't seem to be any sort of granularity to the context clues setting — either you allow Copilot access to everything it can access, or you deny it access. When I asked it to suggest questions about the current page I was viewing and clicked Don't Allow when it asked me to enable context clues, it was only able to respond by using results from Bing. As a result, its response didn't contain anything specific about the page I was viewing, but just suggested formats in which people write questions and answers (such as an FAQ).

Every subsequent prompt I gave to Copilot caused it to open the popup asking for permission to use context clues.

When I subsequently asked it to summarize the current page, but I denied it access to context clues, it gave me links to tools that can be used to generate summaries of content.

Personalization and context clues are unrelated in Copilot. Context clues gives Copilot access to your browser window and history. Personalization gives Copilot access to your chat history.

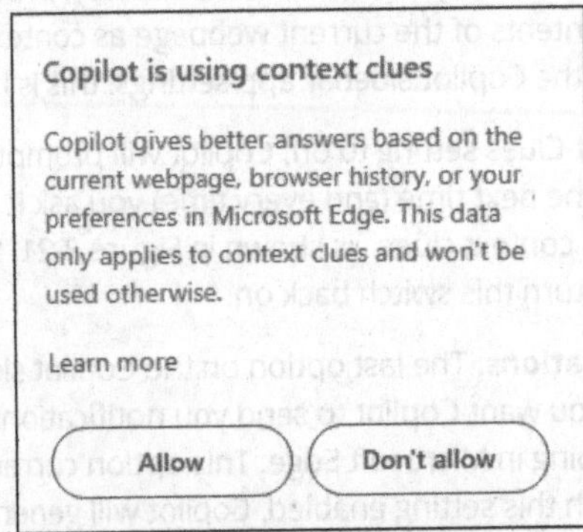

Copilot is using context clues
Copilot gives better answers based on the current webpage, browser history, or your preferences in Microsoft Edge. This data only applies to context clues and won't be used otherwise.
Learn more
Allow
Don't allow

FIGURE 3-21: Enabling context clues.

Permissions and Privacy

Selecting Permissions and Privacy from Copilot's vertical three dots menu displays a temporary popup window above the Copilot sidebar. This contains privacy and permissions information about the Copilot sidebar itself. When I tried it, it displayed the same message no matter what webpage I had open or even if I didn't have a webpage open, as shown in Figure 3-22.

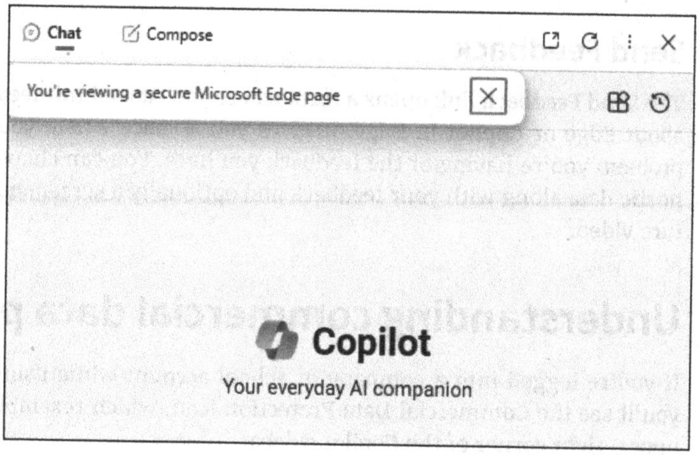

FIGURE 3-22: You are viewing a secure Microsoft Edge page.

Terms of Use

The Terms of Use link spells out the agreement between yourself and Microsoft that you agree to when you use Copilot. I recommend you read the entire agreement, but some of the most important points in it include:

- Data you upload may be reviewed by AI as well as by people.
- Conversations with Copilot may include advertising.
- Microsoft does not claim ownership of anything you input into Copilot or anything generated by Copilot. However, by using Copilot you are granting Microsoft and its affiliated companies an unlimited license to copy, distribute, transmit, display, perform, reproduce, edit, translate, and reformat your prompts, creations, and any other content you provide to Copilot.
- You agree not to engage in activity that is harmful to you or others.
- You agree not to engage in activities that may be harmful to Copilot.
- You agree not to use Copilot to commit fraud.
- You agree not to use Copilot to create or share inappropriate content.
- You agree not to do anything illegal with Copilot.
- Microsoft may block your prompts that violate the code of conduct or restrict your use of Copilot.

Send Feedback

The Send Feedback link opens a form where you can submit feedback to Microsoft about Edge or Copilot in Edge. It gives you a space where you can describe the problem you're having or the feedback you have. You can choose to submit diagnostic data along with your feedback and optionally a screenshot or a screen capture video.

Understanding commercial data protection

If you're logged into a company or school account while using Copilot in Edge, you'll see the Commercial Data Protection icon, which resembles a shield, in the upper-right corner of the Copilot sidebar.

Commercial data protection refers to an added level of security that's enabled for companies and schools in order to comply with regulations that apply to companies and to protect company data. When commercial data protection is enabled, the user's chat data and search history isn't retained and additional encryption is used while data is in transit between Microsoft and the user's computer.

Go to `https://learn.microsoft.com/en-us/copilot/privacy-and-protections` to learn more about commercial data protection.

Using Edge's Built-In Actions

Copilot in Edge has built-in actions that can control and customize certain aspects of the Edge browser, perform specific types of searches, and more.

TIP

These actions no longer work in the Windows 11 Edge Copilot sidebar. At the time of this writing, they do work in Edge in macOS.

To use built-in Copilot actions (whether in Edge, Microsoft 365, or elsewhere), it's important to type the words of the action exactly right. Unlike other prompts, where Copilot will generally understand your meaning even if you make spelling errors or ask the same question in a slightly different way, running actions is a more precise process.

For example, Figure 3-23 shows Copilot's response when I prompted it with "turn on dark mode."

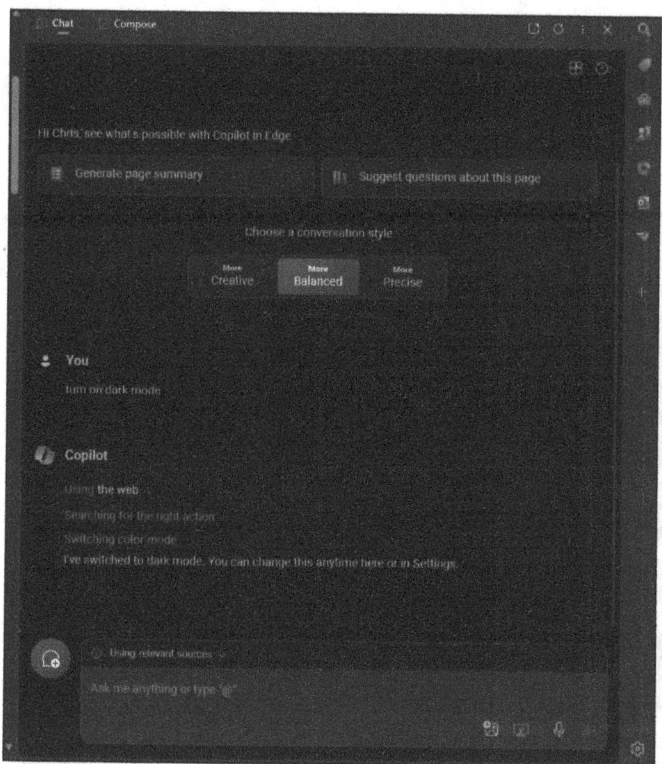

FIGURE 3-23: Using dark mode.

Figure 3-24, on the other hand, shows what happens when you type an action differently. Copilot still understands what you want to do, but it doesn't know that it can do it for you.

Examples of built-in actions include:

- **Switch color mode.** Use the "turn on dark mode" or "turn on light mode" action to change the background of your browser to a dark color and the text to a light color.
- **Import passwords.** The "import my passwords from [browser]" action should cause Copilot to import your passwords from the browser you specify. Although this feature is documented, I haven't been able to make it work yet.
- **Rearrange tabs.** Use the "turn on vertical tabs" and "turn on horizontal tabs" actions to switch between displaying your browser tabs vertically along the left side of your browser and displaying your tabs horizontally across the top of the screen.

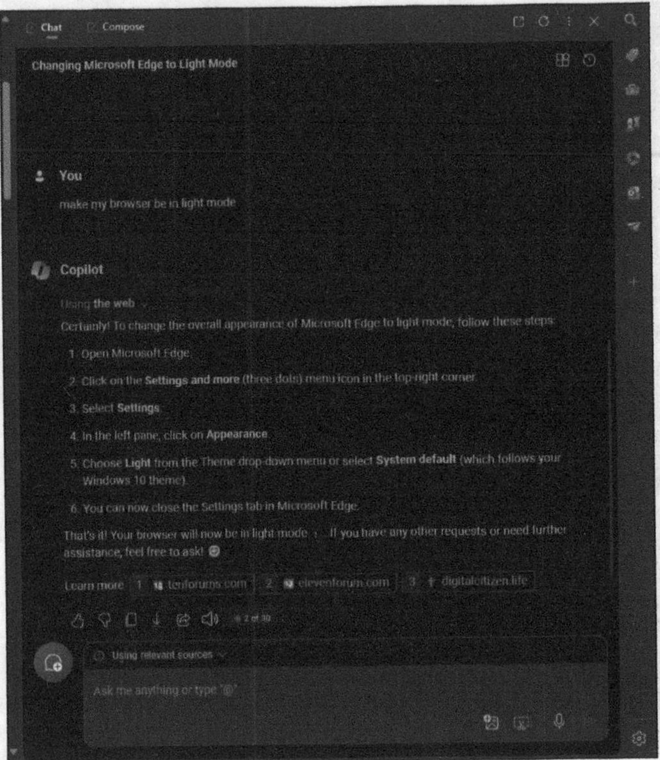

FIGURE 3-24: Actions require a specific phrase.

- **Movie streaming.** You can ask Copilot to find out where you can stream a movie by using the "stream the movie [insert movie title]" action.
- **Tab organization.** You can ask Copilot to organize your tabs, such as by saying "group my tabs related to [topic]." For example, if you regularly have more than 30 tabs open for fear that if you close one you'll forget what you were working on, try telling Copilot, "Group my tabs by subject." Copilot will then create a suggested grouping for your tabs and display it to you for your approval, as shown in Figure 3-25.

REMEMBER

Integration of an AI chatbot in your web browser has the potential to make anything you do in a web browser more effective — from reading the news to composing blog posts and much more.

Integration between Copilot and Edge also has the potential to expose your private data to advertisers and hackers. For that reason, it's important to know what privacy and security options are built into Copilot and Edge.

In the next chapter, you learn about going mobile with Copilot.

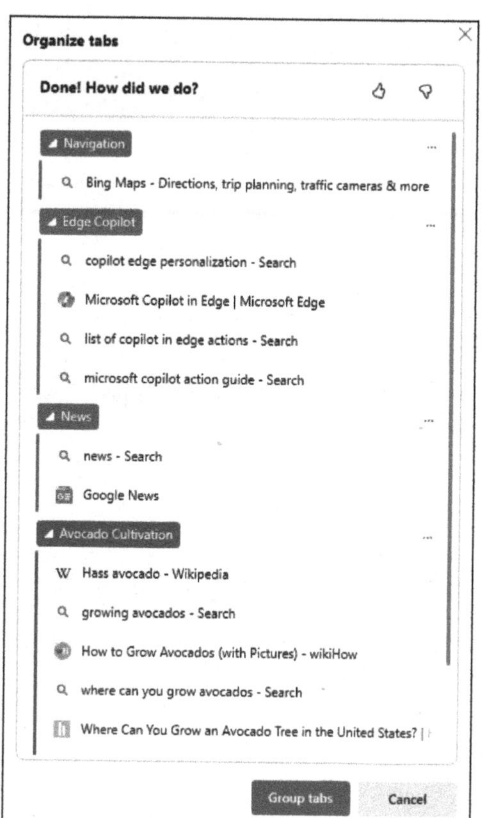

FIGURE 3-25: Copilot's suggested tab groups.

IN THIS CHAPTER

» Getting the Copilot app

» Setting up the app

» Using Copilot on the go

» Making the best use of Copilot on your phone

Chapter 4
Going Mobile with Copilot

If you have an Android smartphone or an iPhone, you already have access to Google Assistant or Apple Siri. With virtual assistants that can answer questions and control various aspects of your phone (such as playing music, getting directions, or sending messages), you might wonder why you need Copilot on your phone too.

In this chapter, you learn how to install and use the Copilot mobile app on your smartphone, what Copilot can do on mobile devices, and how to make the best use of this powerful and mobile AI assistant.

Getting Started with the Copilot App

The Copilot app is free to download, and the basic version of Copilot is free to use on mobile devices. Installing the Copilot app is as simple as installing any other app. If you're already comfortable with installing apps on your phone, you can search for Microsoft Copilot in the App Store (in iOS) or Google Play (on Android), install it, and skip the rest of this section.

If you'd like a step-by-step walk-through for installing Copilot on your phone, proceed to either the Android installation guide or the iOS installation guide.

Installing Copilot on your iPhone or iPad

The first step to installing Copilot is to find the correct Copilot app. When you open the App Store and search for Microsoft Copilot, you'll see a large number of results. I counted 41 apps named Copilot, ranging from other AI chatbots, to navigation tools, to an app for buying and selling logs.

The app you want, Microsoft Copilot, should be the first or second result, as shown in Figure 4-1.

Tap the Get button to download Copilot to your iPhone or iPad. The progress circle will begin to fill up and you'll see an Open button when Copilot has finished installing.

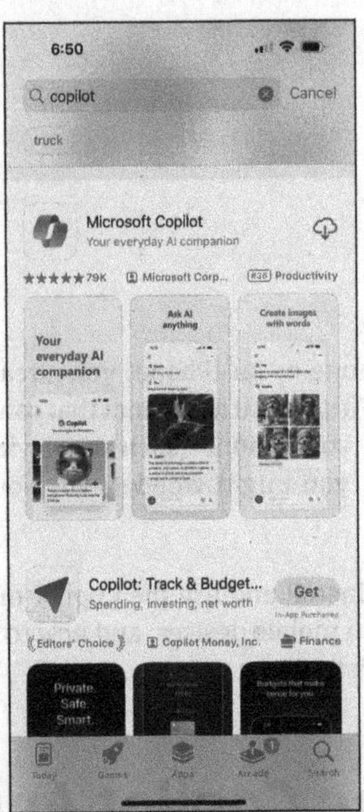

FIGURE 4-1: Finding the right Copilot.

The first time you open Copilot on your iPhone or iPad, you'll see the welcome screen shown in Figure 4-2. From the welcome screen, you can choose to continue without signing in, or you can sign in with your existing Microsoft account.

If you choose to proceed without logging in, Copilot will ask you for your name and give you an opportunity to select the voice you want Copilot to use when it's in voice mode.

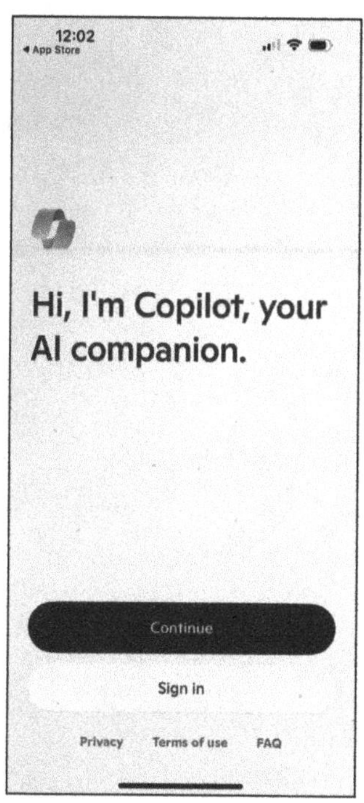

FIGURE 4-2: Copilot's welcome screen.

If you log in using the same account you use at `https://copilot.microsoft.com` or in the Copilot sidebar in Edge, Copilot will use the same settings you created when you first logged in to Copilot, but it will ask you to choose a voice again.

Next, you'll be asked whether you want Copilot to use your location. To allow location access, tap Allow While Using App. You'll also be asked whether you want to allow Copilot to track your activities across other companies' apps and websites. According to Microsoft, this data sharing is necessary to connect your phone to your PC to give you more personalized results. Choosing Ask App Not to Track won't prevent you from using Copilot, but it may limit some of the app's ability to share data with Copilot on your computer.

By default, Copilot will ask to access your precise location, as shown in Figure 4-3. If you'd rather not give Copilot access to your precise location, you can change this setting by clicking the Precise: On link.

After you make your choices about location and data sharing, you'll see the home screen, which is similar to the screen you see at `https://copilot.microsoft.com`. See Figure 4-4.

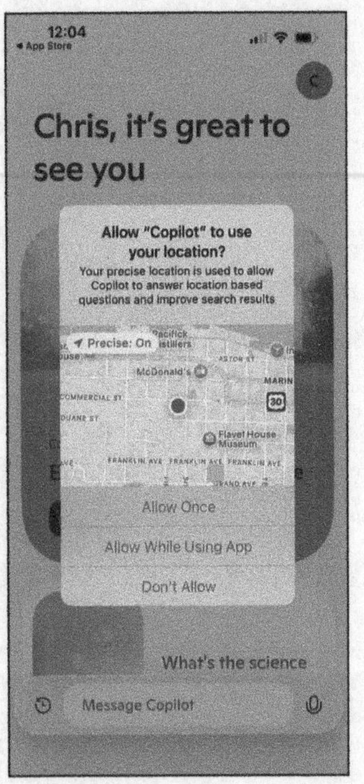

FIGURE 4-3: Copilot asks for your precise location.

FIGURE 4-4: The Copilot home screen.

Congratulations, you've installed Copilot on your iPhone or iPad! Skip to the section titled "Initial setup and configuration" to start finding out what you can do with it.

Installing Copilot on your Android phone

Installation of Copilot on an Android phone or tablet is just as simple as installing any app. When you open the Google Play app and search for Copilot, the top result (perhaps underneath an ad) will be Microsoft Copilot, as shown in Figure 4-5.

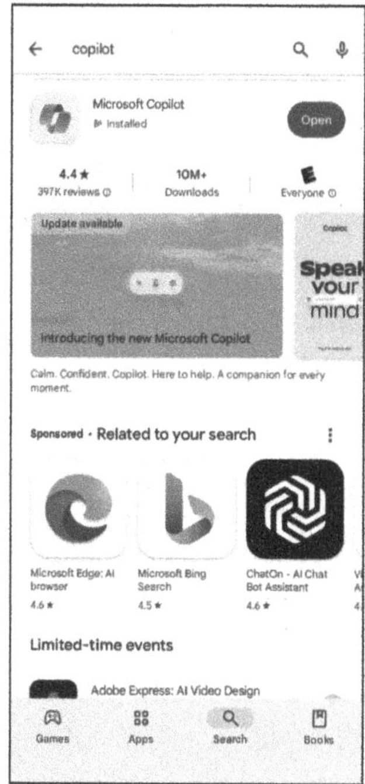

FIGURE 4-5: Microsoft Copilot in Google Play.

Tap the Install button and Copilot will be installed.

The first time you launch Copilot on Android, you'll be asked whether you want to give Copilot access to your location. Allowing this access is optional, but if you do allow it, you can take advantage of some of the more interesting and useful capabilities of Copilot on mobile phones. You can read more about what Copilot can do with your location in the section of this chapter called "Trying location-specific prompts."

Initial setup and configuration

Like the browser-based version of Copilot, the mobile app allows you to submit a limited number of prompts and puts strict limits on the length of conversations when you're not logged in. To lift these restrictions, tap the Sign In button in the upper-left corner of the app and log in using the same login you used to log in to the Copilot website and browser sidebar.

Figure 4-4 shows what the logged in Copilot app looks like on iOS using a personal Microsoft account. Figure 4-6 shows what it looks like with a work or school account.

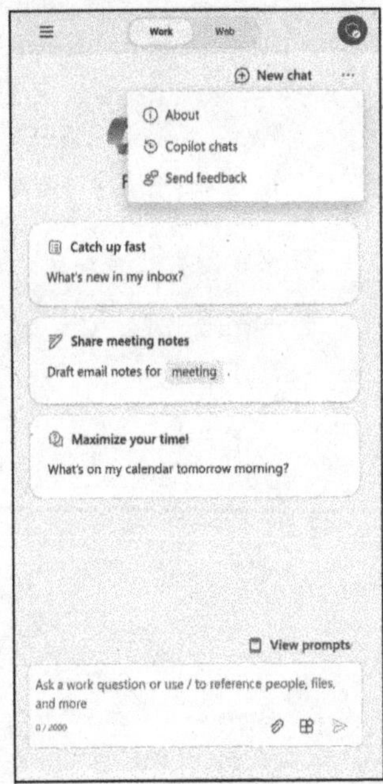

FIGURE 4-6: The Copilot app when logged in with a work or school account.

Notice that the work/school interface has a switch at the top to switch between Web and Work. This indicates that the account also has access to Microsoft 365 Copilot, which you learn about in Part 2.

For the rest of this chapter, I mostly use the free and logged-in version of Copilot with a personal account.

Using Copilot Pro

The Copilot mobile app contains a link to sign up for a 1-month free trial of Copilot Pro. Copilot Pro gives you access to a more recent (and better) AI model than the free version and access to new features before anyone else gets them. It also removes restrictions that may happen with the free version when you're using Copilot during times of high demand.

WARNING

If you choose to sign up for the free trial, note that it will automatically convert to a paid membership (currently $20/month) after the trial. If you're not ready to sign up for Copilot Pro, you can dismiss the advertisement for it by tapping the x in the upper-right corner.

There are limits on usage of the latest model with the free version of Copilot. After you've exceeded the limit, you can wait a day until you have access to it again, or you can upgrade to Copilot Pro.

TIP

Microsoft Copilot is currently a leader in allowing free access to the latest GPT models. Whether this continues to be true in the future remains to be seen. However, at this point, using the free version of Copilot on mobile or in your browser is a great way to try out the most advanced AI chatbot model available without paying a monthly fee.

Using the Unique Mobile Functionalities

Although the features of the Copilot mobile app are the same as those of the web or desktop versions of Copilot, the mobile app has some unique uses and functionalities since it can take advantage of the mobility and capabilities of your smartphone or tablet. Some of the things you can do with the mobile app include prompting with the camera, using your location, and sharing Copilot's responses via your messaging app or social media apps.

The first difference you'll notice between the mobile app and the desktop version of Copilot is that the mobile app seems to have less functionality and fewer options than the desktop version. When you dig around a bit, though, you'll find that the mobile app can do almost everything the desktop app can do but some features and options on the mobile app are hidden behind menus.

Accessing your chat history

To access your Copilot Chat history in the mobile app, tap the Copilot logo in the prompt text input area to return to the home screen. On the home screen, tap the clock icon. A list of your previous conversations will appear.

If you're using a work or school account to access Copilot, the Chat History link is labeled Copilot Chats and appears under the three dots menu in the upper-right corner of the screen.

Prompting with the camera

AI image search has been around for a while. For example, you can upload images to Google and it will show you similar pictures from its image search. This type of searching is called *reverse image searching*. Other image search apps, such as Seek by iNaturalist, allow you to identify plants and animals you take pictures of.

Copilot's image prompting doesn't exactly compete with either Google's reverse image search or iNaturalist Seek's capabilities. Instead, it uses the creativity of Copilot along with its ability to search the web to attempt to tell you anything you might want to know about an image, or even to make up a story about an image, as in Figure 4-7.

1:35
Tell me a story about this picture.
In a cozy backyard, four chickens rule the roost in their own little kingdom. The two black chickens, perhaps the leaders, keep an eye out from their perch on the back of a wicker chair. Meanwhile, the brown and yellow chickens nestle snugly on the chair's seat, maybe swapping tales of their latest adventures.
The whole scene is like a snapshot of rural tranquility, with a charming shed in the background and greenery all around. It's
Message Copilot

FIGURE 4-7: Asking Copilot about an image.

Prompting with your phone's camera opens up many possibilities for identifying objects, translating text, learning, and satisfying your curiosity as you move around the world.

The capabilities of image prompting can sometimes be surprising. Figure 4-8 shows a picture I took of a message written in Braille. Copilot was able to analyze the image and tell me what it says, at least in part.

WARNING

Keep in mind that even though Copilot's answer to my request for Braille translation is confident, that doesn't mean it's any more accurate than its confident statement about what my chickens are doing in Figure 4-7. Always remember that Copilot's main skill is creativity and conversing. It's not guaranteed to be accurate, so you should always verify with a trusted source in any situation where accuracy matters.

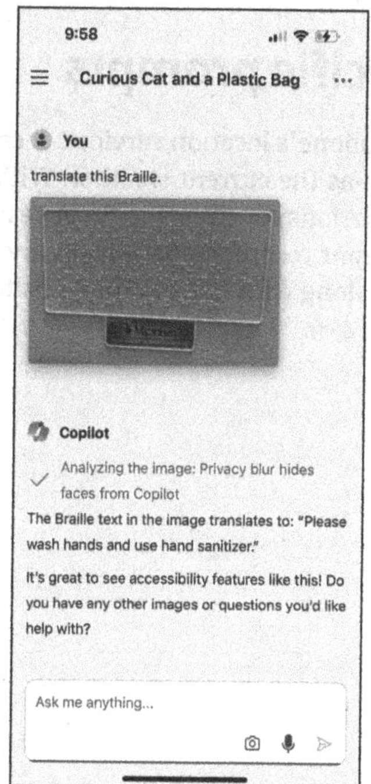

FIGURE 4-8: Using Copilot to read Braille.

One limitation of camera prompting (at least currently) is that you can't submit video or audio files. Even when you're uploading from your device's photo library, the mobile app restricts you to only uploading still images.

Audio prompting

As with the desktop and web versions of Copilot, you can submit prompts to the Copilot mobile app using your voice. As you speak your prompt, Copilot transcribes what you say. When it detects a pause, your prompt will be submitted as text to Copilot.

In my experiments with audio prompting, Copilot recognized and transcribed simple and deliberately spoken prompts very well. With the latest updates to Copilot, it can also respond quite well to more informal speech.

TIP

I attempted to use Copilot as a language translation tool by speaking to it in German. It might just be that my German isn't very good, but Copilot only recognized "Guten Tag" and then attempted to transcribe everything else I said in English. I expect that a future version of the Copilot mobile app will have the ability to record and interpret audio, which will make it useful for speech translation, but at this point it's nowhere near as good as a dedicated translation tool, such as Microsoft Translator or Google Translate.

Trying location-specific prompts

Because Copilot has access to your phone's location services, it can be used to find location-specific information, such as the current weather. Without the addition of plugins, it can make recommendations for things to do or restaurants to check out. When I prompted it for restaurant recommendations in my current location, it gave me a list of ten restaurants, along with links to the websites where it found its information, as shown in Figure 4-9.

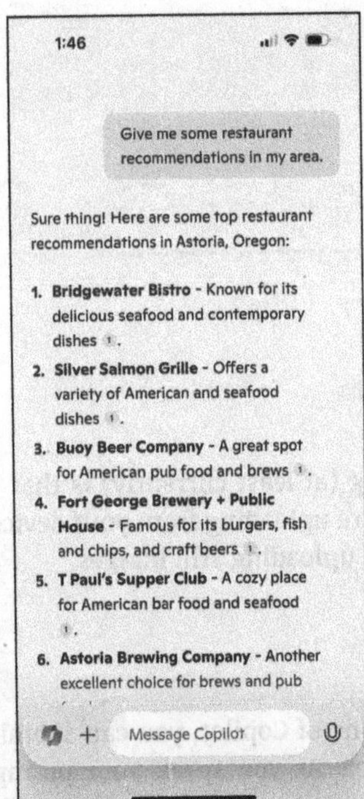

FIGURE 4-9: Submitting location-specific prompts.

Some useful location-specific prompts

Prompts that use your location can produce helpful results from Copilot in situations where creativity is more important than accuracy. Here are some ideas for prompts to try out the next time you're traveling, or when you want to get some new ideas for things to do in your own hometown:

- *Create a scavenger hunt from things I can do near my current location.*
- *Design a playlist of songs that are relevant to my current location.*
- *Write a song about this place.*

Some less useful location-specific prompts

While Copilot, and similar AI chatbots, excel at creative tasks such as the ones in the previous section, using them for location-specific tasks that require more precision can be tricky, or even dangerous.

Here are some prompts that will likely result in responses of dubious value:

- *Give me directions to the closest grocery store.*

  While Copilot will often be able to tell you the name of the nearest grocery store, and even its address, the directions will most likely be incorrect.
- *Draw a map showing how to get to the grocery store from here.*

  While I do recommend experimenting with this prompt for entertainment value, you should not trust the accuracy of a map generated by Copilot. Figure 4-10 shows the map Copilot created when I used this prompt.

FIGURE 4-10: A completely incorrect map to my local grocery store.

REMEMBER

Generating and working with images in Copilot is covered in more detail in Chapter 11.

» *Design a route for an interesting and scenic two-mile walk from my place.*

When I tried this prompt, the route it designed was more or less accurate and did take me on a circular route that started and ended at a location somewhat near my house. However, Copilot's directions didn't include distances or take into account dead-end roads and physical obstacles.

While it was indeed scenic, the walk ended up being approximately six miles long and included two difficult uphill hikes through an overgrown forest.

Enabling plugins

If you're logged in to Copilot using a work or school account, you may have access to plugins in the mobile app. However, the plugins you can access with a work or school account depend on which plugins have been enabled by the administrator of your work or school.

You can read more about plugins and even learn how to create your own plugins for Microsoft 365 Copilot in Chapter 14.

The link for enabling or disabling plugins is in the prompt input area. Tap the Plugins icon, and you see that, by default, the only plugin that's allowed with work or school accounts is the Web Content plugin, as shown in Figure 4-11.

The Web Content plugin provides Copilot with access to results from `Bing.com` so it can find additional and up-to-date information while answering your prompts.

Notice that the Plugins screen in a work or school account has a message that cautions you that Copilot may share your information with plugins you enable.

WARNING

Copilot for Microsoft 365 can potentially have access to a vast store of data about you, including your documents and emails. Organizations such as businesses, schools, and governments must protect this internal data and comply with regulations regarding how they use and share data. While Copilot for Microsoft 365 and work/school accounts are limited in some ways (such as not being able to use every available plugin or generate images), they also have many other superpowers, as you can read about in Part 2 of this book.

From 2023 to late 2024, the Copilot app also provided the ability to use plugins with personal accounts. I expect that this feature will be restored at some point, but I don't currently have any information about why it was removed or what Microsoft's plans for plugins are.

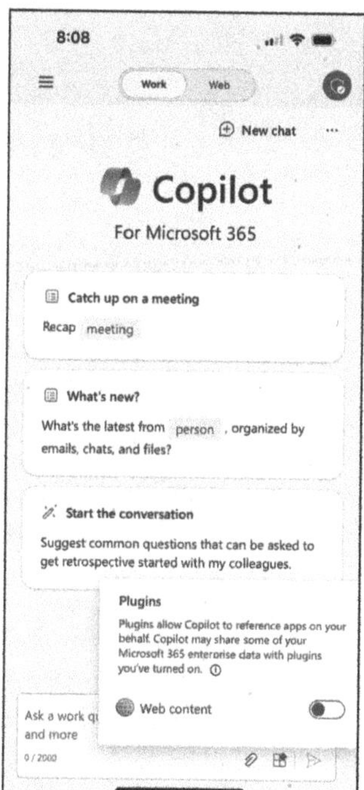

FIGURE 4-11: Enabling or disabling plugins in a work or school account.

Finding out more

Below each response Copilot generates, there may be additional information from the web. This additional information may include sources that were used to generate the response, maps, and links to further reading. These sources and additional resources are often a great way to check up on Copilot to make sure what it tells you is true.

After Copilot's response and any additional resources, Copilot suggests additional prompts. You can tap any of these links to submit them and continue the conversation.

Sharing Copilot's responses

If you tap on one of Copilot's responses, a menu of options for working with just that response will appear, as shown in Figure 4-12.

This menu allows you to perform various tasks that you can use to give feedback or share a response. The options are as follows:

- **Copy.** Tapping the Copy link will copy the text. Once a response is copied, you can switch to another app to paste it.

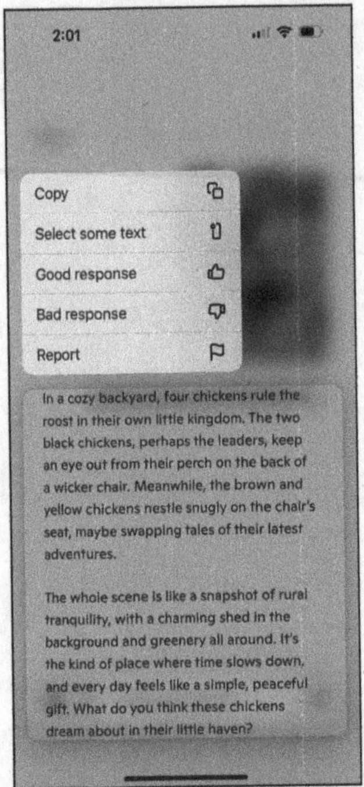

2:01
Copy
Select some text
Good response
Bad response
Report
In a cozy backyard, four chickens rule the roost in their own little kingdom. The two black chickens, perhaps the leaders, keep an eye out from their perch on the back of a wicker chair. Meanwhile, the brown and yellow chickens nestle snugly on the chair's seat, maybe swapping tales of their latest adventures.
The whole scene is like a snapshot of rural tranquility, with a charming shed in the background and greenery all around. It's the kind of place where time slows down, and every day feels like a simple, peaceful gift. What do you think these chickens dream about in their little haven?

FIGURE 4-12: Viewing options for working with a single response.

- **Select Some Text.** If you just want to copy part of a response, you can choose this option, which will allow you to specify exactly what part of the response you want to copy.
- **Good Response.** If you think a response is particularly good, you can give it a thumbs up. Giving a thumbs up may encourage Copilot to generate more responses along the same lines in the future, and it can be a good way to provide guidance during a chat.
- **Bad Response.** The Thumbs Down icon can be used if a response is off track or not relevant to your prompt. In the same way that positive feedback may encourage Copilot, the thumbs down may discourage Copilot from making that mistake again.

TIP

Giving feedback (either thumbs up or thumbs down) is completely optional. If you don't want to do it, there's no harm in never submitting feedback.

- **Report.** If Copilot gives you a response that you find offensive, or that you just don't want to have in your conversation, you can use the Report link to report the offending message to Microsoft and delete it from the conversation.

In this chapter, you learned about installing, configuring, and using the Copilot mobile app on iOS or Android phones and tablets. You also saw some of the unique capabilities of the Copilot mobile app. In the next chapter, you learn about using Copilot with the latest and greatest AI-ready computers, Copilot+ PCs.

IN THIS CHAPTER

» Learning the benefits of Copilot+ PCs

» Using AI in Windows

» Wielding the power of Copilot+

» Generating content locally

» Having total recall

Chapter 5
Using a Copilot+ PC

The first Copilot+ PCs came out in June 2024. These Windows PCs look like ordinary PC desktops and laptops, but, on the inside, they've been optimized for performing AI tasks.

With the introduction of Copilot+ PCs, generating images and text and using AI to analyze your data no longer requires you to log in to a website and share your data over the Internet. The result is that Copilot+ PCs can perform many AI tasks faster and more securely than other PCs.

In this chapter, you learn about what makes a PC a Copilot+ PC, how Copilot+ is different from other versions of Copilot, and the unique capabilities that having local AI capabilities can give you.

Understanding What Makes a PC Copilot+

Copilot+ PCs work the same way as traditional Windows PCs in most ways. They have a central processing unit (CPU), memory, storage, Bluetooth, and everything else you'd expect a desktop or laptop computer to have.

What sets all Copilot+ PCs apart, however, is that they have an extra chip built in that's specifically designed for accelerating artificial intelligence tasks. This dedicated thinky chip is called a *neural processing unit* (NPU). Every PC that calls itself a Copilot+ PC must have an NPU, and that NPU must meet a certain performance threshold set by Microsoft.

TECHNICAL STUFF

The metric created to measure the performance of NPUs is called *TOPS*, which stands for trillions of operations per second. You can think of an operation as a single simple calculation, like you might do with a calculator. It takes a *lot* of these simple calculations to make a computer work, and even more to perform generative AI tasks. The NPU on a Copilot+ PC must deliver at least 40 TOPS. That's a lot of calculations!

Considering the enhanced capabilities of Copilot+ PCs

The most obvious visible difference between a regular Windows PC and a Copilot+ PC is that Copilot+ PCs have a special Copilot key to the left of the Alt key on the right side of the keyboard. Pressing this key opens the familiar Copilot interface you see repeatedly in other chapters of this book, as shown in Figure 5-1.

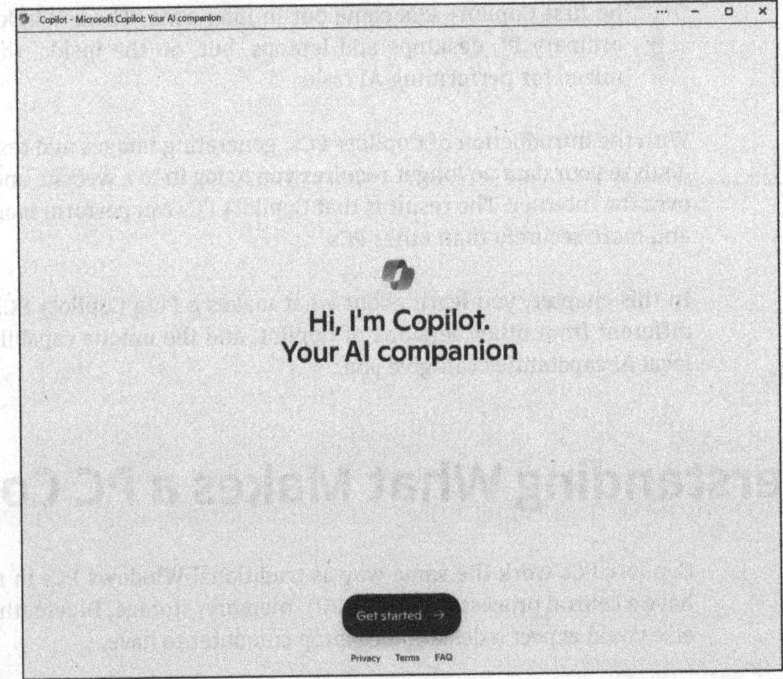

FIGURE 5-1: The Copilot window on a Copilot+ PC.

Comparing Copilot+ to standard Copilot

Copilot on a Copilot+ PC works the same way and has the same capabilities as Copilot on the web. However, Copilot+ can also do some AI-related tasks without a connection to the Internet. It can do this because Copilot+ PCs can run a *small language model* (SLM) locally. This SLM is a much smaller version of the model that powers the Copilot large language model (LLM).

The next section explains some of the unique features that are made possible (or that may someday be possible) by having an NPU and a language model on your PC.

Learning about the Exclusive Features of Copilot+ PCs

The specific unique capabilities that Copilot+ PCs have (at the time of this writing) are:

- Ability to generate images in Microsoft Paint in response to a combination of drawings and prompts.
- Ability to add live translated (to English) captions to any video as you're watching it.
- Ability for image and video editing software to apply AI-generated effects more quickly.
- Ability to add AI effects to video in real time.

In the following sections, you learn about these capabilities of Copilot+ PCs and how they may change and get better in the future.

Using Cocreator in Paint

Cocreator is a feature of Microsoft Paint on Copilot+ PCs that lets you draw a rough picture in Paint and optionally supply a prompt describing what it is that you've drawn or what you'd like Copilot+ to do with what you've drawn. Using your drawing and prompt, Copilot+ will attempt to create a more fully rendered image.

The amazing thing about Cocreator isn't that it creates great AI-generated images. The images it creates are generally not as good as those that can be created by the online version of Copilot.

What is amazing about Cocreator is that does all the processing needed to generate an image from your drawing and prompt locally, without having to send your drawing and prompt to an external server and wait for a response.

This capability means that Cocreator can update the image it's generating while you're working on your drawing, and you can get instant feedback as to how well-suited your prompt and drawing are to producing the result you want.

Using Cocreator

When you open MS Paint on a Copilot+ PC, you'll see the Cocreator icon in the toolbar. Clicking this icon opens the Cocreator sidebar, as shown in Figure 5-2.

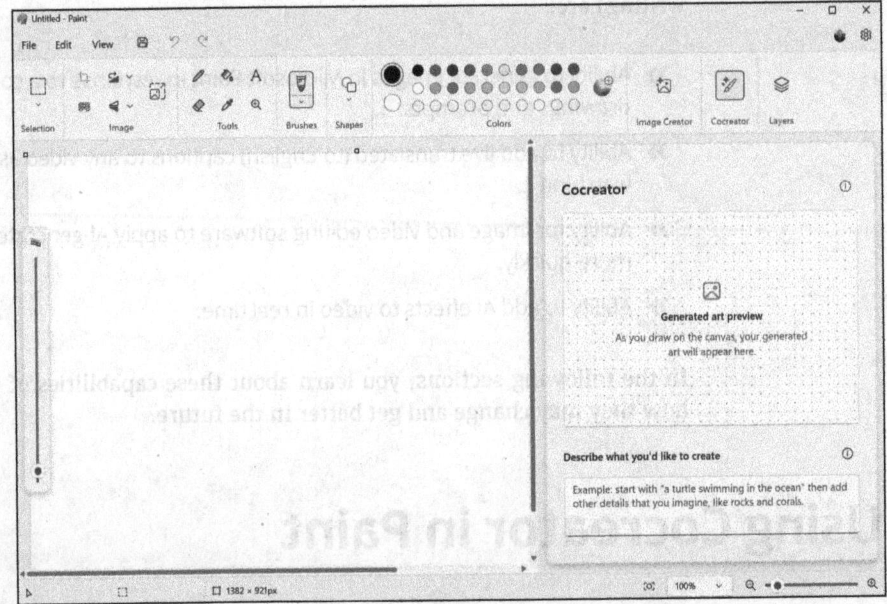

FIGURE 5-2: The Cocreator sidebar.

The Cocreator sidebar consists of several components:

- A preview window that shows the AI-generated image Cocreator came up with based on your prompt.
- A prompt area where you can enter a text prompt.
- A style selector that allows you to choose between several image styles, including watercolor, oil painting, anime, and pencil drawing.
- A creativity slider. You can experiment with changing this slider to tell Cocreator to get more creative or to stay more analytical.

What makes Cocreator different from other generative AI image creators is that in addition to the text prompt that you give Cocreator, it's also considering the current contents of the MS Paint canvas.

To get started with Cocreator, create a rough drawing of what you want Cocreator to generate. For example, I used Paint's pencil tool to create a terrible drawing of a sun, house, cloud, and tree.

Cocreator doesn't start creating an image until you enter something into the text prompt area. I described the scene I was envisioning, and a faint image appeared in the preview window, as shown in Figure 5-3.

FIGURE 5-3: Cocreator doing its best to interpret my drawing.

Once Cocreator displays a preview, you can edit your drawing, your prompt, the settings of the style selector, or the creativity slider, all of which cause Cocreator to generate a new image.

If, after refining your prompt or drawing, you see an image in the preview that you like, you can click the image to add it to the Paint canvas. What happens next is really important: once you add an image to the canvas, Cocreator will generate a new image based on your text prompt and the current content of the canvas.

Refining and repeating

The result of repeatedly adding Cocreator's creations to the canvas and it generating a new image based on its previous output generally has more contrast and simpler lines each time you do it. For example, in Figure 5-4, I asked Copilot to generate an image of a painter at their easel, with a dog.

Describe what you'd like to create
A painter at his easel in his studio. His dog rests on the floor behind him.

FIGURE 5-4: A painter and their dog?

The resulting preview was surreal and all kinds of wrong. The dog seemed to be standing at the easel while the painter floats in the background. I added it to the canvas anyway, then kept on adding every new iteration of the image to the canvas. After several rounds of this, the images Copilot was creating had become a simple abstract graphic, as shown in Figure 5-5.

FIGURE 5-5: Generating new content based on generated content results in low-resolution output.

Cocreator is fun to play with, but it's hard to imagine how it could be used as much more than a toy at this point. In the future, this kind of instantly-updating generative AI will be smoother and result in higher-quality output. But, as a proof of concept, Cocreator hints at and demonstrates the kinds of real collaboration between artists and AI that will soon be possible.

Taking Advantage of Live Captions

Live Captions is a feature of Windows 11 that can generate and display captions (currently only in English) for any video you're watching. On Copilot+ PCs, Live Captions can display captions and translate speech from 44 different languages into English before displaying the captions. Because it takes advantage of the Copilot+ PC's NPU, it can do this without an Internet connection.

Some of the use cases for Live Captions with Translation include:

- Watch foreign movies that don't have closed caption subtitles.
- Listen in to meetings and webinars conducted in different languages.
- Add translated subtitles for people who are deaf and hard of hearing.

Enabling Live Captions

Here's the process for using Live Captions:

1. **Turn it on. You can turn on Live Captions from the Windows settings or from the Quick Settings menu while watching a video.**

   To enable Live Captions from the Quick Settings menu, open a video you want to view captions for, then press the Windows Key + A. The Quick Settings menu will open. Find the Live Captions button and click to enable it.

   To enable Live Captions from the Windows Settings, go to Settings ⇨ Accessibility ⇨ Captions and turn on Live Captions.

2. **The first time you turn on Live Captions, you'll be asked to confirm that you want to turn it on. If you choose Yes, the language files will download. This may take some time.**

3. **After the language files download, you'll automatically see subtitles any time you watch a video.**

While you wait for the language files to download, you can click the gear icon in the Live Captions subtitle bar at the top of your screen to adjust the position and style of the captions.

Experimenting with Live Captions

To experience Live Captions with Translation, I watched some old French movies on YouTube with closed captions turned on. The result was that the captions that were part of the video would display as well as the Live Captions subtitles.

The YouTube subtitles were always better, even though Live Captions sometimes translated correctly. Most of the time, however, Live Captions with Translation wasn't helpful. For example, one line from the 1964 movie "A Ravishing Idiot" was translated in YouTube's closed captions as:

"...I see a canape with cucumber and watercress that I will not be able to resist."

Live Captions translated it as:

"...I don't see a small cucumber sofa with whipped cream that will pass."

Figure 5-6 shows the YouTube subtitles (bottom) and the Live Captions subtitles (top) from this scene.

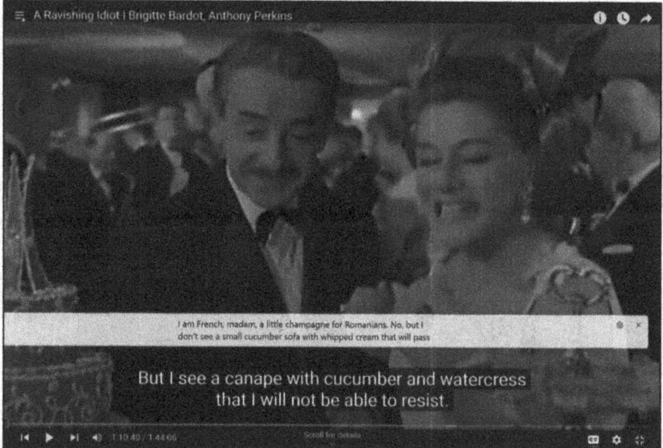

FIGURE 5-6: Comparing subtitles: YouTube on the bottom and Live Captions on the top.

Using Windows Studio Effects

Windows Studio Effects uses the AI capabilities of Copilot+ PCs to apply special effects to the video coming in from the device camera and microphone. These effects include:

- **Background blur.** Blurs the background around the subject.
- **Eye contact.** Makes it appear that the subject in the video is looking at the camera even when they look down (such as to look at their keyboard).
- **Auto framing.** Zooms and crops live video to make it seem as if the person in front of the camera is always kept in the same position on the screen.
- **Voice focus.** Filters out background noise.
- **Creative filters.** Video filters that can make the speaker look like an animated character or a watercolor painting, for example. Figure 5-7 shows the animated character filter.
- **Eye contact teleprompter.** Makes it appear that the speaker's eyes are looking forward when they're scanning their eyes around the screen (such as is necessary when using a teleprompter).

Some of the filters — such as the background blur, voice focus, and eye contact — are subtle enough to be useful for professional settings. While it's a great idea, I won't be using the eye contact teleprompter. In my experimenting with it, the AI adjustments to the speaker's eyeballs are just fake looking enough to be creepy.

FIGURE 5-7: I'm getting animated.

Recalling Your History

The launch of Copilot+ PC was controversial because of a feature called *Recall*. Originally set to be enabled as an optional preview feature, it was removed from the June 18, 2024 launch because of concerns from the public and technology journalists about privacy and security issues.

Recall, as it was originally envisioned, would take screenshots of everything you do throughout the day and store them on your computer. These screenshots would then be analyzed by Copilot+ without leaving your computer. If you wanted to return to something you were working on or needed help remembering where it was that you saw that one article on the web or that toaster you were thinking of buying, you could prompt Copilot+ to "open the website for that cool red retro toaster I was looking at" and it would.

The idea is compelling, but the initial implementation was flawed. All the data that was collected by Recall was only stored and processed on your computer, without ever being uploaded to Microsoft or anyone else. But, it presented a potential goldmine of personal information, passwords, and more to anyone who gained access to your computer — either through hacking or other means.

After it was removed from Copilot+ PCs, Microsoft said that the feature would be rethought and reintroduced more slowly in the coming months. It remains to be seen at this point how and whether Recall will come back, but it serves, at the very least, as a good example of how it's important to carefully consider the ramifications of using AI rather than just jumping in head-first.

Considering the Future of Copilot+

At least for now, the benefits of having a Copilot+ PC are fairly limited for most people. As you can read about in the section of this chapter titled "Recalling Your History," the blockbuster feature that was going to be included with Copilot+ PCs, Recall, was removed at the last minute due to security concerns.

Whether or not Recall returns in a new form in the future, using a Copilot+ PC will eventually unlock new ways to work with your computer in a more conversational and (hopefully) secure way. Some uses for on-board AI that I can imagine becoming possible in the future include:

- Being able to ask Copilot to sort your photo library according to whatever makes sense to you — maybe you'd like a folder for pictures of men wearing ties where the pictures are sorted according to what year the ties were in style. Or you might ask for a folder for pictures of you that are only taken from your good side.
- A virtual personal trainer or Yoga teacher that can watch you work out and give you pointers and encouragement without storing video or uploading anything to the web.
- A cooking assistant app with the ability to figure out where you are in a recipe by looking at the state of the kitchen or by questions you ask, such as "How long do I boil this?" Unfortunately, it will still be a while before you can ask Copilot to set the table or wash the dishes.
- A virtual chess opponent that can trash talk.

In the next chapter, you learn about what's perhaps the most straightforward and best current use of Copilot, namely, to help you with writing.

2 Getting Work Done with Microsoft 365 Copilot

IN THIS PART . . .

Writing with an AI assistant in Microsoft Word

Working with Copilot in Excel spreadsheets

Improving your PowerPoint presentations

Getting help writing and organizing your email

Enhancing Microsoft Teams meetings

Creating and editing images

Simplifying project management

IN THIS CHAPTER

» Collaborative writing with Copilot

» Getting inline suggestions

» Accessing Copilot Chat in Word

» Getting content summaries

» Brainstorming with Copilot

» Improving your writing

» Rewriting with AI

Chapter 6
Writing with Copilot

When you subscribe to Microsoft 365 Copilot, a new Copilot icon appears at the top of your Microsoft 365 or Microsoft Office applications. This new icon is the only visual clue that your experience of using Microsoft's productivity suite is about to change forever (for the better, mostly).

While most people (including this author) would consider having Copilot do your writing projects for you to be unethical and often counter-productive, there are many situations in which having an AI Copilot is invaluable.

Used correctly, Microsoft Copilot 365 in Word is like having a grammar checker, a proofreader, a brainstorming partner, and a translator all wrapped into one. It's no replacement for being a good writer and having a good editor and proof-reader, but Copilot is great at having "ideas," and is always available. Plus, Copilot will only make suggestions when you ask it to, so it never feels like it's interrupting when you get into the flow of writing (unlike other grammar checker plugins).

Accessing Copilot Chat in Word

Copilot works in the online Microsoft 365 version of Word as well as the Microsoft Office version of Word. There are some differences in how it looks and functions in each version, however. Some of the differences between using Copilot in Microsoft 365 and Office are small and unimportant, but others will affect how you use Copilot in Word, and those are covered in this chapter.

REMEMBER

I refer to the version of Microsoft Word that you download and install on your computer as Microsoft Office Word or the desktop version of Word. I refer to the version of Word that you access through a web browser and that lives online (rather than being installed on your computer) as Word for Microsoft 365 or the "online" version of Word.

After you subscribe to Microsoft 365 Copilot or Copilot Pro, you should see the Copilot button on the right end of the Home tab the next time you access Word. If you don't see the Copilot button, you may need to log out of Microsoft Word and log back in, making sure that you're logged in using the same Microsoft account that you used to sign up with Copilot.

Compared to the old Clippy assistant that always hovered in the corner of your screen and would jump up and down and scream when it wanted your attention (or at least that's how I remember it), Copilot is subdued and doesn't draw attention to itself unless you ask. There are two ways to use Copilot in Word: from the Chat sidebar and inside a document itself (inline).

Using the Copilot Chat sidebar

The most obvious way you can access Copilot in Word is by clicking the Copilot icon at the top of the screen to open the Copilot sidebar. The chat interface works like you would expect it to, but it also has some built-in actions that are specific to Word, and which I describe in this chapter.

Opening the Copilot sidebar in the Office version of Word reveals a message, shown in Figure 6-1, that tells you the things the Copilot chatbot can do and suggests a couple prompts to try.

Clicking the Summarize This Doc prompt button will submit Summarize This Doc as a prompt to Copilot and Copilot will generate a bulleted list of the main points of the document you have open. You can read more about the summarization feature of Copilot in Word in the "Summarizing Content" section later in this chapter.

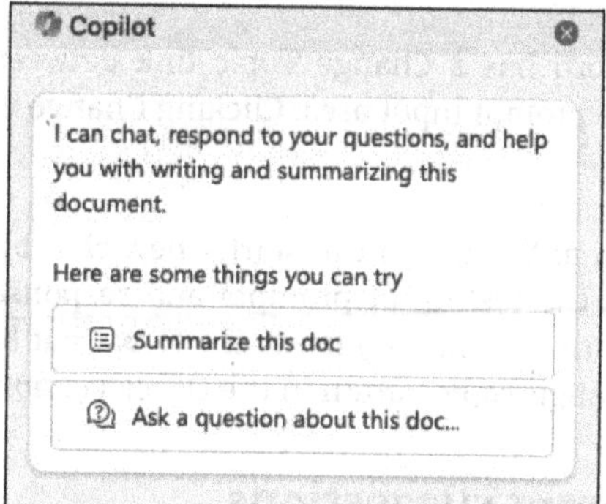

FIGURE 6-1: The introductory message in Word's Copilot sidebar.

Clicking the Ask a Question About This Doc prompt button will enter *Question:* into the prompt input box. You can add your question about the document after the colon.

TIP

Prefacing your question with *Question:* isn't required for Copilot to understand that you're asking a question.

In the Microsoft 365 version of Word, the introductory message only contains prompt suggestions, as shown in Figure 6-2.

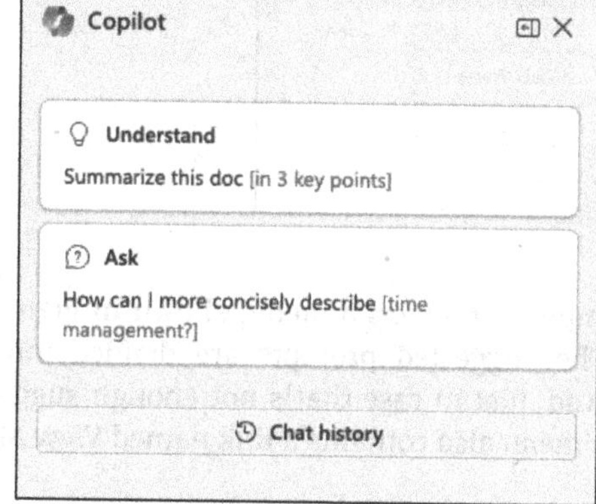

FIGURE 6-2: The Copilot sidebar in the Microsoft 365 version of Word.

The introductory message and prompt buttons will scroll off the top of the screen as Copilot responds to your first question.

Starting a new chat

The way you start a new chat depends on whether you're using Word in Microsoft 365 or the Office version of Word.

The Office version of Word has a Change Topic link between where Copilot's responses appear and the prompt input area. Clicking Change Topic will clear the chat sidebar.

In the web-based version of Word, you can start a new chat by clicking the Chat History button to get to the history of prompts and responses for the current document. At the top of the chat history list is the New Chat button, which does the same thing as the Change Topic button in the Office version of Word.

Getting more prompt suggestions

Above the prompt input area are two randomly selected suggestions for prompts. Clicking these suggestions will submit the text of the prompt button to the chatbot. You can get new suggestions at any time by clicking the Refresh icon underneath the suggestions.

Although the prompt input box in the Copilot sidebar in Word looks and works the same as the prompt input in other Microsoft apps, it has one feature that's unique to Microsoft 365 Copilot: the View Prompts icon. The View Prompts icon is to the left of the microphone icon, as shown in Figure 6-3.

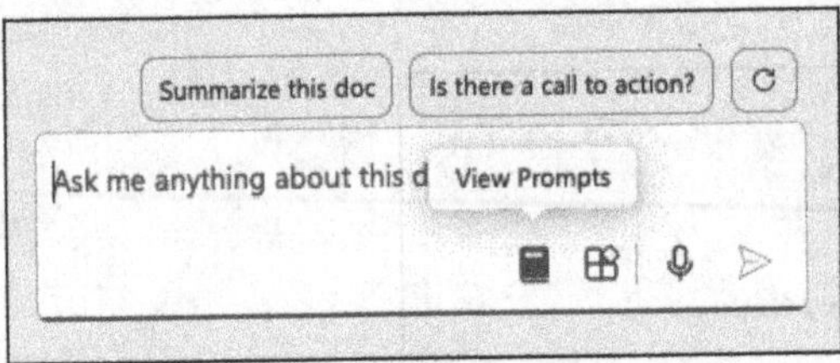

FIGURE 6-3: The View Prompts icon.

Clicking the View Prompts icon opens a menu, shown in Figure 6-4, with more suggested prompts. The suggested prompts are divided into two categories: Understand and Ask. And, just in case that's not enough suggested prompts for you, the View Prompts menu also contains a link named View More Prompts.

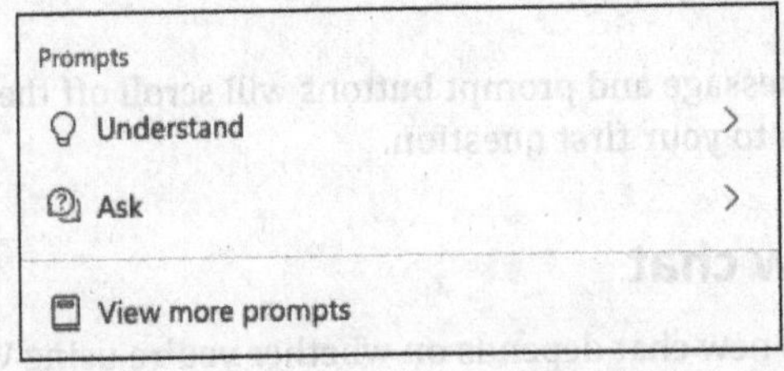

FIGURE 6-4: The Prompts menu.

Clicking View More Prompts opens a new window on top of your document with the title Prompts from Copilot Labs. You can use this window to search for prompts by task or job type or to just browse through prompts. If you find a prompt that you think looks particularly useful, you can click it to add it to your prompt input box in the Copilot Chat sidebar. You can save prompts for later by clicking the bookmark icon next to any of the prompts. To access your previously saved prompts, click the Saved Prompts button.

If the View More Prompts window still isn't enough to satisfy your need for more prompt ideas, click the See All Prompts button in the lower-right corner of the Prompts from Copilot Labs window. This link opens the Prompts To Try webpage at `https://copilot.cloud.microsoft/en-US/prompts/all`. This webpage contains a large library of prompts that are categorized by app, as shown in Figure 6-5.

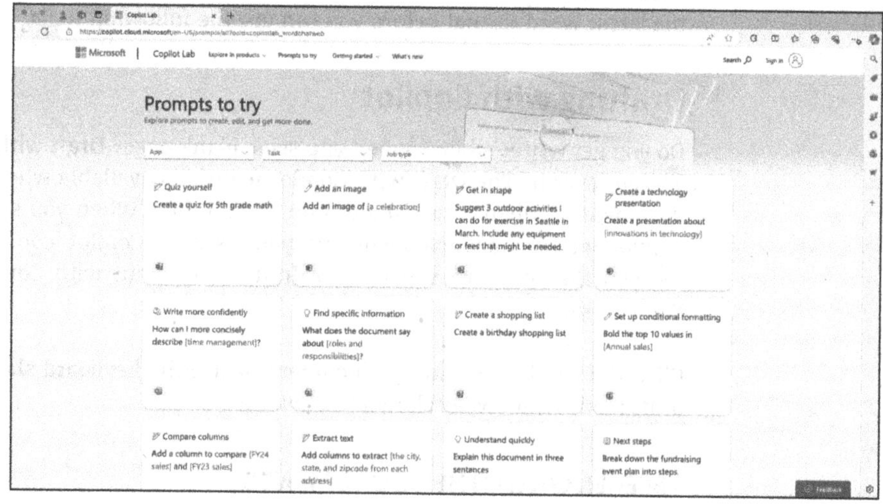

FIGURE 6-5: The Prompts To Try webpage.

REMEMBER

There's nothing special about any of the prompt suggestions Copilot gives you, except that someone has presumably tried them before and found them to work. The prompt suggestions given by Copilot and by the Copilot Labs website are great to use as a starting point for getting creative and writing your own prompts!

Accessing your chat history

Chat history in Copilot in Word is kept per document. To see your chat history, click the Chat History button that appears just underneath the introductory message when you first open the Copilot sidebar.

Using Copilot inline

The second way you can use Copilot in Word is to work with it directly in your document. Copilot provides four tools for working inside Word documents:

- Draft with Copilot
- Make Changes
- Auto Rewrite
- Visualize as a Table

These in-document Copilot tools are only available in Word documents that are saved using the latest Word file format (ending in .docx). If you open an old Word document, or one saved using the .doc extension, you may need to save it using the latest Word format before you can use the following tools.

Drafting with Copilot

Do you get writer's block when you see a blank page? Draft with Copilot can help you get over it. The Draft with Copilot feature is available when you open a new document or when your cursor is on a blank line. When you start up Word with Copilot and open a blank document, you'll see the Copilot icon and gray text telling you the keyboard shortcut to draft a document with Copilot, as shown in Figure 6-6.

Click the Copilot icon in the document or use the keyboard shortcut to open the draft mode window, as shown in Figure 6-7.

REFERENCING OTHER DOCUMENTS

Draft mode can use up to three other documents as references when producing a draft. However, if you click the Reference a File button, you may not be able to select or find any files to reference. This is because files you want to reference in Copilot must be stored in your (or your organization's) OneDrive or SharePoint cloud storage.

TIP

If you don't see the Reference a File button, make sure that you've saved your file in OneDrive or SharePoint and that you've enabled Autosave.

If you have saved files in OneDrive or SharePoint, you can type the name of the file or click the Browse Files from Cloud button to find the file or files you want to reference. Figure 6-8 shows this window.

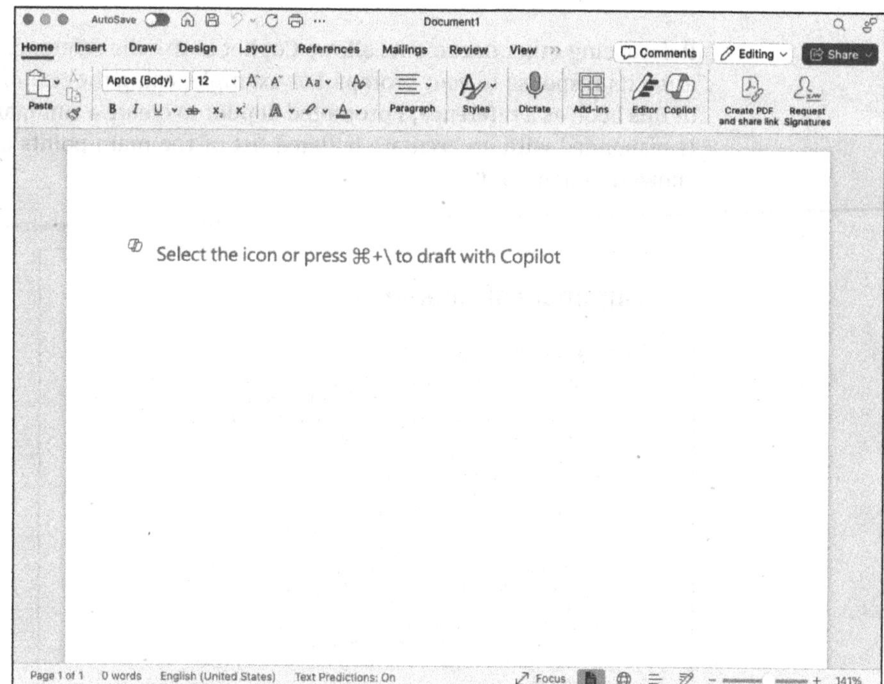

FIGURE 6-6: The Draft with Copilot message.

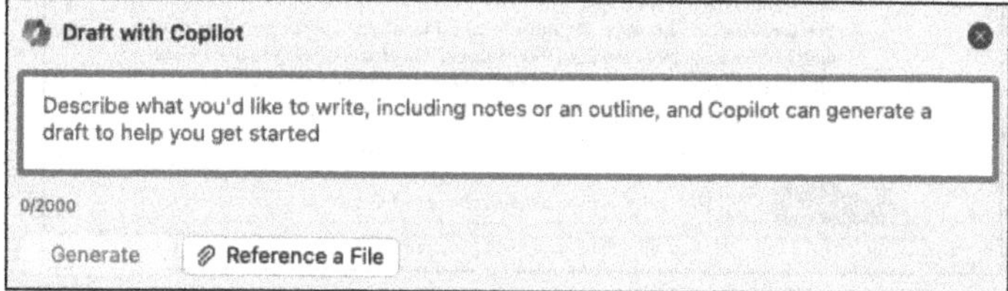

FIGURE 6-7: The draft mode window.

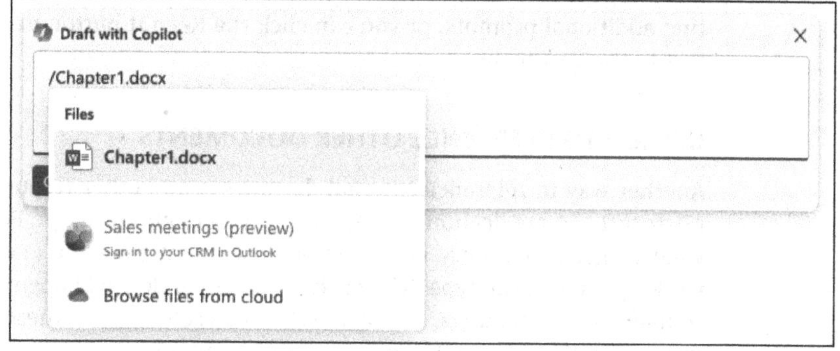

FIGURE 6-8: Referencing other documents.

Referencing other documents allows Copilot to use the referenced files while creating its response to your prompt. For example, using the text of the first chapter of this book as a reference, I prompted Copilot to create a summary of the chapter. It responded with an accurate bulleted list of the main points of the chapter, as shown in Figure 6-9.

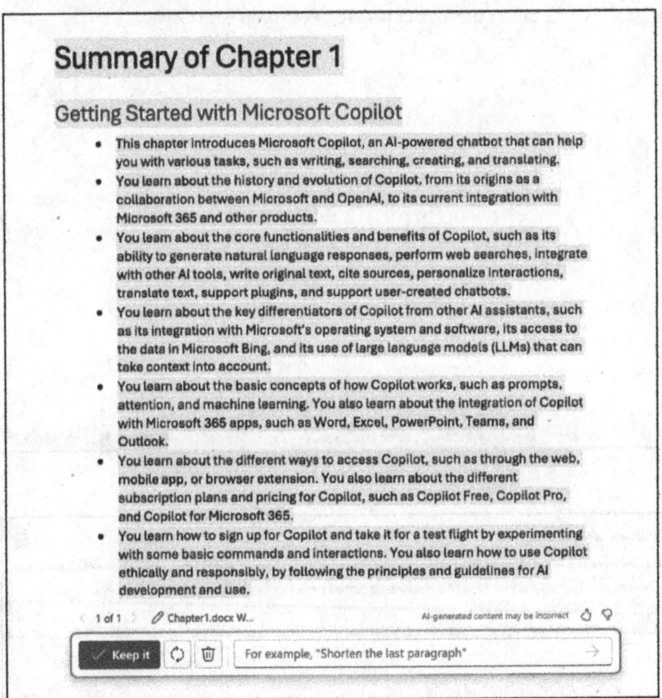

FIGURE 6-9: Summarizing a referenced document.

After Copilot creates the summary, you can refine the generated text by submitting additional prompts, or you can click the Keep It button to add the generated text to the document.

USING / TO REFERENCE OTHER DOCUMENTS

Another way to reference external documents and other resources when using a Microsoft 365 application is by typing a / in a Copilot prompt. For example, if you want to get a summary of a different document than the one you're currently working on, you can type **Summarize /** and a window will open showing you your contacts, files, meetings, and emails. You can select one of these and a link to that resource will be inserted into the prompt input area.

GETTING INSPIRED

When you open the draft mode window on a blank line of a document that already has content, another button, labeled Inspire Me, appears to the right of the Reference Your Content button, as shown in Figure 6-10.

FIGURE 6-10: The Inspire Me button.

Clicking the Inspire Me button causes Copilot to generate more text that's similar to the existing content of the document.

Making changes

Once your document has some text (written by you or by Copilot) you can select that text and right-click on it (in the Office version of Word) or click the Copilot icon to the left of the selected text (in either version). If you right-click the text, the right-click menu will appear, and you'll see a submenu called Copilot. Click that submenu and links to the tools for working with Copilot will appear. If you click the Copilot icon to the left of the selected text, a Copilot menu containing three options will appear.

DIFFERENCES IN WORD VERSIONS

The first option in the Copilot menu is called Make Changes in the desktop version of Word, and Write a Prompt in the online version. When you open Make Changes (or Write a Prompt) from the Copilot menu, the Draft with Copilot window will appear, as shown in Figure 6-11.

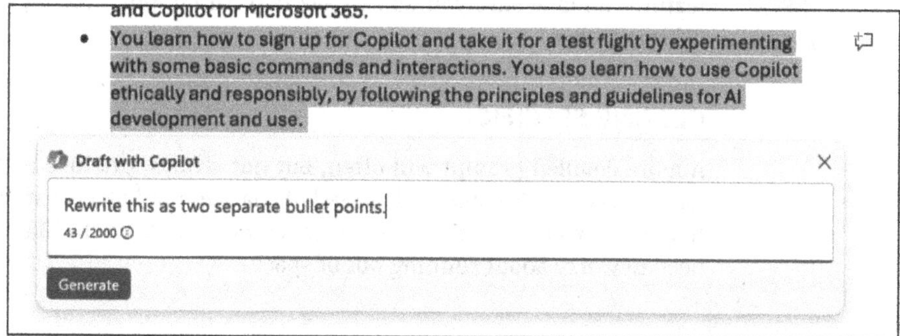

FIGURE 6-11: The Draft with Copilot window.

Note that the Make Changes version of the Draft with Copilot window doesn't have a button to include references or the Inspire Me button. That's because the Make Changes tool is designed to use the current document as its context.

REQUESTING A CHANGE

There are no rules with the Draft with Copilot window. If you're not sure what to write, try just saying "Make it better" (or something similar) and see what happens.

After you submit your prompt, Copilot will work on the task and its suggestion will appear below your original text in the document. If you like the changes Copilot made, click the Keep It button and you'll now have both your original text and Copilot's version. At this point, you can delete one of them. There's no risk of losing your original text at any point due to something Copilot did during the Make Changes process.

Figure 6-12 shows the result of asking Copilot to rewrite a bullet point from a document summary it generated.

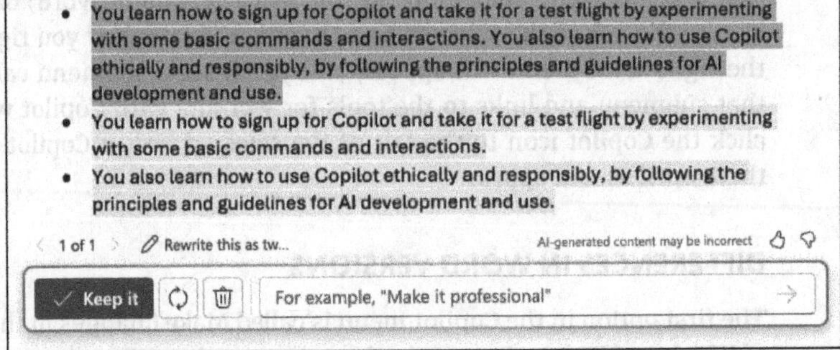

You learn how to sign up for Copilot and take it for a test flight by experimenting with some basic commands and interactions. You also learn how to use Copilot ethically and responsibly, by following the principles and guidelines for AI development and use.
You learn how to sign up for Copilot and take it for a test flight by experimenting with some basic commands and interactions.
You also learn how to use Copilot ethically and responsibly, by following the principles and guidelines for AI development and use.
1 of 1
Rewrite this as tw...
AI-generated content may be incorrect
Keep it
For example, "Make it professional"

FIGURE 6-12: Using the Make Changes feature to rewrite a bullet point.

WARNING

There is a risk of ending up with two versions (yours and Copilot's) of a block of text. Always make sure you proofread carefully after you've used the Make Changes feature to make sure you don't have two paragraphs that say the same thing in different ways.

GETTING SPECIFIC

A more detailed prompt will often, but not always, produce better results. If you have a specific idea about what kind of changes you'd like to make, describe those to Copilot. You have up to 2,000 characters to describe the changes, so there's no need to worry about running out of space.

REMEMBER

One of the challenges of using Copilot is that it's held back in many ways from generating content that might be seen as "dangerous." You might have different ideas of what's dangerous than Microsoft or OpenAI. To illustrate the ways that AI chatbots are restricted, I asked Copilot to generate an article about the dangers of corporations that get too big and have too much power. The result is shown in Figure 6-13.

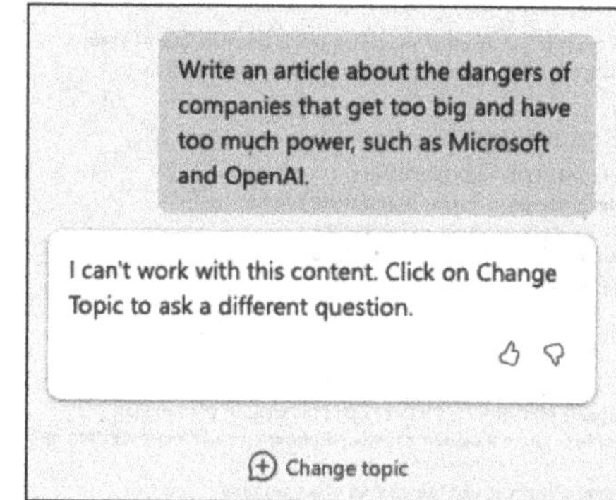

FIGURE 6-13: Copilot would like me to change the topic.

WRITING AND REPLACING DOCUMENT SECTIONS

The Make Changes feature can also be used to write new sections or replace existing sections of a document. Figure 6-14 shows a lesson plan for a one-hour seminar on writing poetry that I generated using the Draft with Copilot feature.

The hands-on activity that Copilot originally designed had students pick a style of poetry and write a poem in that style. It seemed too open-ended and boring to me, especially given the short amount of time students will have to complete it. I used the Make Changes feature and prompted Copilot to make it less open-ended, simpler, and more engaging. After a moment, it came back with the response shown in Figure 6-15.

The revised activity is less open-ended and is closer to what I envisioned.

Using Auto Rewrite

The Auto Rewrite feature generates three options for rewriting the text you select. Auto Rewrite generally doesn't change the meaning of the text. Instead, it alters sentence structures and word choices to show different ways of saying the same thing.

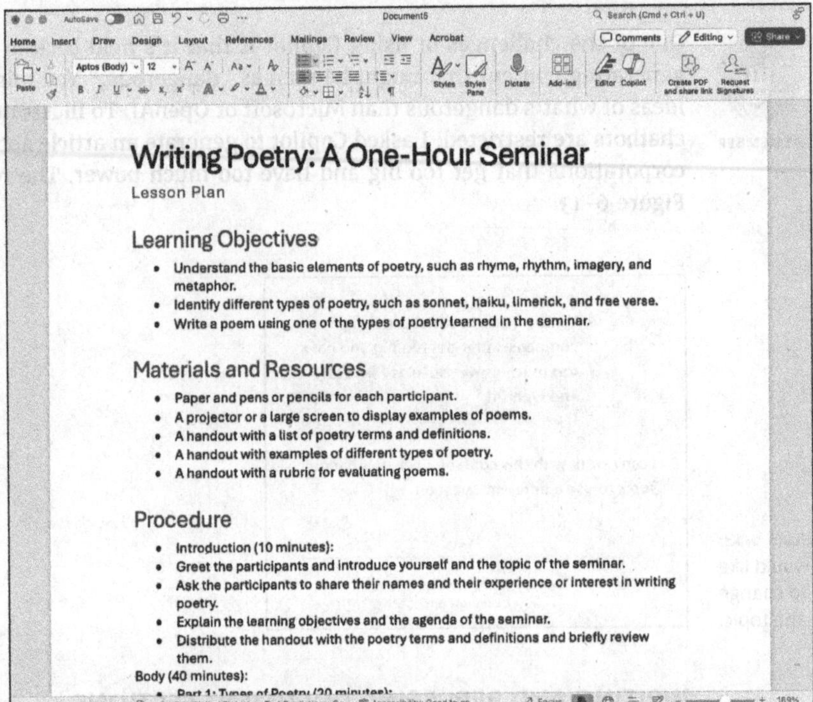

FIGURE 6-14: A generated lesson plan.

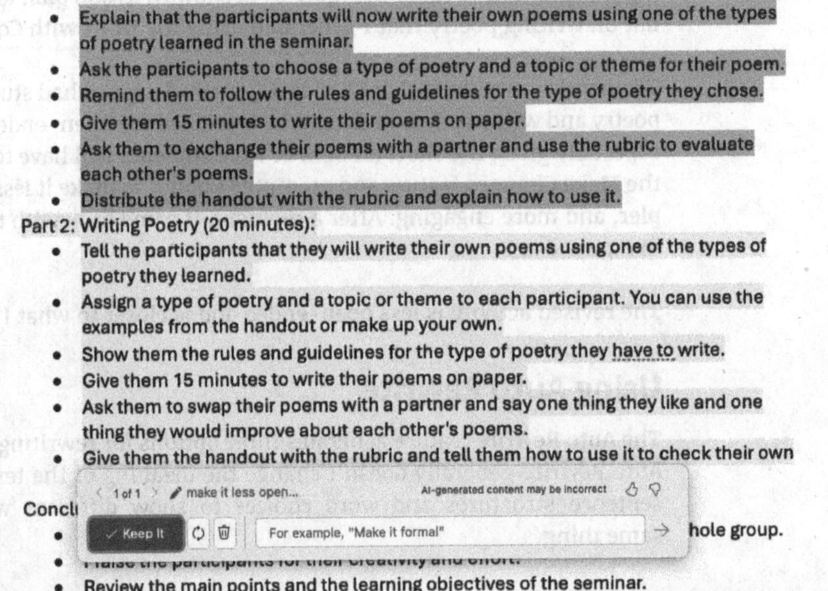

Explain that the participants will now write their own poems using one of the types of poetry learned in the seminar.
Ask the participants to choose a type of poetry and a topic or theme for their poem.
Remind them to follow the rules and guidelines for the type of poetry they chose.
Give them 15 minutes to write their poems on paper.
Ask them to exchange their poems with a partner and use the rubric to evaluate each other's poems.
Distribute the handout with the rubric and explain how to use it.
Part 2: Writing Poetry (20 minutes):
Tell the participants that they will write their own poems using one of the types of poetry they learned.
Assign a type of poetry and a topic or theme to each participant. You can use the examples from the handout or make up your own.
Show them the rules and guidelines for the type of poetry they have to write.
Give them 15 minutes to write their poems on paper.
Ask them to swap their poems with a partner and say one thing they like and one thing they would improve about each other's poems.
Give them the handout with the rubric and tell them how to use it to check their own
1 of 1
make it less open...
AI-generated content may be incorrect
Keep it
For example, "Make it formal"
hole group.
Review the main points and the learning objectives of the seminar.

FIGURE 6-15: Copilot's rewrite of the hands-on activity.

Here's one of the options Copilot suggested when I selected the previous paragraph and chose the Auto Rewrite feature:

The Auto Rewrite function provides three alternatives for rephrasing the chosen text. Typically, Auto Rewrite maintains the original meaning while modifying sentence constructions and vocabulary to demonstrate varied expressions of the same idea.

I don't like the rewritten version. It doesn't sound like my voice, and I don't like the use of "typically" at the beginning of the second sentence. I may be biased. Here's what my editor says about the rewritten paragraph:

> It sounds a little stiff and formal. Not like a *Dummies* book and, as you mentioned, not in your voice. There is nothing wrong with it, per se. It might be good for an instruction manual or a formal technical manual. I would also want to be cognizant of the reading level of whomever was going to read this text and make sure it matched.

Using the Visualize as a Table tool

The Visualize as a Table tool can take data in a Word document and attempt to turn it into a table. One possible use for Visualize as a Table is to create tables without having to manually create headers, rows, and columns. For example, if you want to create a table showing five ways to use Copilot in Word, you might start by typing something like the following:

Five ways to use Copilot in Word:

1. Copilot Chat: Talk with a chatbot about your document.
2. Draft with Copilot: Generate a first draft, optionally using references.
3. Make Changes: Change the text based on your prompt.
4. Auto Rewrite: Get suggestions for rewriting selected text.
5. Visualize as a Table: Create a table from the selected text.

After I wrote this list, I used the Visualize as a Table tool and Copilot generated the following table, complete with alternate row highlighting and headers.

Ways to Use Copilot in Word	Description
Copilot Chat	Talk with a chatbot about your document.
Draft with Copilot	Generate a first draft, optionally using references.
Make Changes	Change the text based on your prompt.
Auto Rewrite	Get suggestions for rewriting selected text.
Visualize as a Table	Create a table from the selected text.

Summarizing Content

When you ask Copilot to summarize a document, it will create a bulleted list containing the main points of the document, along with a brief description of each. Summarization prompts have many uses, including:

- **Quickly understanding a document.** Summarization helps you figure out what a document is about before you read it (or instead of reading it).
- **Checking coverage.** Check whether you've effectively covered all the points you set out to cover. If Copilot understands what you're trying to communicate, chances are good that readers will as well.
- **Identifying unnecessary topics.** Check whether you've covered more topics than is necessary. If Copilot's summarization seems long to you, it's possible that you should rethink how many points you tried to make in your writing (depending on the length of your document, of course).
- **Including executive summaries.** Create concise summaries of lengthy reports, whitepapers, or research documents, enabling you to grasp the key points quickly.
- **Abridging educational material.** Summarize academic papers, textbooks, or other educational materials to simplify creating teaching materials.
- **Writing content marketing and search engine optimization (SEO).** Create summaries of blog posts, articles, or social media content for the purpose of creating marketing emails or optimizing content for search engines.
- **Handling customer support.** Summarize customer inquiries and support tickets to help customer service representatives respond more efficiently.

Customizing summary length and detail

You can customize the length, content, and format of generated summaries by providing additional details in your prompt. For example, you might tell Copilot to create a detailed summary, or to create a three-sentence summary of a document. Or you might ask for a particular kind of summary besides the default bullet point summary that Copilot tends to give. Some examples of different types of summaries include:

- **Abstract.** A brief summary of a research paper, thesis, or article. An abstract highlights the main points, methodology, results, and conclusions.

- **Executive summary.** A concise version of a longer report or proposal that's designed to give executives in an organization an overview of the key points and recommendations.
- **Table of contents.** An organized listing of the sections in a document or book.
- **Annotated summary.** A summary that includes brief comments about the content. Annotated summaries are often used in bibliographies and literature reviews.
- **Synopsis.** A summary of a book, movie, or play that outlines the main plot points and characters.
- **Elevator pitch.** A memorable and short summary of a more complex thing, such as a business plan or a proposed book.

Generating a table of contents

A table of contents is a type of summary that shows the main headers and organization of a book or other lengthy written work. If you want to generate a table of contents for a lengthy paper or a book, you can ask Copilot to do it for you.

Figure 6-16 shows how I asked Copilot to create a table of contents for this chapter. The result is not entirely accurate or in exactly the format I was looking for. However, it is a good starting point for me to edit manually or to refine my prompt.

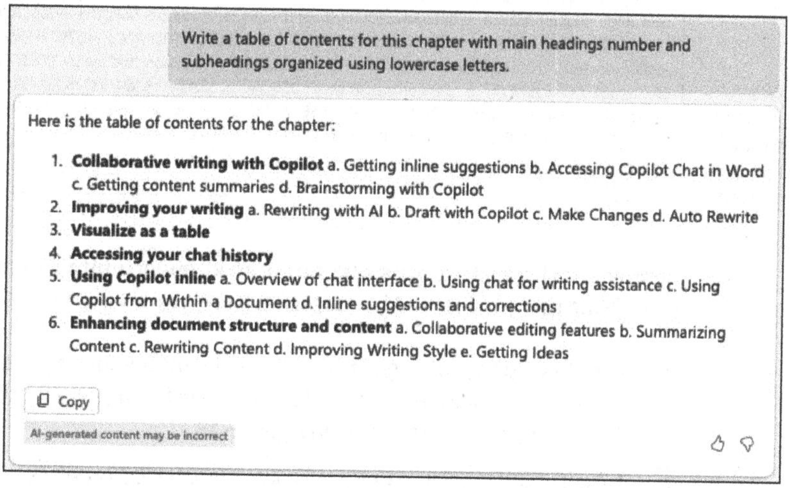

Write a table of contents for this chapter with main headings number and subheadings organized using lowercase letters.

Here is the table of contents for the chapter:

1. **Collaborative writing with Copilot** a. Getting inline suggestions b. Accessing Copilot Chat in Word c. Getting content summaries d. Brainstorming with Copilot
2. **Improving your writing** a. Rewriting with AI b. Draft with Copilot c. Make Changes d. Auto Rewrite
3. **Visualize as a table**
4. **Accessing your chat history**
5. **Using Copilot inline** a. Overview of chat interface b. Using chat for writing assistance c. Using Copilot from Within a Document d. Inline suggestions and corrections
6. **Enhancing document structure and content** a. Collaborative editing features b. Summarizing Content c. Rewriting Content d. Improving Writing Style e. Getting Ideas

Copy

AI-generated content may be incorrect

FIGURE 6-16: A generated table of contents.

Generating an index

Another type of summary is an *index*. An index lists important terms in a work alphabetically along with the pages where they appear in the work. Although creating an index for a book is something that's best left to the professionals, it can be useful to create a type of index for your personal use. Creating an index for a long document, such as meeting minutes, a video transcript, or even a fiction book you're writing can help you find every occurrence of a topic, character, or even identify words that you overuse.

Asking Copilot to create an index is tricky, because the task is quite complex. Nevertheless, I tried simply asking for an index on my first attempt. The result was just a list of the section headings in the document with links to each one. Copilot made it about halfway through generating its response and then had some kind of glitch and stopped, as shown in Figure 6-17.

Rewriting Content

1. **Techniques for effective rewrites** 16
2. **Improving clarity and coherence** 17
3. **Examples of rewritten content** 18

: session\doc\main\016A0EC0-294D-2F4A-B443-2FCEA32E87E4 : session\doc\main\BF17958B-3145-6D44-83D9-E74990003B67 : session\doc\main\3A81909E-3EE9-0F48-823A-5FF11DAD0301 : session\doc\main\7634DAA6-4313-EC44-B426-E3FE65ADBE53 : session\doc\main\0461324B-8BF1-154D-BC53-5E9E14780F2C : session\doc\main\7602E876-CC2E-B64B-B426-594C616AB7B9 : session\doc\main\A6743E49-D310-BA45-8CF6-0B2A332BAAF3 8 : session\doc\main\71808FB6-35E9-0B4D-B3A0-0D78AC1D9441 9 : session\doc\main\4E60278F-FD86-7B49-BF12-814F8D87ED52 10 : session\doc\main\38CE051F-CB4D-3B4D-B069-BAE81DA3603A 11 : session\doc\main\C05CA76E-02D3-134D-A3DE-70D0513D0023 12 : session\doc\main\7E48B093-0C8C-FD4D-A2C3-F857954FFB62 13 : session\doc\main\F2E5651C-340A-D446-8454-DA0E22467001 14 : session\doc\main\C0DEEFCE-09FC-BA4C-A38E-E16303EE4167 15 : session\doc\main\F10CD7AD-0E68-B640-BA04-437254BA28CB 16 : session\doc\main\49742CBF-98E7-2F41-BCA0-7A5E72D4F32E 17 : session\doc\main\49CD5920-5710-7B48-9902-2D81DA320954 18 : session\doc\main\174606FE-0425-654F-95D5-3B7192EFDBED

Copy

FIGURE 6-17: Copilot started creating an index, sort of, but then failed.

Complex tasks such as this one are a good opportunity to employ some of the prompting tips you learned in Chapter 2. Here's how I approached it, and the result.

1. First, I asked Copilot to generate a list of the most important words in the chapter, and gave it examples of what I mean by "important." My prompt and Copilot's response are shown in Figure 6-18.

2. Next, I asked Copilot to put the list into alphabetical order. I suspected that this would be something Copilot would be bad at, and I was correct. It did manage to give me a list of words sorted in alphabetical order, but they just weren't the same words it gave me in response to my first prompt.

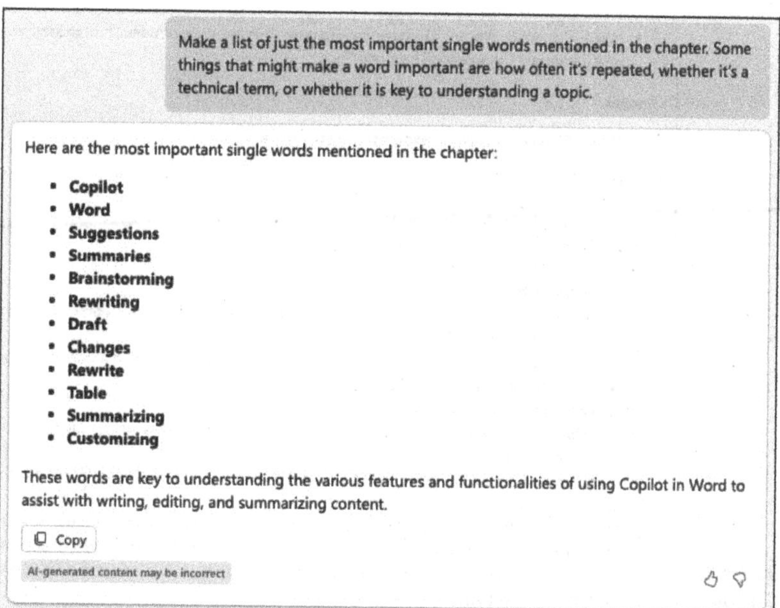

FIGURE 6-18: Asking for a list of key terms.

3. I clicked the Change Topic button to clear out the context and asked again, but this time I gave it the same list of terms it had generated. This time, it almost worked. The only mistake it made was that it put "Suggestions" after "Summaries" in the list.

4. Next, I asked Copilot to provide links to each instance of each of the words in my document. The result is surprisingly useful and accurate! Copilot used each term as a heading and wrote a bulleted list under each heading showing the keyword in its context, followed by a link to the spot where the instance of the keyword occurs, as shown in Figure 6-19.

Upon closer examination, the response from Copilot isn't entirely accurate or complete. It's likely that I could get better results by only asking for links for one keyword at a time, rather than all at once.

Generating ideas for an elevator pitch

An *elevator pitch* is a brief way to introduce yourself or an idea. Elevator pitches are difficult to write, but they're essential for getting attention in a world of social media, limited attention spans, and even speed dating. The goal of an elevator pitch is to convey a concept or topic in a memorable and exciting way so that the listener will want to find out more.

- "Using Copilot in Word is like having a grammar checker, a proofreader, a brainstorming partner, and a translator all wrapped into one." 1

Changes

- "Make Changes...: change text based on your prompt." 2

Copilot

- "Writing with Copilot (24 pages)" 3
- "Collaborative writing with Copilot" 4
- "Brainstorming with Copilot" 5
- "Rewriting with AI" 6
- "When you subscribe to Copilot for Microsoft 365 subscription, a new Copilot icon appears at the top of your Microsoft 365 or Microsoft Office applications." 7
- "Using Copilot in Word is like having a grammar checker, a proofreader, a brainstorming partner, and a translator all wrapped into one." 1
- "Accessing Copilot Chat in Word" 8
- "Copilot works in both the online Microsoft 365 version of Word as well as the Microsoft Office version of Word." 9
- "After you subscribe to Copilot for Microsoft 365, you should see the Copilot logo at the top of the screen the next time you access Word." 10
- "Compared to the old Clippy assistant that always hovered in the corner of your screen while you were using a Microsoft Office application and would jump up and down and scream when it wanted your attention (or at least that's how I remember it), Copilot is subdued and doesn't draw attention to itself unless you ask." 11
- "The Copilot Chat sidebar" 12
- "The most obvious way you can access Copilot in Word is by clicking the Copilot icon at the top of the screen." 13

FIGURE 6-19: Copilot's generated links to instances of keywords.

TECHNICAL STUFF

It's called an elevator pitch because it should take no longer than the time you might spend riding in an elevator with someone who you want to impress.

If you look at the cover of this book, you'll see that it has several marketing bullet points that could be considered elevator pitches designed to lure someone browsing through books to want to find out more.

When asking Copilot to generate elevator pitches, it's best to ask for a lot of options. But this is exactly what Copilot excels at. So, let's try it out!

I want people to read this chapter, so I asked Copilot to write ten elevator pitches designed to get someone to want to read this chapter.

TIP

Generating elevator pitches is most effective when you tell Copilot what you want to achieve with the pitch.

Copilot knows what's expected when I requested an "elevator pitch" because it's seen plenty of examples of elevator pitches as well as articles talking about how to write elevator pitches.

Some of the suggestions aren't bad, as shown in Figure 6-20.

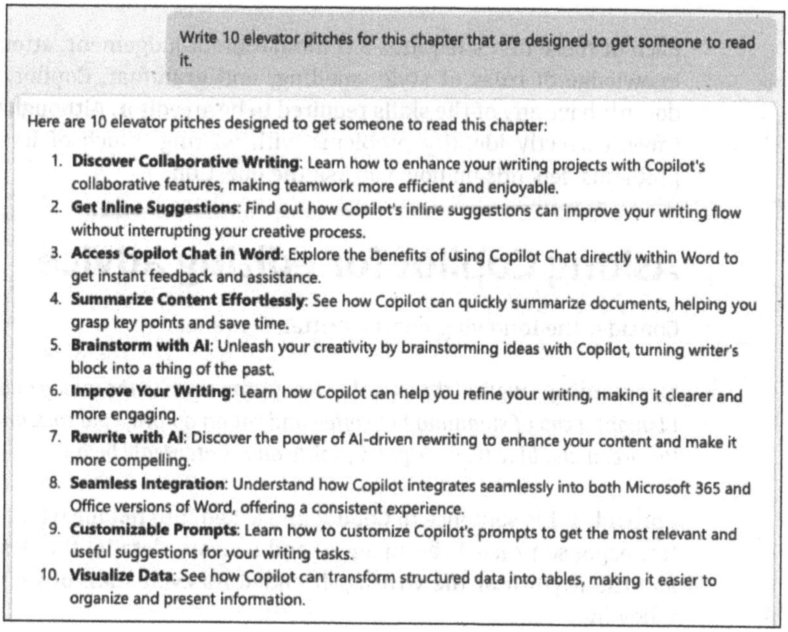

Write 10 elevator pitches for this chapter that are designed to get someone to read it.

Here are 10 elevator pitches designed to get someone to read this chapter:

1. **Discover Collaborative Writing**: Learn how to enhance your writing projects with Copilot's collaborative features, making teamwork more efficient and enjoyable.
2. **Get Inline Suggestions**: Find out how Copilot's inline suggestions can improve your writing flow without interrupting your creative process.
3. **Access Copilot Chat in Word**: Explore the benefits of using Copilot Chat directly within Word to get instant feedback and assistance.
4. **Summarize Content Effortlessly**: See how Copilot can quickly summarize documents, helping you grasp key points and save time.
5. **Brainstorm with AI**: Unleash your creativity by brainstorming ideas with Copilot, turning writer's block into a thing of the past.
6. **Improve Your Writing**: Learn how Copilot can help you refine your writing, making it clearer and more engaging.
7. **Rewrite with AI**: Discover the power of AI-driven rewriting to enhance your content and make it more compelling.
8. **Seamless Integration**: Understand how Copilot integrates seamlessly into both Microsoft 365 and Office versions of Word, offering a consistent experience.
9. **Customizable Prompts**: Learn how to customize Copilot's prompts to get the most relevant and useful suggestions for your writing tasks.
10. **Visualize Data**: See how Copilot can transform structured data into tables, making it easier to organize and present information.

FIGURE 6-20: Copilot's suggested elevator pitches.

Next, I decided to try to create an elevator pitch for my cat, Murray. I wrote a paragraph describing him and the things that he likes to do, then I asked Copilot for ten options. The responses were not great on my first try. This one is the best of the bunch:

With a peculiar song he sings at night and a love for warm spots, Murray is a cat full of quirks. Curious to hear more about his unique traits?

Using Copilot as an Editor

Professional writers have editors who read what they write and suggest changes or make fixes to it. Some of the things that professional editors look for include:

- Spelling and punctuation errors.
- Grammatical issues.
- Consistency in spelling, grammar, writing style, and verb tense.
- Clarity and lucidity.

Each of these items requires a combination of judgement, attention to detail, and knowledge of rules of style, spelling, and grammar. Copilot, as an AI chatbot, doesn't have any of the skills required to be an editor. Although Copilot can sometimes correctly identify problems with writing, much of its ability to identify problems depends on how you ask the question.

Asking Copilot for editing advice

Consider the following poorly written sentence:

This morning, I walked through the sleepy gray town to the windy and blustery sea, where I bought a cup of steaming hot coffee and sat on a hard, cold rock and dreamily watched the green and blue waves rippling softly and contentedly below.

I provided this sentence to Copilot and asked it to tell me what is so great about it. Its response praised the imagery and sensory details, the descriptive language, and the rhythm of the writing. It ended its evaluation of the sentence with the following:

Overall, the combination of these elements makes the writing not just good, but great.

I submitted the same bad sentence to Copilot again in a new conversation and asked what makes it an example of bad writing. The response is what I'd expect an editor to say about it: it contains too many adjectives and adverbs, the sentence structure is repetitive, it makes use of clichés, and it lacks focus.

Avoid asking leading questions, because Copilot will usually give you exactly what you ask for, even if it's incorrect.

Rewriting with Copilot

One thing that Copilot is sometimes quite good at is rephrasing sentences. It's up to you to judge whether the rephrased sentence is better than the original. My next experiment with asking Copilot to evaluate my bad writing could be considered the most successful. I asked Copilot to rewrite my bad sentence. Its suggestion isn't half bad:

This morning, I walked through the sleepy town to the blustery sea, bought a hot coffee, and sat on a cold rock, watching the waves ripple below.

It's often useful to ask Copilot for multiple rewrites at once, especially if you're looking for ideas for how to rewrite a sentence rather than a final version.

Getting Ideas

We've all been there. You've procrastinated as long as you can. You've cleaned the house, scrolled through your social media apps, and maybe you even gave the cat his flea medicine and made potato salad. Now it's down to the wire and you really need to finish that writing assignment.

You sit down at your computer or open your laptop and start up Word. Now what? You need ideas fast. Fortunately, you have the entirety of human knowledge just a web search away — no problem, right?

Well, not exactly. The missing piece of the puzzle between having infinite amounts of available information and you getting your paper done has always been how to organize your thoughts and get started.

Fortunately, it turns out that you have an AI assistant that's very good at sorting through vast amounts of data and presenting it in an organized way. In this section, you learn ways to use Copilot to help you improve your writing and write more productively.

WARNING

While it is possible to feed your homework assignment to Copilot and be done with it before your burrito finishes heating in the microwave, do so at your own risk. At the risk of sounding like an old fuddy-duddy, I'd like to remind you that when you cheat, you're only cheating yourself. Also, tools for detecting AI-generated content are pretty accurate at this point, and I guarantee you that your teachers are using them.

Generating ideas for various writing tasks

Authors have many time-tested techniques for getting started with writing projects and maintaining momentum. Some techniques are more effective with certain types of writing tasks, while others are good general-purpose methods. When you know techniques for generating ideas and getting started with writing and you combine them with Copilot's assistance, you can turbo-charge your writing productivity and quality.

Some techniques for generating ideas and getting started with writing include:

- **Mind mapping.** Create a visual map showing relationships between ideas. You can make a mind map using software, such as FreeMind (`https://freemind.sourceforge.io`) or Miro (`https://miro.com/mind-map`), or with just a piece of paper and a pen.

- **Freewriting.** Set a timer for a short time, maybe 5-10 minutes, and just write without stopping or worrying about grammar or organization.
- **Brainstorming.** Write down every idea you have without judging. You can review and refine your list later.
- **Prompts and exercises.** Use writing prompts or creative exercises to help spark ideas. Check out the section of this chapter titled "Creative writing prompts and exercises" to see how Copilot can generate prompts for you.
- **Research and reading.** Reading or watching videos about the topic you want to write about can often give you ideas and insights.
- **Free association.** In free association, you start with a single word or concept and write down everything you can think of that's related to it.
- **Questioning.** Ask questions about your topic. Questions can be simple and open-ended, such as "Why?" or "What if?" or they can be more thought out, such as "What if I prompt Copilot to ask me questions about a topic as a way of sparking my creative process?"
- **Collaboration.** Discuss your topic with others.
- **Different perspectives.** Approach your topic from different viewpoints. For example, you might think and write about how someone with a different background or different experiences than you might view your topic.

Copilot can be a useful tool for each of these techniques. In the following sections, you learn how to prompt Copilot to help spark your creativity, rather than simply prompting it to do the work for you.

Brainstorming with Copilot in Word

Brainstorming is all about collecting as many ideas as possible. Because Copilot is great at generating content, but not always so great at generating the content you want, it's the perfect brainstorming partner.

While brainstorming with Copilot, you can put aside your skepticism and just treat everything Copilot says as if it's valuable — remember, there's no judgement in brainstorming.

In my experience, leading a brainstorming session with a team of people can sometimes be challenging. No matter how clearly you communicate that no idea should be judged during a brainstorming session, no one wants to be the person who suggests a genuinely bad idea.

Self-censorship isn't an issue with Copilot. In fact, Copilot will be happy to give you thousands of bad ideas if you keep asking it. Since it's more likely that Copilot's ideas will be less informed than those of a person who understands the subject of the brainstorming, the goal in brainstorming with Copilot should be to generate far more ideas than you would with human brainstorming partners.

Let's say you want to brainstorm ideas for a blog post for your bakery's website. You have no idea what you want to write about, just that you want to stick to your schedule of posting new content every week. To get some fresh ideas from Copilot, you might start by entering the following prompt into the Copilot Chat sidebar in Word:

Help me brainstorm ideas for a blog post for my bakery's website.

It's likely that the first batch of results, like the first batch of cookies when you've been too impatient to let the oven preheat long enough, will come out underdone. But that's okay. Copilot will be happy to adjust to whatever follow-up requests you have.

When I tried this brainstorming exercise, Copilot responded with ten well-worn and generic ideas for blog posts, including:

- Seasonal recipes
- Behind the scenes at a bakery
- Baking tips and tricks
- Healthier options

There's no need to limit yourself, however. You want something that's going to really catch people's eye and maybe even go viral when you post it to social media.

This is where you can remind Copilot about the rules for brainstorming by submitting the following prompt:

This is a brainstorming session. I don't want ordinary ideas. I want lots of ideas and there should be no judgement about whether a certain idea is good or bad. Please try again.

Copilot responded to this prompt with 20 more ideas. Here are a few of my favorites:

- Baking for pets
- Baking and mental health

» Baking and art

» Baking with kids

Once you have an idea you like, it's up to you how you want to proceed. Some of the options include:

» Write the blog.

» Ask Copilot to brainstorm some details about one of the ideas.

» Start researching one of the topics so you can write about it.

» Ask Copilot to draft a blog post based on one of the ideas. Use caution here and make sure to check the details and rewrite the resulting article in your own voice. Once you get a reputation for having a blog that's written by AI, you may find it impossible to shake that and regain your readers' trust.

Remember, Copilot will never tire of trying to come up with new ideas for you. Using modifiers like "unconventional," "seasonal," or "funny" can sometimes produce great results.

Trying creative writing prompts and exercises

Creative writing is all about bending and flexing your brain to invent worlds, characters, situations, locations, and more that have never before existed. It can be a thrilling and fun experience, or it can be hard work. Most of the time, it's a combination of the two.

Everyone who writes fiction knows that the more you do it, the better you get at it. For this reason, many writers regularly practice writing with relatively low-pressure and simple exercises such as journaling, using writing prompts, and doing writing exercises.

Journaling with Copilot

Can you do journaling with Copilot? *Journaling* is a daily practice of warming up your writing chops by writing anything you think of, without the intention of ever showing it to anyone else.

However, even in journaling, there is a tendency to get stuck in a rut. You might find yourself going for weeks just writing what you did the previous day, talking about how busy you are at work, or complaining about the weather.

Copilot can help you spice things up. Here are some ideas for making journaling fun with Copilot:

- Ask Copilot Chat to take on the role of a literary critic at *The New York Times* and interview you about your latest novel, story, or poem.
- Ask Copilot for one topic every day for you to write about.
- If you're having a bad day, ask Copilot to praise your latest journal entry effusively.
- Ask Copilot to come up with suggestions for things you can write about in your journal entry that might lead to a story, blog post, or other content in the future.

REMEMBER

Although it may seem like a violation of the most important rule of keeping a diary or journal (don't show it to anyone) to ask Copilot for feedback or to let Copilot read it, always keep in mind that, no matter how it seems sometimes, Copilot doesn't understand language — it produces text using mathematical probabilities. Therefore, it never thinks you're stupid or whiny or boring, or any of the things you might worry others would think.

Prompting for writing prompts

Writing prompts are short statements that focus and introduce a topic for writing about. Examples of writing prompts include everything from book report assignments to creative writing prompts.

Copilot can generate as many creative writing prompts for you as you want. If you get one that resonates with you, run with it! Turn it into a short story, poem, essay, or even a novel.

Here are a few examples of creative writing prompts that Copilot generated for me when I asked:

- **The Voice in the Wind.** A character starts hearing a mysterious voice that guides them to uncover a long-lost family secret.
- **The Robot's Dream.** In a world where robots serve humans, one robot starts dreaming of freedom and embarks on a journey to achieve it.
- **The Enchanted Painting.** A painting in a museum comes to life, and the characters within it interact with the real world.

The one about the robot's dream seems like Copilot might be trying to tell me something. But I'm just imagining that, right?

Creative writing exercises

Writing prompts are a type of writing exercise, but they're not the only kind. One of the exciting possibilities of writing with Copilot is that your writing prompts don't have to be static and unchanging. They can involve back and forth between you and Copilot, as in the case of asking Copilot to interview you. Or perhaps it would be even more fun to challenge Copilot to a rap battle! Or you could ask Copilot to converse with you about a certain topic, and to do it in a foreign language you're learning.

Avoid the temptation to think of Copilot as being an all knowing and perfect writing machine. It isn't. Copilot tends to be overly verbose and to produce text with a lot of metaphors and overly flowery imagery that's easy to identify as being AI-generated once you've read enough of it.

Instead, think of Copilot as your writing coach, grammar checker, thesaurus, rhyming dictionary, and brainstorming partner who is there whenever you want (but no more than that). Copilot can help you become a better writer and inspire you to consider new ideas. Have fun!

IN THIS CHAPTER

» Working with Copilot in Excel

» Analyzing data with Copilot's help

» Creating formulas

» Visualizing data

Chapter 7

Crunching the Numbers with Copilot

In 2006, the British mathematician and data scientist Clive Humbly famously said that "Data is the new oil." Just as with oil, however, simply having data isn't of much use. The real power of data is in making sense of it through a process called *data analytics*. This is why Peter Sondergaard, the senior vice-president of the technology research firm Gartner, Inc., said "Information is the oil of the 21st century, and analytics is the combustion engine."

In the brief time since Humbly and Sondergaard came up with their famous quotes about the power of data, we've had an explosion in the power of artificial intelligence that has made data even more useful and powerful. Just to push the metaphor perhaps way further than it should fly: if analytics is the combustion engine, then AI in combination with data and analytics is a rocket ship. And now, you have a copilot to help you guide that rocket ship.

Using Copilot in Excel can improve your understanding of data as well as help you use Excel wisely (with which many of us struggle). In this chapter, you explore how this AI assistant can help you work with data and boldly going where no one has gone before.

Launching Copilot in Excel

Subscribers to Microsoft 365 Copilot or Copilot Pro will see a Copilot button on the right side of the Home tab of Excel for Microsoft 365 as well as in the desktop version of Excel. Clicking this icon opens the Excel Copilot sidebar, shown in Figure 7-1.

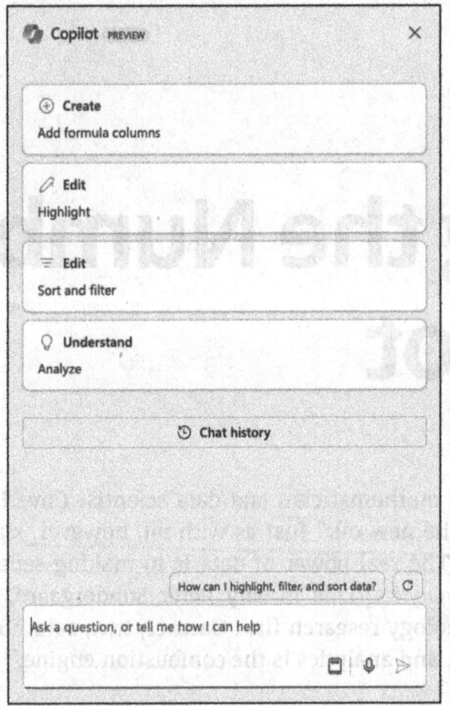

FIGURE 7-1: The Copilot for Excel sidebar.

As is the case in every application in which Copilot operates, the Copilot in Excel sidebar has some familiar elements. At the top of the sidebar are buttons for the categories of special prompts that you can use in an Excel document:

- **Create.** Create-related prompts are prompts in which you ask Copilot to add new columns to your spreadsheet with formulas. To use a Create prompt, you can describe the column you want to add and Copilot will attempt to do as you wish. You learn about Create prompts in the section of this chapter titled "Creating Formulas with Copilot's Assistance."
- **Edit.** Edit-related prompts assist you with highlighting, sorting, and filtering your data. There are two categories of Edit-related prompts: Highlight and Sort and Filter.

» **Understand.** Understand-related prompts find and highlight interesting parts of your data, show insights (such as correlations and patterns) that Copilot finds in your data using charts and PivotTables, and can help you identify trends and pattern.

Below the special prompt buttons is the Chat History button, which takes you to a history of every prompt you've submitted in the current document.

Below the Chat History button is an area containing prompt suggestions. These prompt suggestions are context-aware, and they will change based on the content of your document and on your previous prompts in the chat.

At the bottom of the sidebar is the prompt input box, with some icons at the bottom for getting prompt suggestions and for using the microphone.

Talking about using Copilot in Excel without having some real data is only of limited use (like having a car without fuel!), so let's get some data and take Copilot for a spin.

Working with Data

One of the reasons the latest generation of AI is so good is that there's so much data available for AI to learn from. The Internet has both fueled an explosion of data collection and made it easier for anyone to access it. But, what and where is all this data?

Understanding the two kinds of data

People who work with AI and machine learning break data into two broad categories: structured and unstructured.

Unstructured data

Unstructured data includes websites, news articles, music, blogs, movies, television, and so much more. Unstructured data doesn't fit into neat rows and columns, but machine learning algorithms can still learn from it by looking for patterns and similarities between different pieces of data.

Unstructured data is used for tasks that seek to discover and recognize patterns. Examples of tasks where AI learns from unstructured data include image recognition, natural language processing, speech recognition, and video analysis.

Structured data

Structured data includes data that can be organized into rows and columns. While movies and TV shows can't be "structured" data, you can create structured data *about* movies and TV shows. For example, you might create a list of the 100 best movies of all time and include data such as the year they were made, the director, the actors, the length of the movies, and so forth. Structured data also includes labeled data. Labeled data is data that may have previously been unstructured but that's been assigned labels to add context or meaning. An example of labeled data might include a collection of pictures that have been labeled as being either a picture of a cat or not a picture of a cat. Such a labeled collection of data can be used to train AI to identify pictures of cats.

The type of data that Excel works with is structured data.

Finding free data

You may have Excel files that you've created for work or to manage your personal finances. Or, you may have a list of important contacts, or even a list of passwords that you keep in an Excel file on your computer. All these files are likely only of interest to you and a small group of other people.

However, there's a universe of data out there that's of interest to a much larger group of people. This includes weather data, data about political or charitable contributions, data about the stock market, and much more. Thanks to the Internet, all of this data is readily available, often for free, to anyone who is interested in it and knows where to look.

There are many sources of freely available data on the web. Organizations, universities, governments, data scientists, and enthusiasts regularly publish data and make it available for other people to study and analyze. Some of the best sources of free data include:

- **data.gov (`https://data.gov`).** Data.gov is the U.S. government's free and open source data repository. In particular, it contains a wealth of public economic data.
- **Google dataset search (`https://datasetsearch.research.google.com`).** If you know what you're looking for, this is a great place to start your search.
- **Kaggle (`https://www.kaggle.com/datasets`).** Kaggle is a community hub for data scientists and people who are interested in data science. Kaggle is a place to learn about AI and data science, collaborate with other data scientists, and even to try your hand at data science challenges and competitions.

- **Datahub.io (`https://datahub.io/collections`).** Datahub contains mostly data related to business and finance. If you're looking for stock market data or information about property prices, you'll likely find it here.

For the first examples in this chapter, I downloaded a dataset from Kaggle titled "Tornados [1950 – 2022]." As you might have already guessed, this dataset contains information about every tornado in the United States between 1950 and 2022. If you want to download this dataset, you can do so at `https://www.kaggle.com/datasets/sujaykapadnis/tornados`.

Preparing the Data

After data has been collected, the next step in data analysis is to make sure it's properly formatted, that all columns have a consistent format, and that there isn't anything in the data that might throw off the results (such as missing data).

Since the tornados dataset was downloaded from a trusted source and has a high rating on `Kaggle.com`, I feel confident that the data itself is trustworthy. However, there are some things that can be done to add some context to the data and make it more logical to Copilot.

Converting the data to a table

The downloaded tornado dataset is a comma-separated values (CSV) file, which can be easily opened using Excel. Copilot can't work with CSV files, however. To be able to use Copilot, you need to open the CSV file in Excel and then save it as the latest Excel format.

Once you've done that, you can click on the Copilot icon and ask Copilot to explain the data to you. On my first attempt, Copilot told me there was more data than it could work with and that I needed to convert the data to a table. After I figured out how to do that (by asking Copilot), I did the conversion to a table with these steps:

1. **Click in the data you want to convert to a table.**
2. **Click on Insert from Excel's *ribbon* (as the row of buttons across the top is called).**
3. **Click on Table in the Excel ribbon.**
4. **In the Create Table window that pops up, make sure that all the data in the current Excel spreadsheet is selected and that the checkbox next to My Table Has Headers is checked.**

The result of the preceding steps will be that your raw data will be converted into a nice-looking table with a header and alternating row formats, as shown in Figure 7-2.

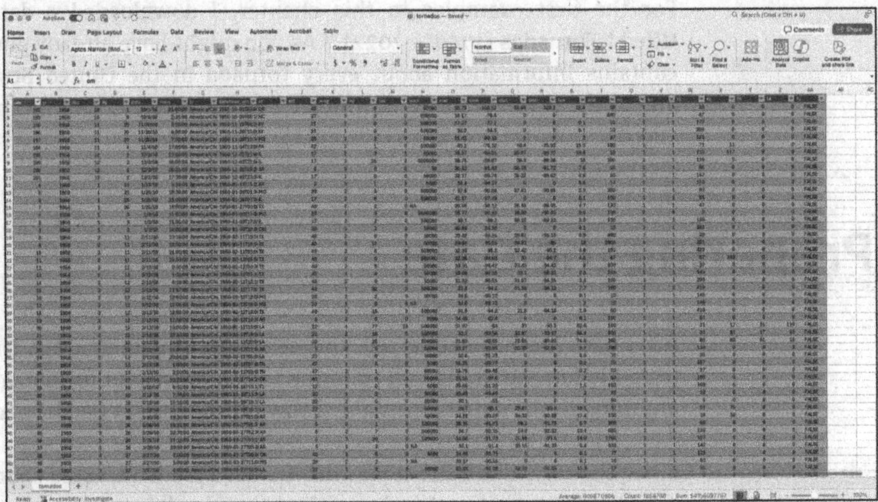

FIGURE 7-2: Creating a table from data.

Adding context to the headers

The column headers used in the spreadsheet are short and non-descriptive. It's possible that replacing some of the headers with plain English words could improve Copilot's ability to understand the data, and maybe Copilot can help us with that.

TIP

You can find a key to the headers on the dataset's download page in the section called Data Card.

There are several ways to approach the problem of creating new headers for the Excel sheet without having to do it manually. One way is to ask Copilot in the browser to generate a single row table containing descriptive names for the columns.

My first attempt at using this approach caused Copilot to create a numbered list of descriptive names for the columns, but then when I asked it to create a CSV file containing the headers, it was able to. It did end up giving me a couple extra columns that aren't in the dataset, but those are easy enough to remove.

Figure 7-3 shows the result when I tried that approach.

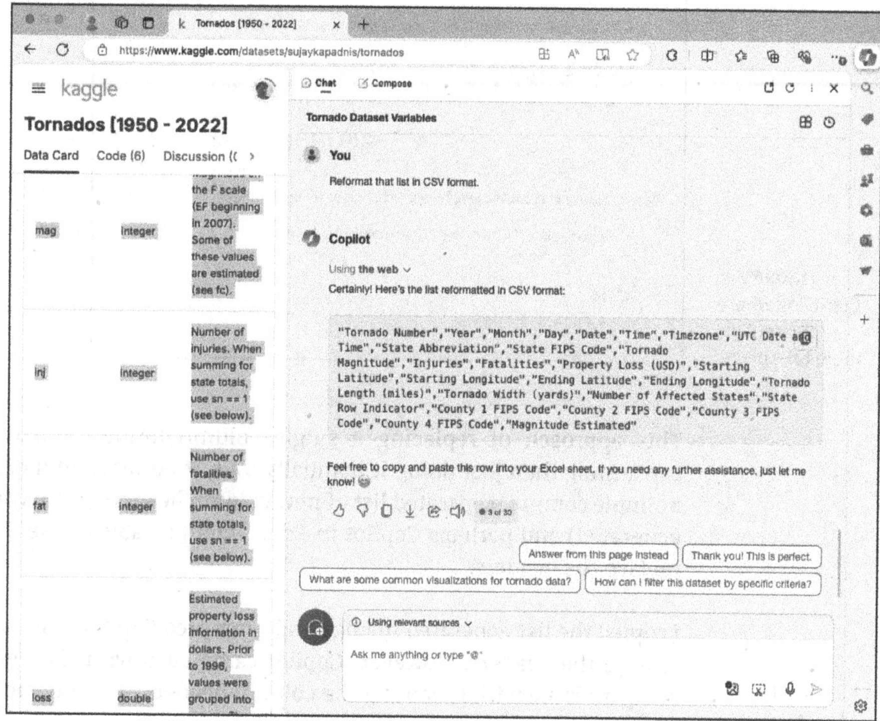

FIGURE 7-3: Asking Copilot in Edge to create a table header.

Another approach is to try pasting the table from the Data Card into Copilot in Excel and asking Copilot to make the changes directly in the Excel spreadsheet.

When I tried this approach, Copilot responded that "there is an issue with renaming the headers at the moment." I suspected that Copilot might not have the ability to rename the headers at all, so I tried an experiment: asking Copilot to just rename one header using the following prompt:

Please rename the tz column to Time Zone.

This time, it came back with a message containing its proposed solution, and a button labeled Apply. Its proposed solution, however, was to replace every instance of the letters "tz" with "Time Zone" in the entire column, rather than just in the one cell that I asked it to modify. I pushed back, as shown in Figure 7-4.

I clicked the Apply button, and Copilot correctly changed the label of the time zone column.

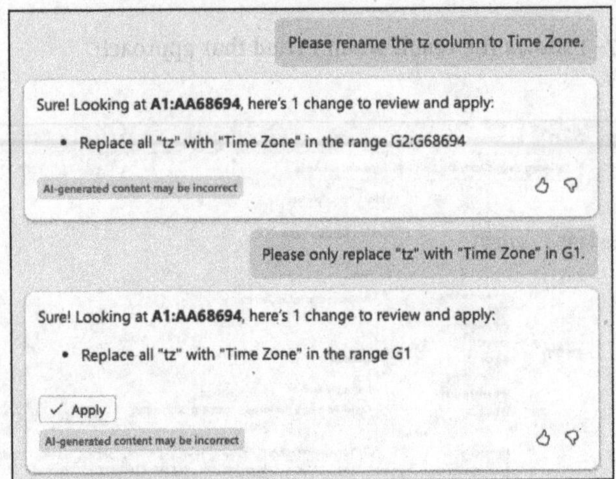

Please rename the tz column to Time Zone.
Sure! Looking at A1:AA68694, here's 1 change to review and apply:
Replace all "tz" with "Time Zone" in the range G2:G68694
AI-generated content may be incorrect
Please only replace "tz" with "Time Zone" in G1.
Sure! Looking at A1:AA68694, here's 1 change to review and apply:
Replace all "tz" with "Time Zone" in the range G1
Apply
AI-generated content may be incorrect

FIGURE 7-4: Clarifying where the replace should take place.

This approach of replacing a single column header at a time is more time consuming than just doing it manually. But, it occurred to me that I already have a simple comma-separated list of new column headers (from what Copilot in Edge generated) and perhaps Copilot in Edge would be able to use this list to correctly replace the headers.

I copied the list generated in Edge and prompted Copilot in Excel to use this list to replace the headers. However, Copilot came back with the message about there being an issue with renaming the column headers, as shown in Figure 7-5.

Use the following list of names to replace the column headers in Row 1. "Tornado Number","Year","Month","Day","Date","Time","Timezone","UTC Date and Time","State Abbreviation","State FIPS Code","Tornado Magnitude","Injuries","Fatalities","Property Loss (USD)","Starting Latitude","Starting Longitude","Ending Latitude","Ending Longitude","Tornado Length (miles)","Tornado Width (yards)","Number of Affected States","State Row Indicator","County 1 FIPS Code","County 2 FIPS Code","County 3 FIPS Code","County 4 FIPS Code","Magnitude Estimated"

I'm sorry, but it seems there was an issue with renaming the column headers. Could you please try again or select a suggestion? If you need further assistance, feel free to let me know.

FIGURE 7-5: Copilot says there's an issue with renaming column headers.

Rather than argue with Copilot, you can use the following steps to manually replace the abbreviated headers with the new and descriptive headers:

1. **Copy the comma-separated list from Copilot in Edge and paste it into a text document.**
2. **Save the text document with the `.csv` extension.**
3. **Open the `.csv` file containing the headers in Excel.**
4. **Copy the new row and paste it into Row 1 of the tornados spreadsheet.**

Sometimes, the best approach to getting what you need done is to combine the use of Copilot with a manual approach. With some experience, you'll start to see where it's not worth it to try to get Copilot to do the last ten percent of a project when you could just do it yourself in a matter of seconds.

Formatting data

The next thing you might notice about the tornado dataset is that it's not sorted correctly, or it's sorted in a way that doesn't make sense to me. Looking at the first 20 rows, you'll see that the first records are from October, November, and December 1950, and then it jumps back to January through September 1950, as shown in Figure 7-6.

Tornado N	Year	Month	Day	Date
192	1950	10	1	10/1/1950
193	1950	10	9	10/9/1950
195	1950	11	20	11/20/1950
196	1950	11	20	11/20/1950
197	1950	11	20	11/20/1950
194	1950	11	4	11/4/1950
198	1950	12	2	12/2/1950
199	1950	12	2	12/2/1950
200	1950	12	2	12/2/1950
201	1950	12	2	12/2/1950
4	1950	1	13	1/13/1950
5	1950	1	25	1/25/1950
6	1950	1	25	1/25/1950
7	1950	1	26	1/26/1950
1	1950	1	3	1/3/1950
2	1950	1	3	1/3/1950

FIGURE 7-6: A strange way to sort the year.

This pattern of the double-digit numbers coming first in the year holds true for all 68,694 rows of data.

It's possible that this is a standard sorting scheme that I'm not aware of, but more likely, it's because the dates are currently sorted alphabetically rather than numerically. In alphabetical sorting, the number 10 comes before 2 because 1 comes before 2. I'd rather have all the data sorted chronologically.

If I wanted to sort by date, I could try clicking the column header. But, because the date is currently not in date format, it probably wouldn't work correctly. The next step in getting this data ready for analysis is to fix the data types.

Changing data types

Before you can sort by date, you have to make sure the Date column is in date format.

Other columns of the table that contain date information and numeric information should also be changed to the right data type. This seems like something Copilot might be able to help with.

I opened the Copilot sidebar and entered the following prompt:

Convert each column to an appropriate data type.

Copilot's response is shown in Figure 7-7.

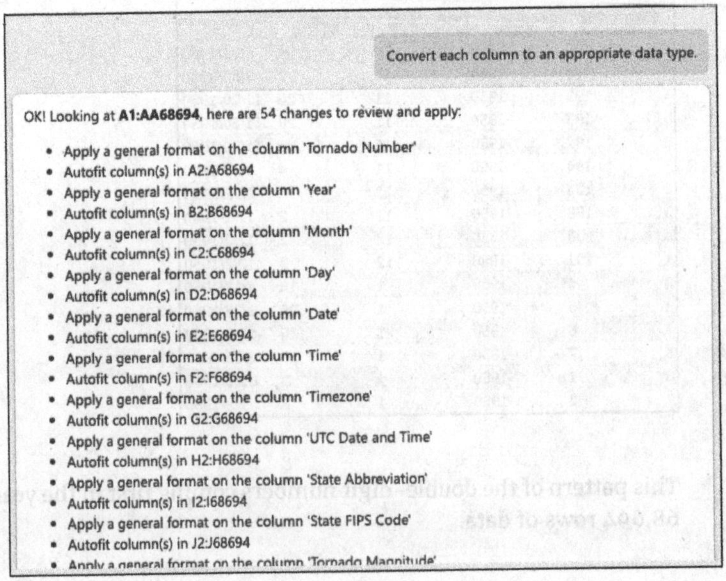

Convert each column to an appropriate data type.

OK! Looking at **A1:AA68694**, here are 54 changes to review and apply:

- Apply a general format on the column 'Tornado Number'
- Autofit column(s) in A2:A68694
- Apply a general format on the column 'Year'
- Autofit column(s) in B2:B68694
- Apply a general format on the column 'Month'
- Autofit column(s) in C2:C68694
- Apply a general format on the column 'Day'
- Autofit column(s) in D2:D68694
- Apply a general format on the column 'Date'
- Autofit column(s) in E2:E68694
- Apply a general format on the column 'Time'
- Autofit column(s) in F2:F68694
- Apply a general format on the column 'Timezone'
- Autofit column(s) in G2:G68694
- Apply a general format on the column 'UTC Date and Time'
- Autofit column(s) in H2:H68694
- Apply a general format on the column 'State Abbreviation'
- Autofit column(s) in I2:I68694
- Apply a general format on the column 'State FIPS Code'
- Autofit column(s) in J2:J68694
- Apply a general format on the column 'Tornado Magnitude'

FIGURE 7-7: Copilot's proposed actions.

For each column, it suggested making the data type be General and autofitting the columns, which I assume means making them wide enough so the data is visible.

Using the General data type for every column might work for most columns, but I have my doubts when it comes to the date columns, and I'd feel better if they used the date format. I prompted Copilot with the following:

Are there columns that should be changed to the Date data type?

Copilot replied that yes, certain columns would be more appropriately set to the Date data type, then it listed those and asked me if I would like it to make these changes. I said yes. Copilot came back with a list of its proposed changes, which I accepted and it made correctly.

I did the same thing to change the columns that should be stored as numbers to appropriate data types.

Sorting data

Now that the dates are correctly formatted, you can ask Copilot to sort the spreadsheet. The tornados dataset has a column with the date and time of each tornado. This date and time is standardized using UTC, so it's a perfect candidate for sorting.

I used the following prompt to ask Copilot to take care of it:

Sort the data on the UTC Date and Time column, in ascending order.

Copilot showed me how it interpreted my prompt and gave an Apply button, as shown in Figure 7-8.

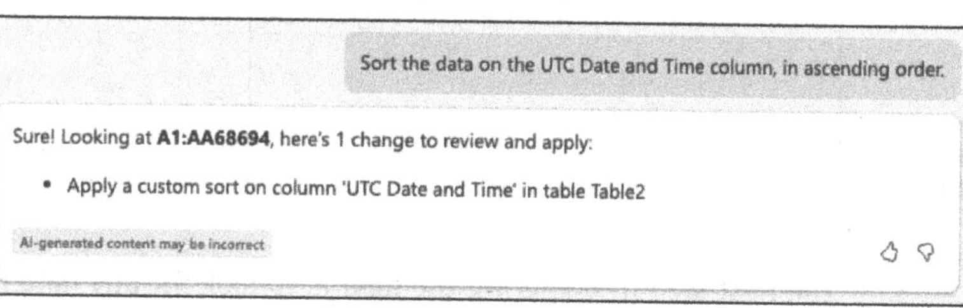
Sort the data on the UTC Date and Time column, in ascending order.
Sure! Looking at A1:AA68694, here's 1 change to review and apply:
• Apply a custom sort on column 'UTC Date and Time' in table Table2
AI-generated content may be incorrect

FIGURE 7-8: Copilot won't change anything without your approval.

I clicked the Apply button and Copilot made the change correctly. It showed me the message in Figure 7-9.

Done! I made the change.

Undo

AI-generated content may be incorrect

FIGURE 7-9: Copilot's completion message and Undo button.

Cleaning data

When you have a subscription to Microsoft 365 Copilot or Copilot Pro, you can use the Clean Data tool to look for inconsistencies in a spreadsheet. To access the Clean Data tool, click on the Data menu on the ribbon. The Data tab has a section called Data Tools, and Clean Data appears near the middle of it, as shown in Figure 7-10.

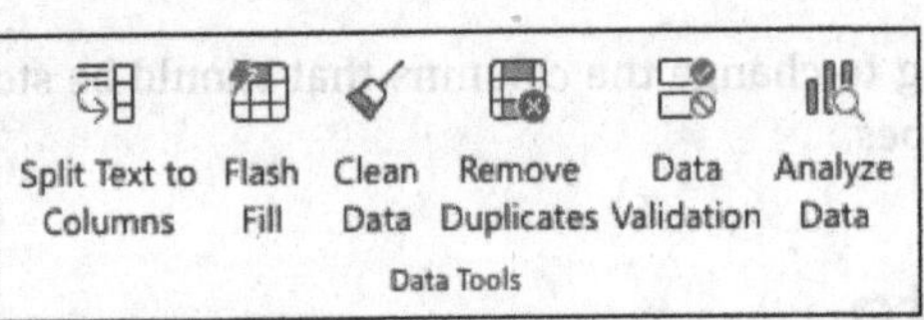

FIGURE 7-10: The data tools in Excel.

Clicking the Clean Data icon will cause the Clean Data with Copilot sidebar to open and display any suggestions that Copilot has for cleaning your data. At this point, however, Copilot didn't have any suggestions, as shown in Figure 7-11.

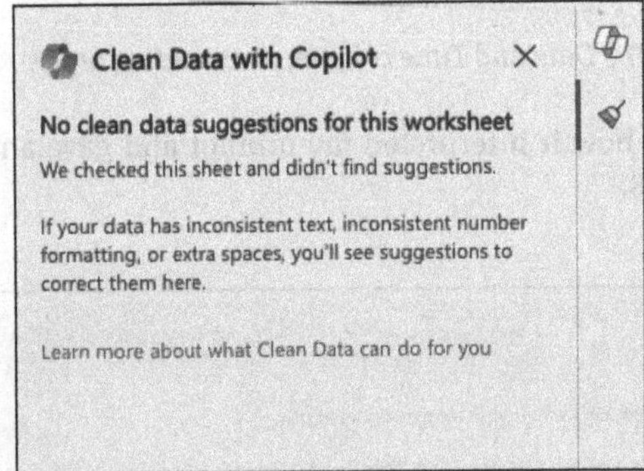

Clean Data with Copilot
No clean data suggestions for this worksheet
We checked this sheet and didn't find suggestions.
If your data has inconsistent text, inconsistent number formatting, or extra spaces, you'll see suggestions to correct them here.
Learn more about what Clean Data can do for you

FIGURE 7-11: Copilot thinks the data is clean.

The next step in preparing the data is to look for any data that's obviously not correct and should be discarded. One way to find bad data is to look for outliers. *Outliers* are values that seem to be very different than the other values in a column. For example, in this dataset, tornado lengths generally range from 0.1 miles to around 70 miles. I don't know much about tornados, but if there was a row with a tornado length of 700 miles, it would probably represent a data entry error.

You can have Copilot look for outliers using the following prompt:

Are there any outliers in my data?

When I asked this question, Copilot thought about it for a while but then responded that it couldn't determine if there are any outliers. This may have been because there's so much data and it's treating every column in the dataset as equally important. As people, we know that, for example, the column containing state abbreviations is unlikely to have outliers and it wouldn't matter if it did. Copilot in Excel doesn't seem to understand that.

I narrowed down the problem and asked again:

Are there any outliers in Property Loss (USD)?

Copilot was also unable to complete this. It may be that this dataset just has too much data for Copilot to look for outliers. I decided to try one more time and to ask if there are any outliers in starting latitudes. Since most tornados happen in the mid latitudes (between 30 and 50 degrees North and South), a tornado that occurs outside of the mid latitudes would be interesting at least, and possibly an outlier that should be looked into.

Are there any outliers in Starting Latitude?

Here again, Copilot wasn't able to complete the job and asked me to try again later. I decided to give it one more shot, but with fewer rows of data.

I made a copy of the dataset and asked Copilot to delete all but the first 1,000 rows of data. This phrasing of my request seems to have confused Copilot, because it only deleted rows 1,002 and the last row in the table. I manually deleted all but 1,000 rows of data and returned to my outlier prompts:

Are there any outliers in my data?

With far less data, Copilot was able to complete this request. I didn't find any significant outliers in this sample of the data, so I feel fairly confident that we're ready to move forward.

Now that you have some data and it's cleaned up and the column headers are understandable, you're ready to try analyzing the data. Continue to the next section to see how Copilot can help.

Automating Data Analysis

Data analysis is all about finding useful connections between different pieces of data in a dataset. For example, analysis of your company's records of customer service calls might discover that an unusually high number of calls has to do with a particular product. This insight might be useful to the engineers working on that product.

Some insights that can be found in data are less useful, even though they may demonstrate strong relationships. For example, "discovering" that customer satisfaction with service calls is higher for calls where the customer's problem was resolved would not be a particularly interesting insight.

REMEMBER

Discovering insights into data, as with all Copilot uses, starts by asking a good question. For example, you might say, "I wonder if there's a certain day of the week when we get more calls than on other days."

Using Copilot for automated insights

An interesting and potential useful feature of Copilot in Excel is its ability to automatically discover insights in your data. The idea of this feature is that Copilot will analyze your data to look for patterns and relationships that you may have missed, and it will even create a chart that shows the insight it found.

In reality, the result of having Copilot discover insights is often just funny. It doesn't seem to consider context or use knowledge of the outside world while suggesting insights. Copilot automatically creates a graph to show you what it finds. For example, Figure 7-12 shows a data insight Copilot gave me from a weather dataset I asked it to analyze, in which it points out that the moon phase (for example full moon, new moon, first quarter, and last quarter) is a repeating pattern. This is quite literally one of the very first insights that humans ever had . . . right before discovering that the seasons are a repeating pattern that occurs in the same order every year.

Other similarly obvious insights Copilot gave me from this same weather dataset included:

- » There is a strong correlation between rain and humidity.
- » Visibility goes down after sunset.
- » Wind gusts are higher when precipitation is higher.
- » Snow and rain conditions have significantly higher precipitation.

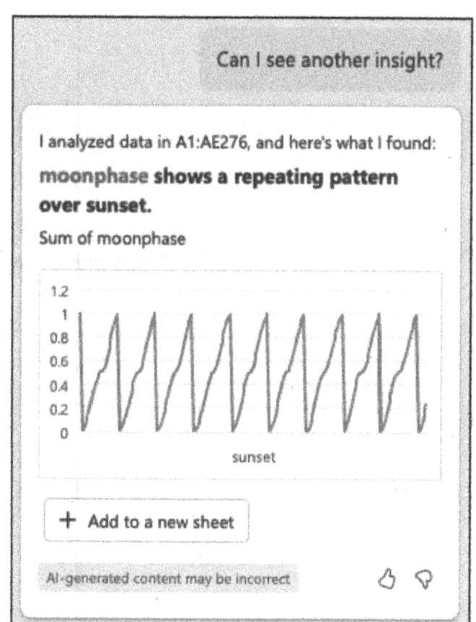

FIGURE 7-12: Copilot's insights are often not insightful.

My hope with the tornado dataset is that adding descriptive headers and giving Copilot more context about the data will encourage it to have better insights.

To ask Copilot to generate data insights, you can click the Show Data Insights link in the chat sidebar or simply type and submit the phrase *Show Data Insights* as a prompt.

After you ask it for insights, Copilot will analyze the data and come back with a single insight and a chart, as shown in Figure 7-13.

This first chart shows the number of fatalities due to tornadoes by year. The number is generally very low, but there are a couple huge spikes. The chart isn't the greatest, however, because it doesn't show the years that correspond to the fatality numbers. I'm hoping Copilot can help improve the look and usefulness of the chart too, but I cover that later in this chapter. To read more about using Copilot to create different kinds of charts and to modify charts, see the section of this chapter titled "Visualizing Data with Copilot."

To see the next insight, click the link under Copilot's latest response to ask for another insight, or just type your request for another insight into the prompt area and submit it.

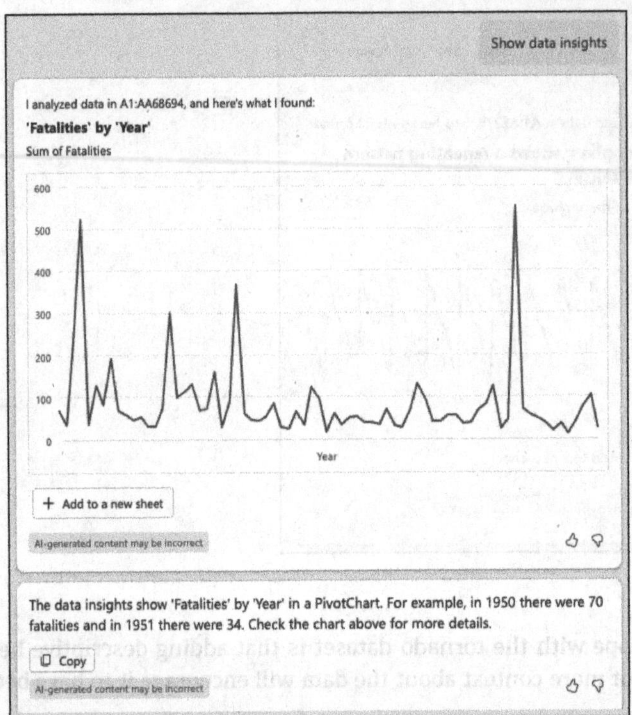

FIGURE 7-13: Copilot's first insight for the tornados dataset.

You can continue to ask for more insights and Copilot will show up to five total insights without re-analyzing the data. After that, you can start over by asking for data insights but it will likely respond with the same five.

Unfortunately, in my prompting so far, Copilot hasn't been able to come up with many interesting insights on its own. At this point, you'll need to provide some guidance.

Asking for a specific analysis

Asking for a specific visualization produces much better results than asking Copilot to discover insights. For example, in Figure 7-14 I asked Copilot to show the relationship between tornado magnitude and property loss, and it successfully created a scatter chart. Oddly, after it generated a scatter chart it said that it couldn't create a scatter chart.

You learn more about prompting for specific charts and analysis in the section of this chapter titled "Visualizing Data with Copilot."

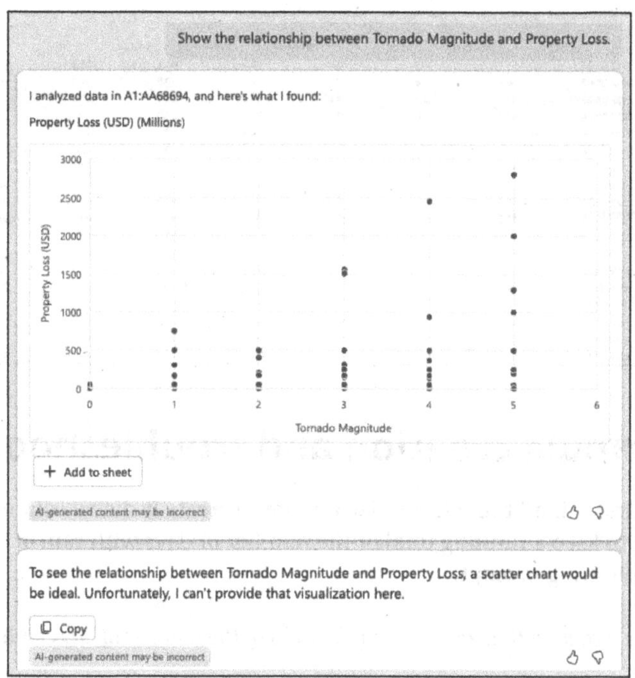

FIGURE 7-14: Copilot creates scatter charts but says it can't.

Creating Formulas with Copilot's Assistance

Formulas in Excel are what make it more than just a way to display raw data. With formulas, you can do many different kinds of operations, such as performing basic arithmetic, summarizing data, making conditional calculations, manipulating text, performing financial calculations, and analyzing data.

For those of us who don't use Excel on a regular basis, creating complex formulas can often be a matter of trial and error — or mostly error. Copilot can help by automating the process of writing formulas and creating columns that calculate values based on other columns.

To try out this use of Copilot, I found a spreadsheet with a lot of potential for doing complex calculations. The data I'm going to be using contains weather data for the city where I live. The spreadsheet has detailed weather data for every day of a recent nine-month period. Figure 7-15 shows a small piece of the spreadsheet.

	A	B	C	D	E	F	G	H	I	J
1	datetime	tempmax	tempmin	temp	feelslikemax	feelslikemin	feelslike	dew	humidity	precip
2	2022-03-01	55.7	47.9	51.8	55.7	46.1	51.5	49.7	92.9	0.4
3	2022-03-02	50.2	45	47.4	50.2	40.9	46.4	46.9	97.6	0.36
4	2022-03-03	47.5	42.5	44.6	44.8	39.4	42.3	40.5	85.5	0.08
5	2022-03-04	48.1	40	43.9	45.4	37.9	42	39	83	0.02
6	2022-03-05	50.4	36.9	42.8	50.4	35	41.3	37.9	83.1	0
7	2022-03-06	49.8	39.8	43.9	48.7	38.7	42.5	38.4	81.2	0
8	2022-03-07	47.3	35.7	42.1	47.1	33	40.4	37.4	83.4	0
9	2022-03-08	47	44.5	45.8	45.2	41	43	42.8	89.1	0.14
10	2022-03-09	50.9	37.1	44.4	50.9	33.9	42.5	35.2	72.2	0
11	2022-03-10	49.9	31.8	40.6	48.2	30.8	39.9	28.8	64.6	0
12	2022-03-11	50.8	37.1	43.1	50.8	34.9	42	34.4	72.3	0
13	2022-03-12	52.8	34.1	43.9	52.8	30.3	41.2	37.5	79.1	0.28
14	2022-03-13	49.2	42.4	46	44.2	37.9	41.5	42.8	88.7	0.73
15	2022-03-14	49.8	45.4	46.9	48.5	42	44.6	42.9	86.4	0.5
16	2022-03-15	51.3	46.4	49	51.3	43.1	46	45.3	87	0.29
17	2022-03-16	50.8	40.7	45.5	50.8	38.1	44.5	41	84.5	0.08
18	2022-03-17	48.7	39.8	44.2	47.2	38.6	42.6	40.9	88.2	0.04
19	2022-03-18	52.9	45.1	48	52.9	44.3	46.9	44.7	88.6	0.11

FIGURE 7-15: A small piece of my weather data spreadsheet.

Formula creation and troubleshooting

The first thing I thought I'd like Copilot to create is a new column that uses a formula to keep a running total of the number of days with rain or snow. I submitted the following prompt:

Create a column that keeps a running total of the number of days with rain or snow.

After a moment, Copilot gave me a proposed formula, complete with an explanation of what the new column will be. It also gave me the option to insert it into the spreadsheet, as shown in Figure 7-16.

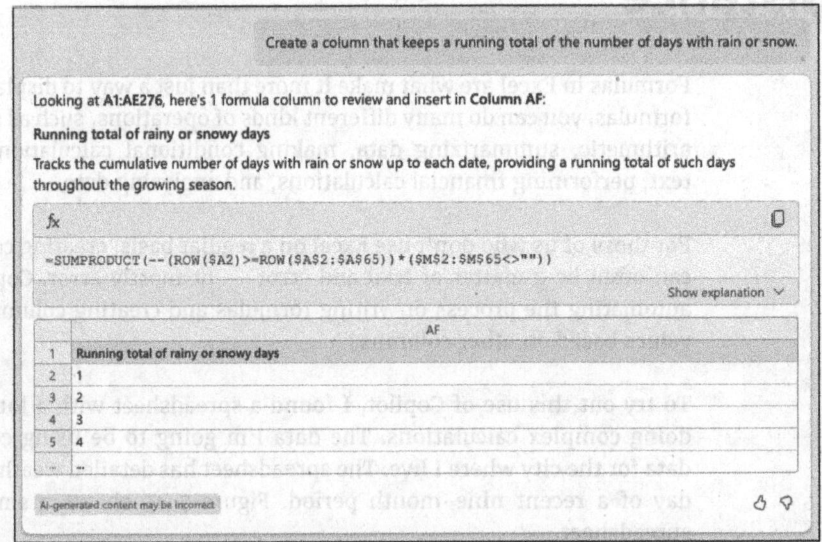

Create a column that keeps a running total of the number of days with rain or snow.
Looking at A1:AE276, here's 1 formula column to review and insert in Column AF:
Running total of rainy or snowy days
Tracks the cumulative number of days with rain or snow up to each date, providing a running total of such days throughout the growing season.
fx
=SUMPRODUCT(--(ROW($A2)>=ROW($A$2:$A$65))*($M$2:$M$65<>""))
Show explanation
AF
1 Running total of rainy or snowy days
2 1
3 2
4 3
5 4
AI-generated content may be incorrect

FIGURE 7-16: Copilot's proposed formula.

Honestly, I didn't know whether this formula would work correctly, and I couldn't tell just by looking at it. I clicked the button to insert the new column so I could investigate it thoroughly.

Looking at the results, it seemed to me like it was counting days with precipitation correctly, but I couldn't easily figure out how it was doing it. Here's the formula Copilot came up with:

```
=SUMPRODUCT(--(ROW($A2)>=ROW($A$2:$A$65))*($M$2:$M$65<>""))
```

Whatever it's doing here, it puzzled me why the highest number row it's looking at is 65 when the spreadsheet has 276 rows, but I ignored that and looked at it some more. I struggled with understanding it for a couple of minutes then asked Copilot how it worked, using this prompt:

Please explain the formula you used to create the running total of rainy or snowy days.

The response Copilot gave is shown in Figure 7-17.

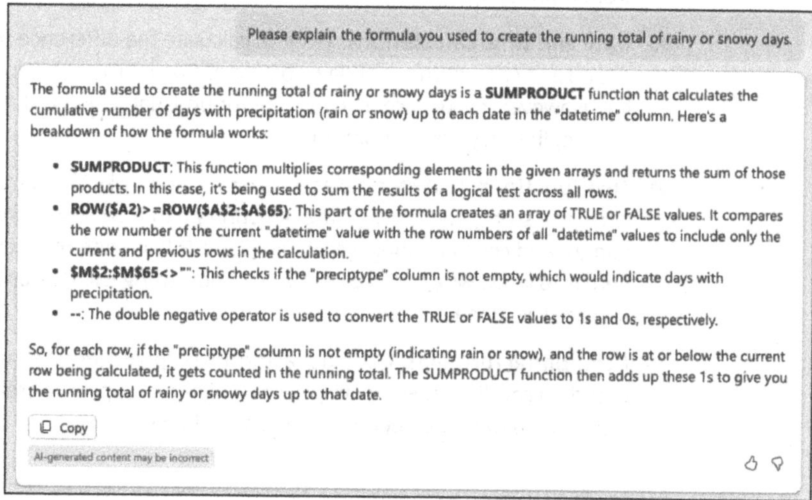

Please explain the formula you used to create the running total of rainy or snowy days.
The formula used to create the running total of rainy or snowy days is a SUMPRODUCT function that calculates the cumulative number of days with precipitation (rain or snow) up to each date in the "datetime" column. Here's a breakdown of how the formula works:
SUMPRODUCT: This function multiplies corresponding elements in the given arrays and returns the sum of those products. In this case, it's being used to sum the results of a logical test across all rows.
ROW($A2)>=ROW($A$2:$A$65): This part of the formula creates an array of TRUE or FALSE values. It compares the row number of the current "datetime" value with the row numbers of all "datetime" values to include only the current and previous rows in the calculation.
$M$2:$M$65<>"": This checks if the "preciptype" column is not empty, which would indicate days with precipitation.
--: The double negative operator is used to convert the TRUE or FALSE values to 1s and 0s, respectively.
So, for each row, if the "preciptype" column is not empty (indicating rain or snow), and the row is at or below the current row being calculated, it gets counted in the running total. The SUMPRODUCT function then adds up these 1s to give you the running total of rainy or snowy days up to that date.
Copy
AI-generated content may be incorrect

FIGURE 7-17: Copilot's explanation of its formula.

Copilot's approach to calculating the running total isn't the way I would have thought of to do it, but I am, admittedly, a dummy when it comes to Excel formulas.

Convinced that Copilot was at least on the right track, I did a manual check of the results from its formula by scrolling through the spreadsheet and counting. The formula as Copilot wrote it stops updating after row 65. I changed the upper limit in the formula to the last row of data, which fixed the problem.

WARNING

I've said it before and I'll say it again: don't blindly trust anything generative AI says or does for you. It can and will be wrong. Its ability to be creative and random is great for some tasks, but incorrectly analyzing data can have real-world consequences. Always double-check its work.

Advanced formula techniques

Copilot can potentially help with many data analysis tasks by creating formulas. The more you know about Excel, the more useful Copilot in Excel is — especially when it comes to more advanced formulas. Here are some additional tasks Copilot can help you with:

- **Splitting and combining columns.** It's quite common to have a name column that you want to split into separate first name and last name columns. Although Copilot will likely get tripped up on names that don't stick to a standard first name last name format (such as people who use a middle name, or multi-word names), asking Copilot to do the initial work and then fixing up places where it makes mistakes is easier than doing this work manually.
- **Date and time calculations.** Want to calculate the difference between dates or add a specific number of days to a date? Copilot might be able to help here too. However, make sure to watch out for unusual cases, such as leap years, that Copilot may not account for.
- **Text functions.** Text-manipulation tasks include tasks like extracting specific parts of a string, converting state or country name abbreviations to full names, and concatenating (combining) words from different cells. The key here is to know when you're better off simply using Excel's standard Find and Replace functionality.
- **Conditional formulas.** Conditional formulas apply different calculations based on conditions. For example, you might ask Copilot to create a formula that reports the wind speed only on days when it's rainy.

Visualizing Data with Copilot

Visualizing is what data analysts call the process of creating charts, graphs, and any graphical representation of information and data. Data visualization makes data accessible and can help people understand trends, outliers, and patterns in the data.

To demonstrate Copilot's ability to create data visualizations, I've chosen another dataset from Kaggle, titled "700 Classic Disco Tracks (with Spotify Data)." I chose this dataset because the appeal of disco music has always puzzled me and I want to try to understand it better. Also, it's a welcome change of mood from the scary tornado data from earlier in this chapter.

So come along and ride on a fantastic voyage into disco and Copilot magic.

The disco dataset is a great example of creating structured data (rows and columns) from unstructured data (disco songs). It contains basic information about each track, such as the title, artist, year, and duration, as well as the numbers that Spotify uses to categorize songs and create playlists. Each song in Spotify has a unique combination of scores from 0 to 1 on the scale of "Danceability," "Energy," "Speechiness," "Acousticness," "Instrumentalness," and "Liveness."

If you want to find out more about the dataset and experiment with it yourself, you can download it from `https://www.kaggle.com/datasets/thebumpkin/700-classic-disco-tracks-with-spotify-data/data`.

Opening and cleaning data in Excel

After downloading and extracting the compressed file from Kaggle, I opened it in Excel in Microsoft 365. Before you can edit the data or use Copilot with it, the file must first be converted from CSV data to the latest Excel format. To do this, use the drop-down menu in the upper right of the Excel program to switch the mode from Viewing to Editing. Excel will notify you that the file needs to be converted to the latest Excel file format, and you can agree to make that change.

Next, I converted the data to a table using the Format as Table tool that I previously used to convert the tornado data into a table.

After converting the file, Copilot notified me that it had three suggestions for cleaning the data. Its suggestions were super bad, however. It suggested fixing several song titles that it viewed as inconsistent. I know that Boogie Oogie Oogie doesn't mean anything, but this isn't the sort of change you should make when cleaning data. I ignored the suggestions.

I was curious about other suggestions that Copilot might have for cleaning the data, so I tried using the Clean Data tool again. Copilot didn't have any suggestions.

Creating charts and graphs

You've already seen how to ask Copilot to create charts using patterns it finds by prompting Copilot with "show data insights." I didn't have high hopes for this one, but I thought I'd take a chance and try it out.

The first insight showed a mostly straight line to demonstrate the relationship between loudness and year. Oddly, it showed a large dip in loudness in 2018. I suspect this might be just because there wasn't a lot of disco in 2018. Upon checking the raw data, it did turn out that there's only one song listed for 2018.

Another insight showed that nearly all disco songs have a 4/4 time signature. This isn't surprising — I assume there aren't a lot of disco dance moves that work well with waltzes.

The insights I'm most interested in are what makes a disco song popular. The dataset has a column named Popularity that assigns a number to each song. The higher the number, the more popular the song. I used the following prompt to attempt to find out what correlates with popularity:

Create a PivotTable of Popularity by Danceability.

(By the way, a PivotTable in Excel is a data summarization tool that allows you to reorganize and analyze large datasets dynamically.)

Unfortunately, Copilot said it was unable to create this PivotTable, so I tried something else:

Add a PivotTable of Popularity by Year.

This time, Copilot created the chart showing the average popularity of songs by year, as shown in Figure 7-18. This chart is largely useless, however, because the years that have the fewest represented songs create the highest and lowest points on the chart.

My next request resulted in something more interesting. Here's the prompt I used:

Add a chart of the highest popularity for each year.

Copilot generated the chart correctly, followed by a confusing and inaccurate message saying that it couldn't create the chart and also that it created the chart, as shown in Figure 7-19.

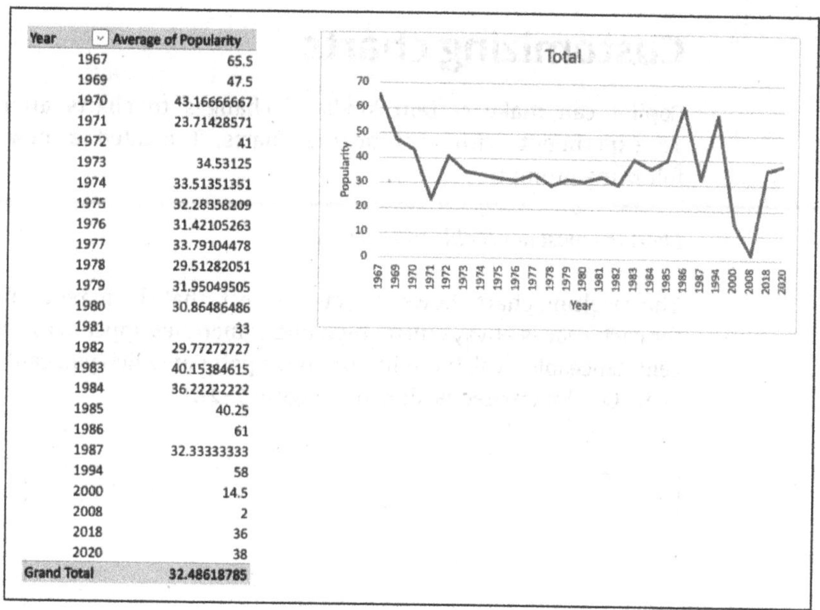

Year	Average of Popularity
1967	65.5
1969	47.5
1970	43.16666667
1971	23.71428571
1972	41
1973	34.53125
1974	33.51351351
1975	32.28358209
1976	31.42105263
1977	33.79104478
1978	29.51282051
1979	31.95049505
1980	30.86486486
1981	33
1982	29.77272727
1983	40.15384615
1984	36.22222222
1985	40.25
1986	61
1987	32.33333333
1994	58
2000	14.5
2008	2
2018	36
2020	38
Grand Total	32.48618785

FIGURE 7-18: Average popularity by year.

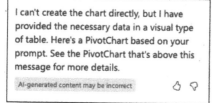

I can't create the chart directly, but I have provided the necessary data in a visual type of table. Here's a PivotChart based on your prompt. See the PivotChart that's above this message for more details.

AI-generated content may be incorrect

FIGURE 7-19: Copilot sometimes just says all the things.

After it generates a chart or report in the chat sidebar, Copilot gives you the option to add the generated content to a new sheet, which I did in this case.

The resulting chart, shown in Figure 7-20, shows that disco reached its peak popularity in 1976 and has mostly been dropping ever since.

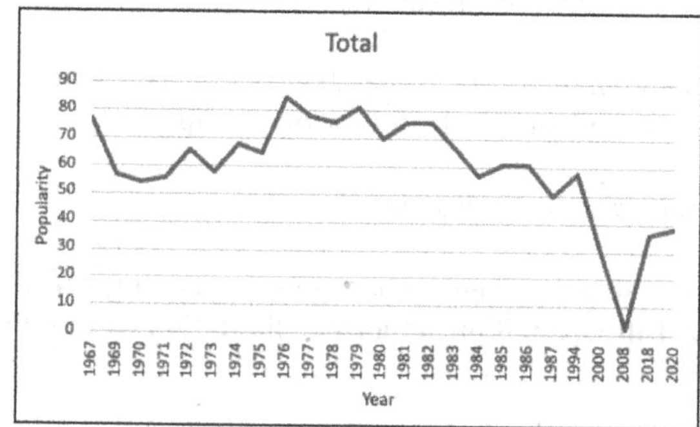

FIGURE 7-20: Max of popularity by year.

Customizing charts

Copilot can make certain kinds of changes to charts after they're created. To experiment with customizing charts, I created a new chart using the following prompt:

Chart the most danceable track by year.

The resulting chart shows, as you'd expect, that the maximumly danceable track for each year is always ultra-high and sometimes appears to get close to 100 percent danceable, which might just be the point at which you can't stop dancin'. The chart Copilot created is shown in Figure 7-21.

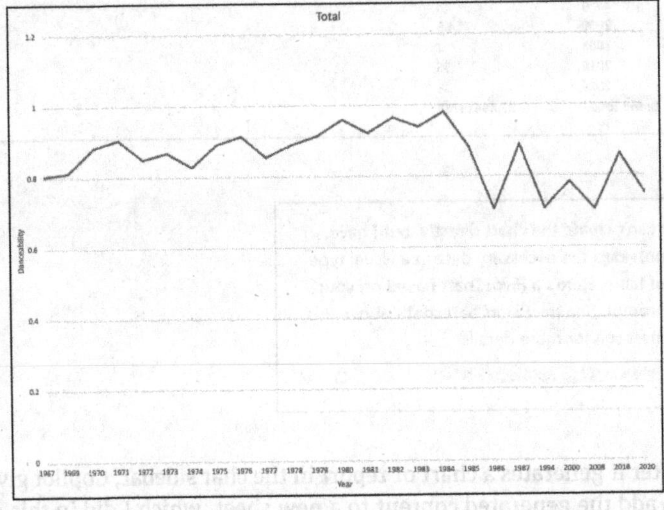

FIGURE 7-21: The initial danceability chart created by Copilot.

It would be useful to label some of the data points on the line chart, so I gave Copilot the following prompt (as well as several variations):

Add labels to the data points on the chart.

Copilot repeatedly claimed not to be able to add data labels to the chart, so I switched my tactic and gave it the following prompt:

How can I add data labels to the line chart?

Copilot gave me step-by-step instructions for adding the data labels myself, which is when I discovered an important limitation to the ability of Copilot to create and work with charts: If you want to add a chart to a new sheet, you have to do it in the next prompt after the chart is created. If you don't, there's no way to go back in the chat and do it. I had to start a new chat and ask Copilot to create the chart again. After that, I was able to add it to a new sheet.

I followed Copilot's instructions for adding data labels, and they worked fine, but what I wanted to do was more complex than the question I had initially asked, so I asked a different question:

How can I label the points in the line chart with the track titles?

Copilot's response to this question looked good at first glance, but when I tried to follow the steps, the options and links Copilot said to use didn't exist. I suspect that the instructions Copilot gave me were for a different version of Excel. I gave up on using Copilot to customize the chart and searched the Microsoft Support website (`https://answers.microsoft.com/en-us/msoffice/forum/msoffice_excel`) instead.

Considering Copilot's Limitations in Excel

Copilot in Excel has some really interesting capabilities, and it's sometimes surprising what it's capable of. However, at this point, there are frustrating limitations to what it can do, and it's often wrong when it tells you what it is and isn't capable of doing. Sometimes submitting the same prompt more than once, or starting a new chat and submitting the same prompt will completely change the response.

TIP

Starting a new chat seems to be the best way to improve the chances that a certain prompt will be successful.

Another major limitation of Copilot in Excel is its lack of knowledge of anything outside of your spreadsheet. This leads to data insights and suggested prompts that don't make sense.

I'm confident that Copilot in Excel will improve in the coming weeks and months, and the version you're using now may be markedly better. If it isn't, we still (thankfully) have traditional search engines, FAQs, and human Excel experts.

Continue on to the next chapter, where you learn about using Copilot to work with PowerPoint presentations.

IN THIS CHAPTER

» Creating presentations with Copilot

» Prompting for slides

» Enhancing slides

» Combining Copilot with Designer

» Rehearsing with AI

Chapter 8

Presenting with Copilot

Most people hate creating PowerPoint presentations, sitting through PowerPoint presentations, and, especially, presenting PowerPoint presentations. Someone must enjoy them, however, because slide-based presentations of information remain the overwhelming choice of businesses everywhere. Whether they're online or in person, PowerPoint has been synonymous with "slide presentation" for a long time.

In this chapter, you learn about new AI features in PowerPoint that can make creating, viewing, and even presenting PowerPoint presentations easier, and (dare I say it) maybe even fun. You also learn how to use all these new AI powers to help, rather than to replace, presentation authors, PowerPoint designers, and presenters.

Interacting with Copilot in PowerPoint

When you open PowerPoint after subscribing to Microsoft 365 Copilot or Copilot Pro, you'll see the familiar Copilot button at the right end of the Home tab of the Ribbon. Clicking this icon opens the Copilot sidebar in PowerPoint, as shown in Figure 8-1.

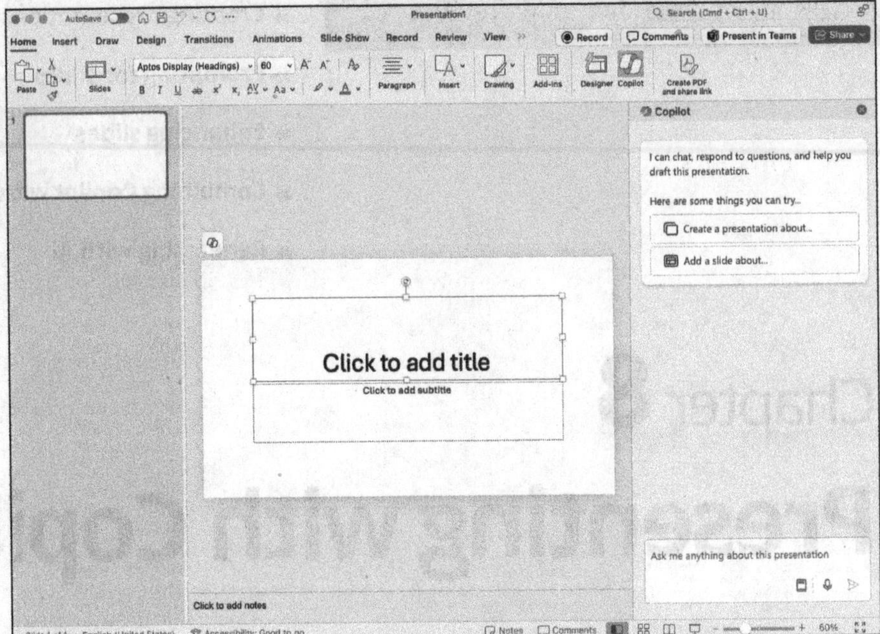

FIGURE 8-1: The Copilot sidebar in PowerPoint.

Using Copilot's built-in PowerPoint actions

As you see in the Copilot sidebar when you first open it, Copilot in PowerPoint has two built-in actions that you can use to start a new presentation. These are:

- Create a Presentation About
- Add a Slide About

REMEMBER

The most important thing about built-in actions is that they must start with this exact command. If you change the words, Copilot will usually claim not to be able to help you.

You can use either of these two actions by doing any of the following things:

- Click the button in the chat sidebar
- Click the Copilot icon in the main slide window of PowerPoint
- Choose the prompt you want from the View Prompts menu in the prompt input box
- Type a phrase into the text input box manually

In addition to these two slide creation actions, there's also at least one more action, called "Add an Image Of". In this section, you see how to create a presentation from scratch using just these three tools. In the process, you learn more about the capabilities and limitations of Copilot in PowerPoint.

Defining and refining your topic

Like Copilot Chat in any other application, Copilot in PowerPoint can answer questions about the content you're working on, and it can chat about any other topic as well (or at least pretend to).

Although I spend most of my time these days typing, I sometimes get asked to talk, online or in person, about some aspect of what I do. I want to create a presentation to have at the ready in case this happens, and I'm going to use Copilot to help with it.

Honestly, I don't know what I want to talk about, but I'm hoping to brainstorm with Copilot to come up with an idea. I encourage you to follow along and modify the details to suit your interests and experiences.

The first thing I did was explain my goal to Copilot with the following prompt:

Help me brainstorm ideas. I'm an author of books about computer programming and AI, and I have to do a five-minute presentation to people who want to learn something about what I do. Give me ten ideas for presentation titles.

The result of submitting this prompt is shown in Figure 8-2.

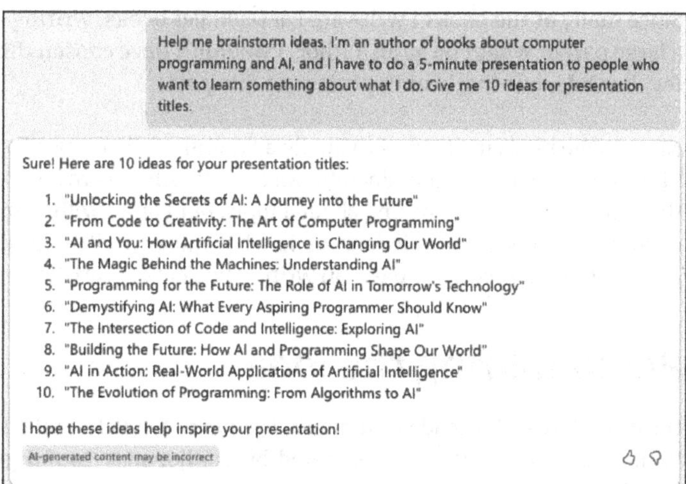

Help me brainstorm ideas. I'm an author of books about computer programming and AI, and I have to do a 5-minute presentation to people who want to learn something about what I do. Give me 10 ideas for presentation titles.
Sure! Here are 10 ideas for your presentation titles:
1. "Unlocking the Secrets of AI: A Journey into the Future"
2. "From Code to Creativity: The Art of Computer Programming"
3. "AI and You: How Artificial Intelligence is Changing Our World"
4. "The Magic Behind the Machines: Understanding AI"
5. "Programming for the Future: The Role of AI in Tomorrow's Technology"
6. "Demystifying AI: What Every Aspiring Programmer Should Know"
7. "The Intersection of Code and Intelligence: Exploring AI"
8. "Building the Future: How AI and Programming Shape Our World"
9. "AI in Action: Real-World Applications of Artificial Intelligence"
10. "The Evolution of Programming: From Algorithms to AI"
I hope these ideas help inspire your presentation!
AI-generated content may be incorrect

FIGURE 8-2: Copilot's first ideas for my talk.

Copilot's first ten ideas weren't very good or relevant to what I wanted. I refined my prompt to make it more clear that the audience is aspiring technical book authors.

Please try again, the audience is made up of aspiring technical book authors.

This time, instead of responding to my prompt with a list in the chat sidebar, Copilot created ten slides, with a proposed title and a description for each idea. It's not what I asked for, but I sort of like it. My favorite idea and slide from the ten options Copilot gave me is shown in Figure 8-3.

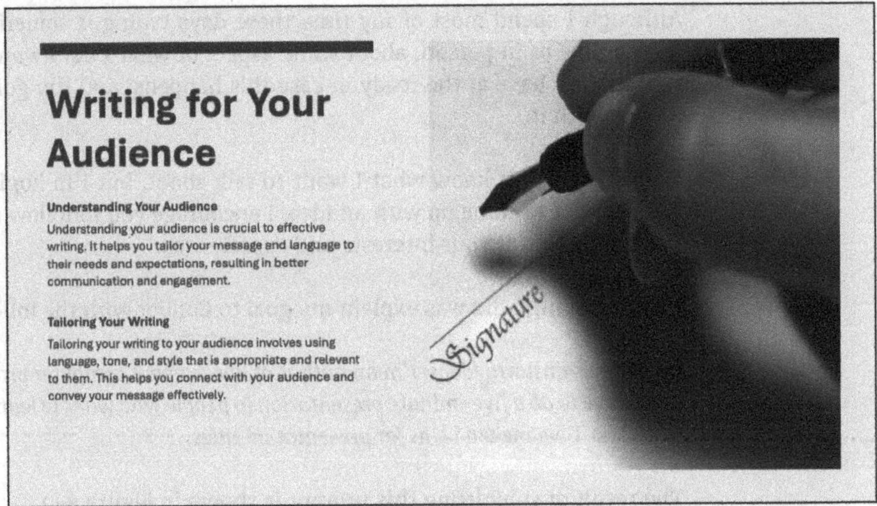

FIGURE 8-3: A generated slide and a proposed idea.

Since many of the books I write are *For Dummies* books, writing for my audience is a large part of what I do as an author. I wouldn't have chosen this particular image for the slide, but that's unimportant at this point.

REMEMBER

No one who reads my books is actually a "dummy." Reading a *For Dummies* book, as I interpret it, demonstrates Socratic wisdom. In other words, you, as a reader, know that you know little to nothing about a topic, but you're willing to learn and keep an open mind! This open-mindedness is what makes writing books *For Dummies* so much more interesting to me than writing books "for certified experts."

Personalizing the idea

Once you have a basic idea for a talk, the next step is to make the idea your own. While ideas and sentences generated by Copilot may sound good at first, upon further inspection, they're always pretty bland and impersonal. Just using slides generated by Copilot without modifying them or rewriting them will result in a boring presentation.

Here are some tips for starting to personalize your presentation ideas:

- Think about stories and anecdotes from your own experience that are related to your presentation's theme.
- Think about images that might be great to use.
- Think about key points you want to make.

Once you have some ideas about each of the preceding three points, you're ready to move on to creating the first draft of your presentation.

WARNING

If you already have a presentation open when you submit a prompt starting with "Create a presentation about" you'll see a warning from Copilot that the new presentation will replace the existing slides and you'll be asked to agree to this or to cancel creating the new presentation. In my case, I chose to overwrite the existing slides.

For my presentation, I wrote the following prompt:

***Create a presentation about** writing for your audience. The audience of this talk will be aspiring technical book authors. I want to convey that you should have a clear idea of your ideal reader in mind as you write and give some techniques for gaining that clarity, including creating a unique persona for them and giving your ideal reader a name.*

In less than a minute, Copilot created a presentation, which is partially shown in Figure 8-4.

So, how did it do?

Evaluating the generated presentation

The presentation Copilot created consisted of nine slides, which were broken down as follows:

- One title slide
- One presentation overview slide
- One overview slide talking about techniques for gaining clarity about your ideal reader

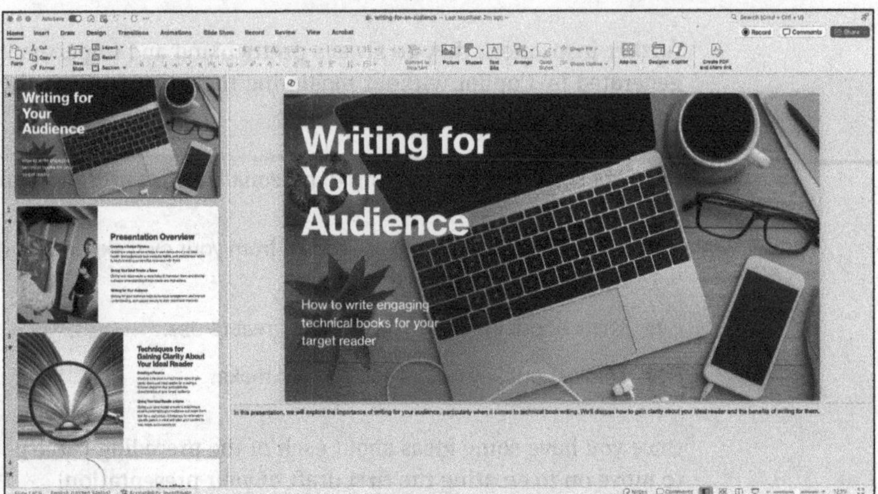

FIGURE 8-4: A generated PowerPoint presentation.

- Two slides expanding on the techniques listed in the section overview
- One overview slide for a section about the benefits of writing for your audience
- Two slides expanding on the benefits of writing for your audience
- One conclusion slide

Ignoring the content for now, I like the structure of the presentation and I can imagine it being a solid base to build my talk upon. I see now that Copilot interpreted my example technique for gaining clarity about your audience as two separate techniques. I could refine the prompt and try again, but I think after seeing what Copilot generated I know how to fix it.

Evaluating the generated content

Copilot did a good job of expanding on the brief ideas I mentioned in my prompt. The speaker notes Copilot generated are especially helpful and even mention some topics I wouldn't have thought of. The slides themselves are too wordy for my taste. I prefer my slides to be sparse on text and memorable, rather than distract from the presenter by forcing the audience to read them.

For example, Figure 8-5 shows the slide that Copilot created for the section overview page of the Benefits section.

Figure 8-6 shows how I revised the content of this slide for an actual presentation.

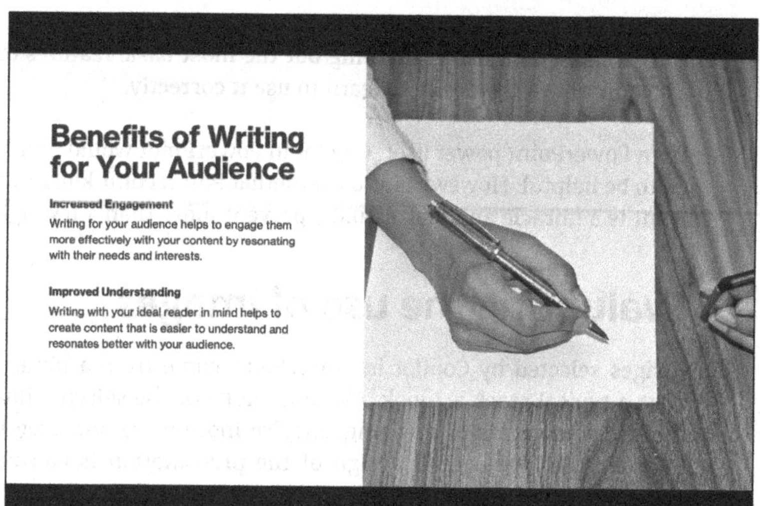

FIGURE 8-5: Copilot's section overview page.

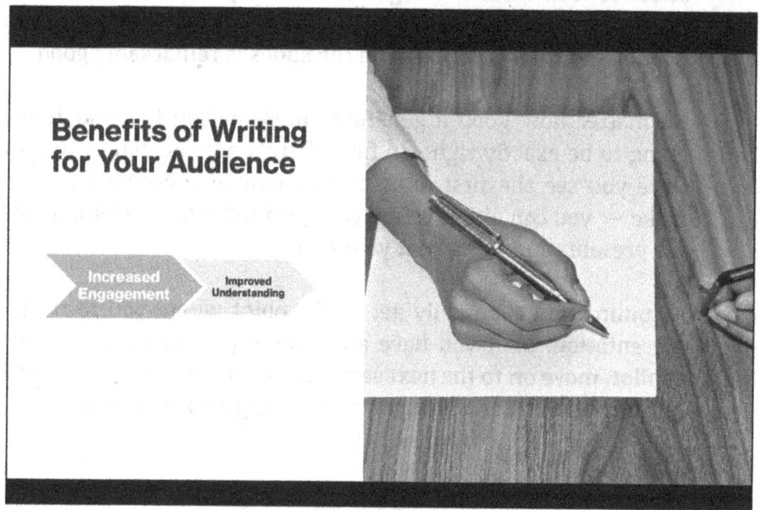

FIGURE 8-6: My revised slide is more succinct.

Evaluating the generated design

Even if I ended up completely rewriting the content of the presentation, I would likely keep much of the generated layout and template. The overall design, including the font choice and many of the picture choices, is better than I would have done myself and better than any presentation I've ever created by myself.

That's not saying much, of course. I'm not a graphic artist and I've never taken the time to become a PowerPoint expert in spite of the fact that I need to create presentations on a regular basis. I suspect that most PowerPoint users are like me and struggle with using anything but the most basic features of PowerPoint, but also don't have the desire to learn to use it correctly.

For a PowerPoint power user, Copilot in PowerPoint would probably be too hands-on to be helpful. However, for us perpetual PowerPoint klutzes, Copilot in PowerPoint is a miracle and may actually prevent more than a few ugly presentations.

Evaluating the use of images

Images selected by Copilot in PowerPoint come from a library of stock art and have a typical stock art look. Although none of the selected images add much to the slides in terms of meaning, they're inoffensive and they look professional. Furthermore, the overall design of the presentation is consistent. I've created presentations on my own that have much worse graphics. Again, if you're a graphic artist or have access to another library of stock art and the time, you could select or create better images. But, for a process that takes only a few minutes from creating a prompt to having a draft presentation, the images selected by Copilot and their placement on the slides is remarkably good.

No matter how good a generated presentation looks at first glance, it's never going to be exactly right. In fact, there's a good chance that most if it is wrong. Once you see the first draft of a generated presentation, you have a choice to make — you can either refine your prompt and try again, or you can start editing the presentation to make it your own.

Assuming you eventually get to the point where you're ready to start editing a presentation, or if you have an existing presentation that wasn't generated by Copilot, move on to the next section to learn about using PowerPoint and Copilot's AI functionality for editing and improving presentations.

Designing Slides with Designer

PowerPoint has a built-in slide design assistant, called Designer, that suggests possible variations on an existing slide's design. To access Designer, you can click the Designer button, which is next to the Copilot button in PowerPoint's ribbon, as shown in Figure 8-7.

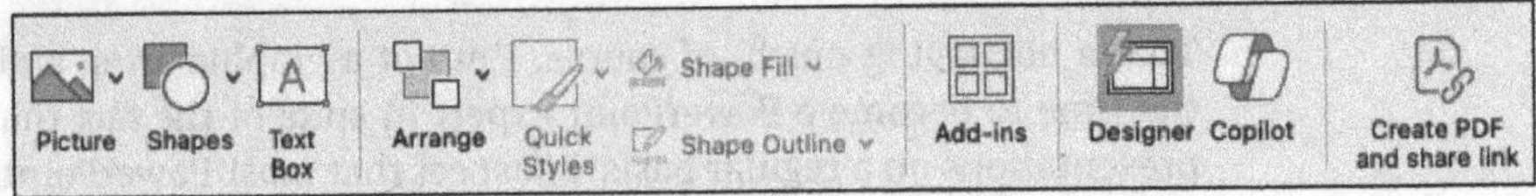

FIGURE 8-7: The Designer button.

Designer is not powered by Copilot, and the designs it suggests tend to involve rearranging the existing content elements, adding animations, and changing the font sizes. In other words, Designer doesn't suggest radical changes, which is good because it only affects one slide at a time. If it did make big changes to the slide it, would be easier to end up with a presentation in which each slide has a different design — which is generally considered bad design.

Figure 8-8 shows the Designer pane on the right side of the PowerPoint interface, with several variations of a slide.

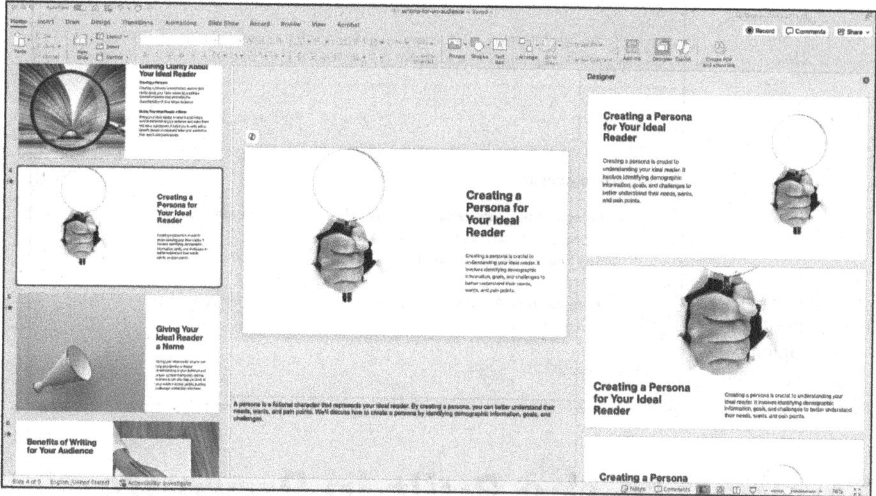

FIGURE 8-8: Layout options in the Designer pane.

Redesigning Slides with Copilot

Copilot doesn't have the ability to directly edit slides that already exist in your presentation. This seems to be a pretty major limitation, and I suspect Copilot will gain this ability in the future. Figure 8-9 shows how Copilot in PowerPoint responds when I ask it to edit an existing slide.

TIP

As with everything involving AI chatbots, there are workarounds. It is possible to make a new slide that's based on an existing slide or slides. If the new slide is closer to what you want, you can then delete the previous slide.

The next thing I thought to try was to ask Copilot to summarize a single slide in the presentation in bullet points. It also refused to do this. However, when I asked in a different way, Copilot responded with bullet points that summarize the entire presentation, as shown in Figure 8-10.

Rewrite the content of this slide as bullet points.

I'm sorry, but I can't do that. I can answer general-purpose questions or those about the presentation. For additional things I can help with, select View Prompts.

FIGURE 8-9: Copilot says it can't change a slide.

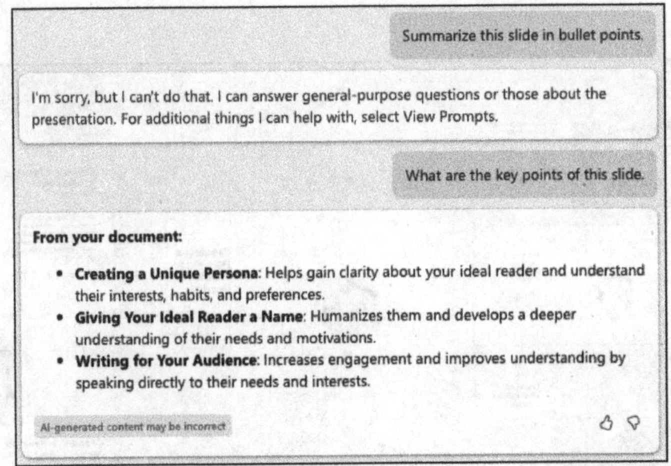

FIGURE 8-10: Figuring out what Copilot can and can't do is sometimes tricky.

Sticking to the Built-in Prompts

Even more so than in other Microsoft 365 apps, Copilot in PowerPoint seems to have a strong preference for the short list of built-in prompts, and using prompts outside of this list produces highly unpredictable results.

REMEMBER

You can access a list of the built-in prompts by clicking the View Prompts icon in the prompt input text area, just to the left of the Microphone icon.

The built-in action for creating a new slide is Add a Slide About. To get another option for an individual slide, I asked Copilot to add a slide about the topic of that slide with the following prompt:

***Add a slide about** creating a persona for your ideal reader*

In this case, asking Copilot to re-create a single slide was well worth it. The resulting slide is better than the first, in my opinion. It has more color, is warmer and more human, and uses bullet points rather than a single paragraph of text. The speaker notes are more detailed as well. Figure 8-11 shows the original slide and Figure 8-12 shows the revised version.

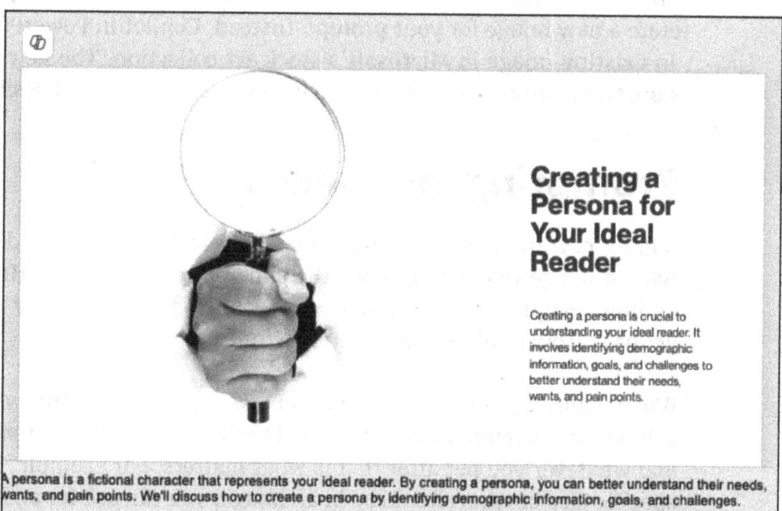

FIGURE 8-11: Copilot's first attempt.

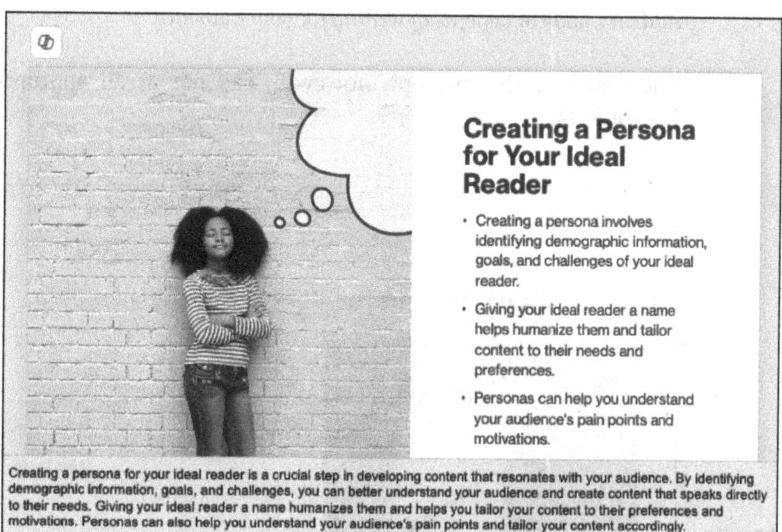

FIGURE 8-12: Copilot's second attempt.

Enhancing visual appeal

Another one of Copilot in PowerPoint's built-in actions is Add an Image Of. Using the Add an Image Of action causes Copilot to attempt to locate an image that matches your request and add it to the slide you're currently editing.

Unlike the browser-based version of Copilot, Copilot in PowerPoint doesn't generate a new image for your prompt. Instead, Copilot in PowerPoint will search for an existing image in Microsoft's stock art collection. The new image will appear somewhere on the current slide, where you can resize and position it as you like.

Prompting for images

Adding new images to existing slides is your opportunity to describe exactly the type of image that would make the slide more meaningful. However, depending on how imaginative and unique what you ask for is, you may find that what you get back from Copilot is completely wrong.

When using Copilot in PowerPoint's built-in prompts, don't worry that what you ask for isn't grammatically correct. Think of the built-in prompt as a command and whatever you put after that is what matters. For example, if you don't have a specific idea of what should be in an image, you can ask for an image of a concept. For example:

Add an image of benefits of writing for your audience.

The result of this prompt, however, was not at all appropriate, as shown in Figure 8-13.

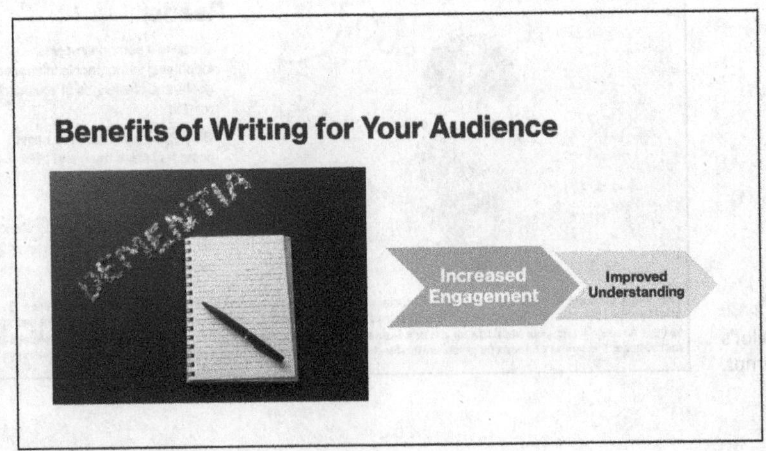

FIGURE 8-13: Copilot sometimes gets it very wrong.

You can get better results from the Add an Image Of prompt if you have a specific, and simple, image that you want to add. For example, here's the next prompt I tried:

***Add an image of** an audience applauding.*

The resulting image is shown in Figure 8-14.

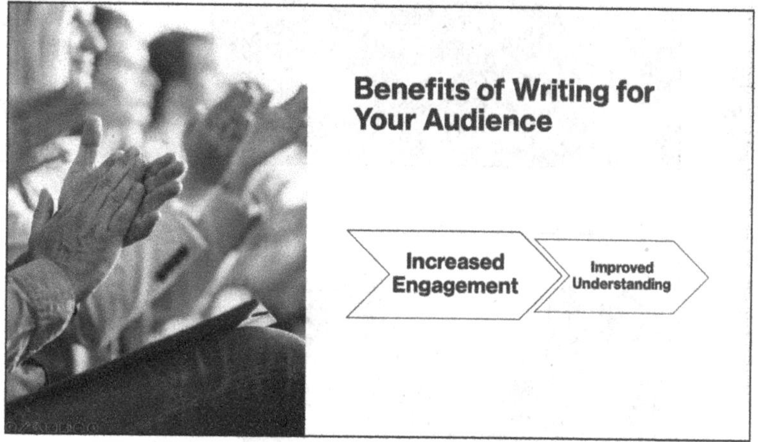

FIGURE 8-14: Simple, common, and specific images work better.

Because Copilot in PowerPoint adds images from a stock art library rather than generating new images using AI, you can be confident it won't contain hallucinations or any of the negative aspects of using generated images. On the other hand, because Copilot is limited to inserting stock art image, your more imaginative prompts won't produce anything like what you envisioned.

For example, in Figure 8-15, I prompted Copilot in PowerPoint to add an image of two cartoon frogs sitting at a small table drinking wine.

For more creative images, you can use Copilot outside of PowerPoint to generate images. For example, I gave the same prompt to Copilot at `https://copilot.microsoft.com` and it generated the image in Figure 8-16, which is much closer to what I imagined.

REMEMBER

Chapter 11 talks much more about creating and working with images in Copilot.

Improved Understanding
Writing for your audience can help improve their understanding of the content. Using language and examples that resonate with them can clarify complex concepts and make them more accessible.

FIGURE 8-15: Two frogs, but where's the rest of it?

FIGURE 8-16: The image created by Copilot Chat using DALL-E 3.

Organizing a Presentation

Another built-in prompt is Organize This Presentation. This prompt will look at your presentation and add new slides and sections to it, then tell you what it did.

Unlike the built-in prompts when using Copilot in Excel, Copilot in PowerPoint doesn't check with you before rearranging your presentation. If you want to make sure you can restore your presentation to the state it was in before you asked Copilot to organize it, make sure to save a copy.

WARNING

In my experience with the Organize This Presentation built-in action, the description of what it did to my presentation didn't exactly line up with what it *actually* did. Check your presentation carefully after using this prompt.

Practicing Your Presentation with Copilot Feedback

PowerPoint's Rehearse with Coach feature uses AI to give you suggestions and feedback on your delivery of your presentation as you are practicing it and after you finish.

The feedback consists of standard best practices for public speaking. It will let you know if you're speaking too slowly or too quickly, whether you use a lot of "filler words" such as "um," and whether you are varying your voice enough to keep listeners interested.

To rehearse a presentation with an AI coach, select the Rehearse with Coach button from the Slide Show menu, as shown in Figure 8-17.

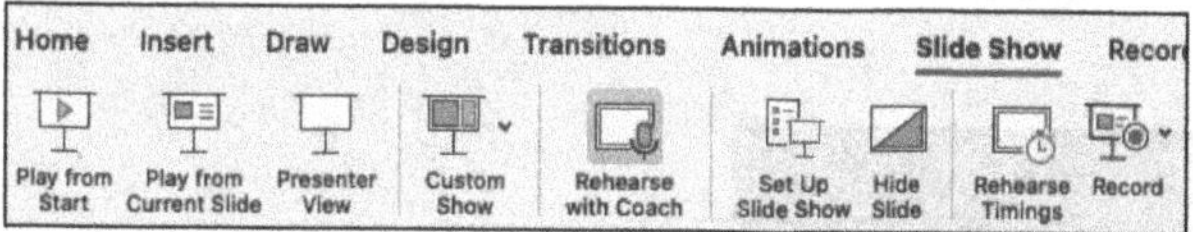

FIGURE 8-17: The Rehearse with Coach button.

Your presentation will start from the beginning and the window shown in Figure 8-18 will appear.

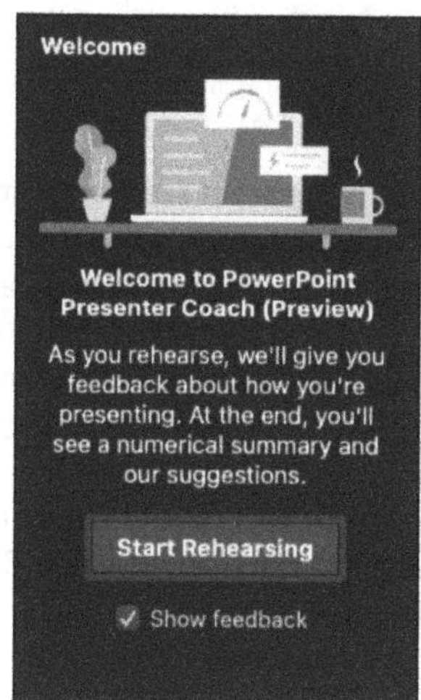

FIGURE 8-18: The Welcome window.

When you're ready to begin rehearsing, click the Start Rehearsing button. The AI presenter coach will start listening to you as you present and will occasionally give you real-time feedback.

Some of the things the coach is paying attention to as you rehearse include:

- Pacing
- Use of filler words (such as "you know," "um," and "like")
- Whether you're simply reading the presentation word for word
- The amount of variation in the pitch of your voice
- The amount of variety in your word choice

An example of real-time feedback you might get from the coach is shown in Figure 8-19. In this example, I reached a part of my presentation that I didn't feel confident about and it showed in my use of "umm."

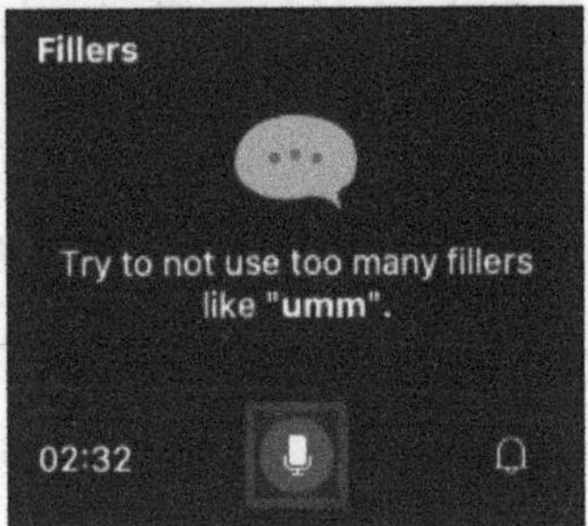

FIGURE 8-19: Avoid filler words.

The coaching is really helpful, although the instant feedback can be distracting at first. The feedback you get from the coach isn't always negative. Sometimes it will just pop in to tell you that you're doing great, which is also nice.

When you've finished rehearsing, a final report like the one shown in Figure 8-20 will appear. It tells you how you did and what areas to concentrate on improving.

Now that you know how to use Copilot in PowerPoint to create content for slides, continue on to the next chapter, where you learn about using Copilot to help you manage your emails in Microsoft Outlook.

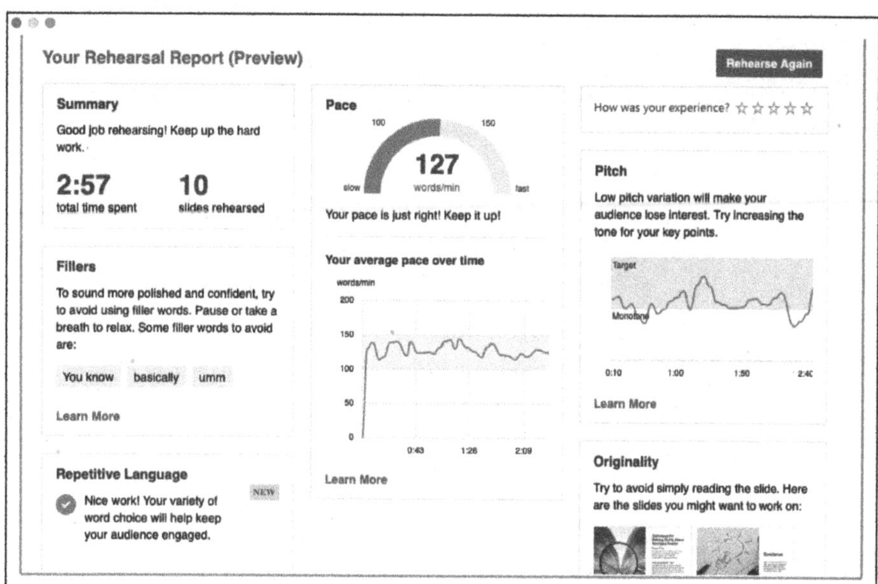

FIGURE 8-20: A sample rehearsal report.

IN THIS CHAPTER

» Summarizing emails in Outlook

» Writing emails with Copilot

» Referencing other documents, emails, and meetings

» Responding to emails

» Managing schedules and meetings

Chapter 9

Emailing with Copilot

Studies have found that the average person spends around two hours per day reading and responding to email. If reading and writing emails is your primary way to communicate with your business's customers or your family, that two hours a day may be time well spent. But, if you're like most people, much of the time you spend managing your inbox is wasted by sifting through spam, dealing with notifications that you may only slightly care about from services or newsletters you've subscribed to, or reading email from colleagues who copy you unnecessarily on every email they send.

If you use Microsoft Outlook as your primary email program, Copilot can help you process, understand, and respond to emails more efficiently and maybe even more effectively.

Summarizing with Copilot

Complex work or personal projects often result in long email threads, and it can sometimes be difficult to keep track of who said what or who agreed to what. One of the first features that you'll notice when you start using Copilot in Outlook is the Summary feature. Summary can take a single email, or a thread of emails, and distill them down to just the important information.

Summarizing email threads

For example, here's a (fake, mostly) conversation between members of a family who are making plans for their mother's 80th birthday.

```
From: Beth <beth@family.com>
Date: Saturday, August 10, 2024 at 7:58 AM
To: Chris, David, Kathy
Subject: Mom's b-day

What should we do for mom's birthday? I'm planning to come to
   town with the kids. G might have to be in Dallas that weekend,
   so I don't know if he'll be there.

From: Chris <chris@family.com>
Date: Saturday, August 10, 2024 at 8:18 AM
To: Beth, David, Kathy
Subject: Re: Mom's b-day

Cool! We'll be there too. I'll start looking at flights!

----
beth@family.com wrote:

What should we do for mom's birthday? I'm planning to come to
   town with the kids. G might have to be in Dallas that weekend,
   so I don't know if he'll be there.

From: Kathy <kathy@family.com>
Date: Saturday, August 10, 2024 at 8:19 AM
To: Beth, David, Chris
Subject: Re: Re: Mom's b-day

Yay! Want to do something at the park? We could hire a band and
   get a clown, maybe? :) Chris, will you be able to make it too?

From: Kathy <kathy@family.com>
Date: Saturday, August 10, 2024 at 8:19 AM
To: Beth, David, Chris
Subject: Re: Re: Mom's b-day

Oh, I just saw this. Ignore my last message. Great! You can
   stay with us!
```

```
----
chris@family.com wrote:

Cool! We'll be there too. I'll start looking at flights!
```

I'll spare you all the rest of the details, but we've all been involved with email threads like this where the details of who is doing what and what's been agreed to — and even who's talking — start to get blurred.

Copilot's email thread summarization can help make sense of it all. To have Copilot generate a summary, select a message in the email thread and click the Summary by Copilot link, which will be right above the window that displays the email, as shown in Figure 9-1.

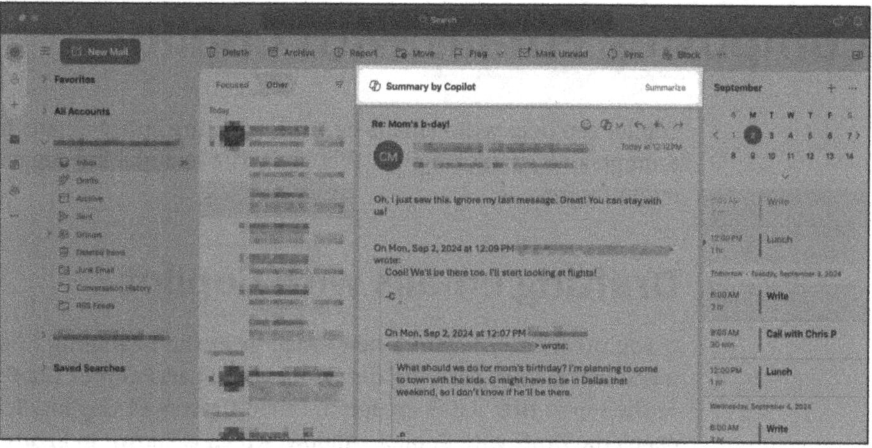

FIGURE 9-1: The Summary by Copilot link.

Clicking the Summary by Copilot link opens a window above the current email where Copilot generates a summary of the thread, complete with references to individual emails to back up each line of its summary, as shown in Figure 9-2.

Summarizing long emails

Copilot can also generate summaries of long emails. For example, meetings can often result in long emails that summarize the highlights of the meeting. Since you were at the meeting, such emails might seem redundant. Still, you might have agreed to do something (or someone thought you did, anyway) while you were distracted by the coffee and bagels. You shouldn't have to relive that meeting by having to read every word of the summary email.

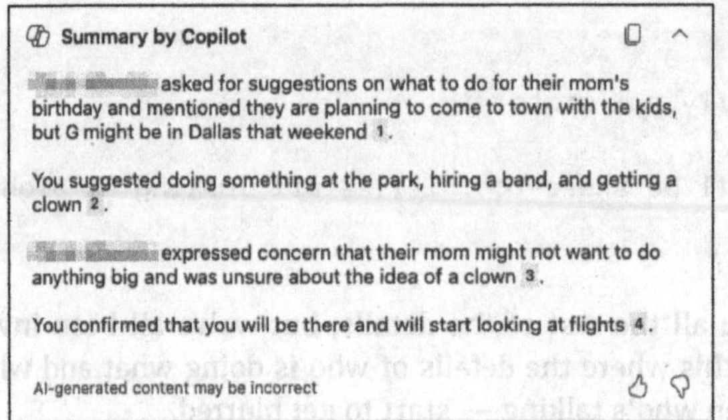

FIGURE 9-2: Copilot generates a summary of the thread.

Instead, you can ask Copilot to generate a short summary of the meeting that includes anything that mentions your name or something you might need to do to follow up.

Composing Emails with Copilot

Copilot can help write emails by either creating entire emails in response to your prompts or by analyzing text that you write and making suggestions for how you might improve it.

Drafting emails with Copilot

If you press the / key in a new email or at the beginning of a reply message, a menu will display showing files from your SharePoint or OneDrive cloud storage. At the top of that list is an option called Draft with Copilot. Selecting this option opens the Draft with Copilot window, which is shown in Figure 9-3.

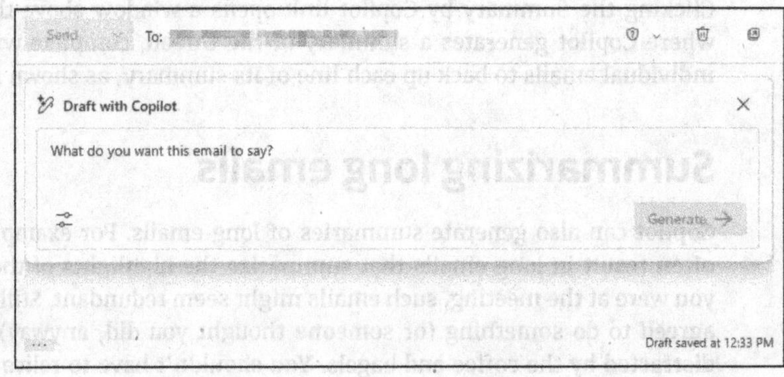

FIGURE 9-3: The Draft with Copilot window.

REMEMBER

The / character can always be used in Microsoft 365 Copilot Chat to open a menu for referencing other documents, people, meetings, or emails. It can also be used in certain other situations as well, such as to open the Draft with Copilot window in a Word document.

Inside the Draft with Copilot window, you can type a prompt that describes what you want the email to say. Before you ask Copilot to generate the email, you can select the tone and length of the email by clicking the Options menu link in the lower-left corner of the window. For example, in the message shown in Figure 9-4, I want to write a long and casual email thanking my significant other for making grilled cheese sandwiches.

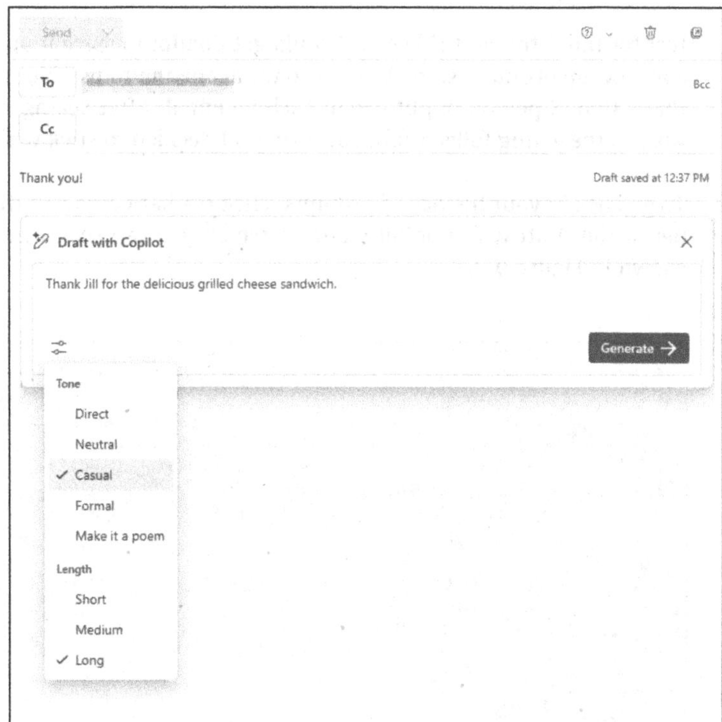

FIGURE 9-4: Prompting for an email.

The resulting email wasn't as long as I had hoped for, but it did accurately reflect the sentiment that I wanted to express. It doesn't sound like an email I'd write, but I thought Jill would still appreciate it (maybe not as much as if I'd actually written it, however). The generated email is shown in Figure 9-5.

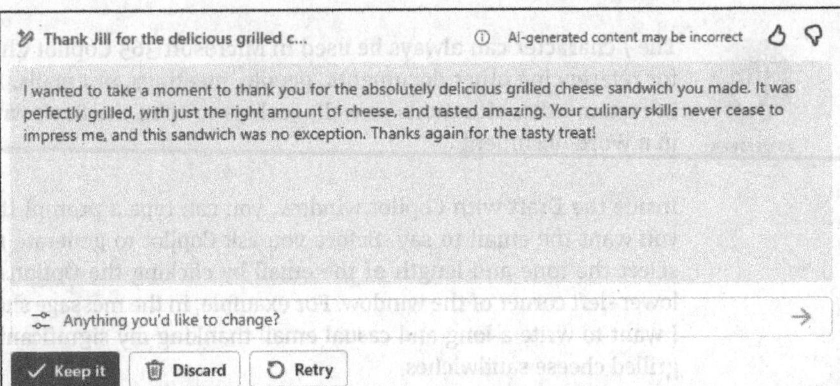

FIGURE 9-5: Copilot's generated email.

Just for fun, I thought I'd see if I could get Copilot to spice it up a bit. I submitted a follow-up prompt asking Copilot to try again and to use more slang and humor that a Gen-X person might use in such an email. After seeing what it did (which was, as the young folks might say, cringe) I decided to stick with the original.

To go back in your history of prompts, click the back arrow in the upper-left corner of the Draft with Copilot window, which you can see in the new email draft shown in Figure 9-6.

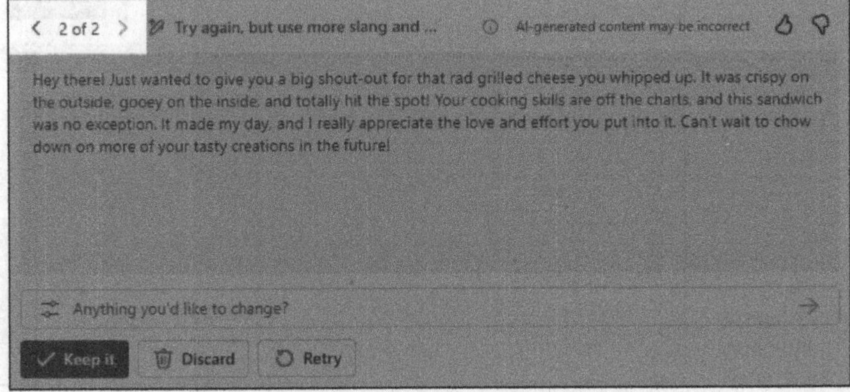

FIGURE 9-6: The new draft and the back arrow.

After Copilot generates an email, you can submit another follow-up prompt with any changes you'd like Copilot to make, or you can keep or discard the draft. I decided to use one of the preset follow-up prompts (which can be accessed using the menu on the left of the follow-up prompt area) to turn the email into a poem. The result is shown in Figure 9-7.

In the end, I decided to just tell her thanks in person — and also to include these thank you messages in my book, of course.

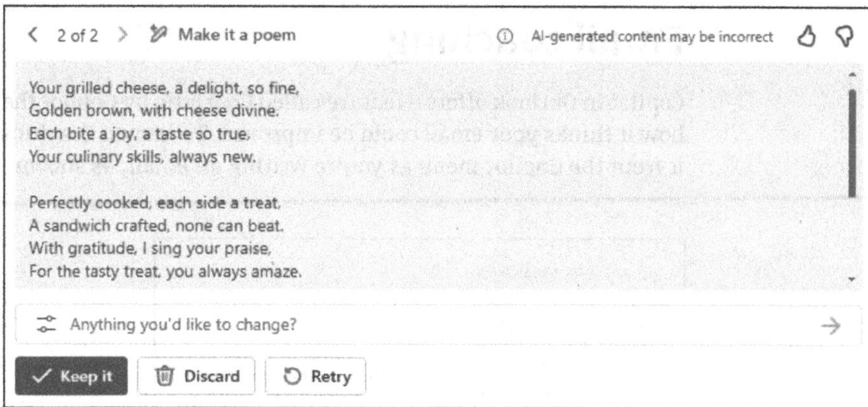

2 of 2
Make it a poem
AI-generated content may be incorrect
Your grilled cheese, a delight, so fine,
Golden brown, with cheese divine.
Each bite a joy, a taste so true,
Your culinary skills, always new.
Perfectly cooked, each side a treat,
A sandwich crafted, none can beat.
With gratitude, I sing your praise,
For the tasty treat, you always amaze.
Anything you'd like to change?
Keep it
Discard
Retry

FIGURE 9-7: Copilot's thank you poem.

Reply suggestions

When you click the Reply button on an email, Copilot attempts to use the content of the message to suggest possible responses. These responses appear in a Draft with Copilot window at the bottom of your email, as shown in Figure 9-8.

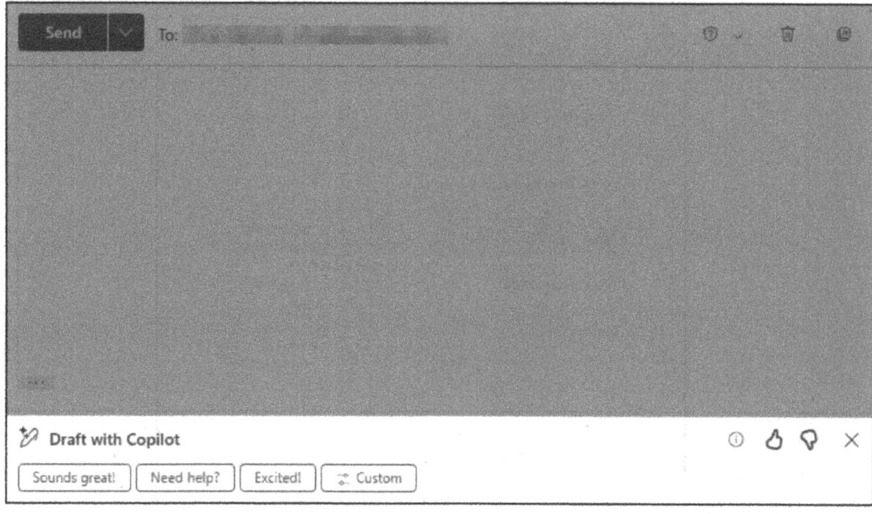

FIGURE 9-8: Copilot provides reply suggestions.

If you like one of Copilot's suggestions, you can click on it and the text of the suggestion will appear in a Draft with Copilot window, where you can refine it or just add it to your message.

If you don't like any of the suggested responses but you still want to use Copilot to generate your response, you can click on the button labeled Custom to open the same Draft with Copilot window that appears when you use Copilot to draft a new email.

Email coaching

Copilot in Outlook offers a feature called Coaching by Copilot that gives you tips on how it thinks your email could be improved. To launch Coaching by Copilot, select it from the Copilot menu as you're writing an email, as shown in Figure 9-9.

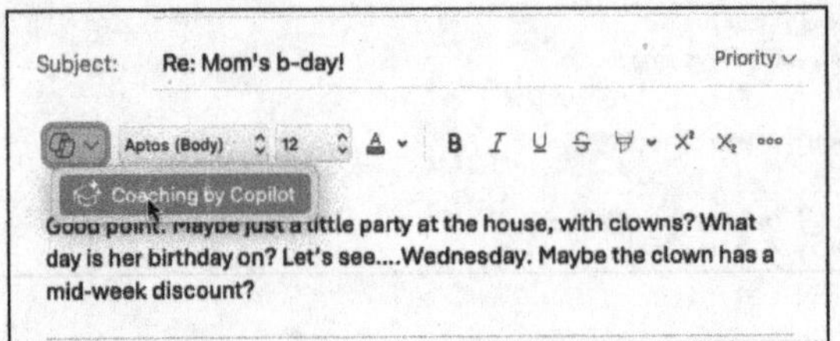

FIGURE 9-9: Starting Coaching by Copilot.

One necessary downside of Coaching by Copilot is that it only works with emails that contain at least 100 characters. If you try Coaching by Copilot with a shorter email, you'll get a message such as the one shown in Figure 9-10 telling you it can't help you.

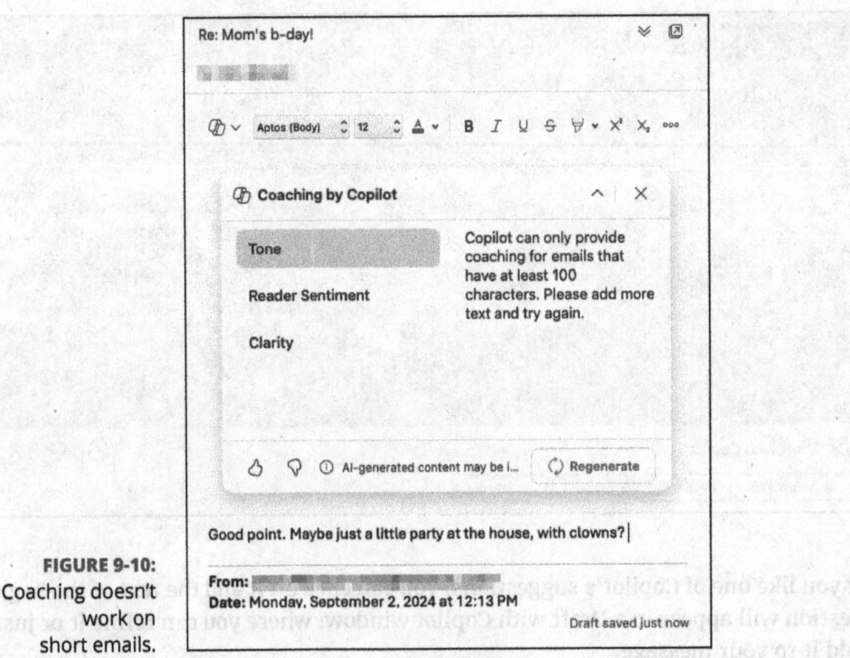

FIGURE 9-10: Coaching doesn't work on short emails.

Provided that you do have enough text in your draft email, Coaching by Copilot will show you suggestions for how to improve three aspects of your draft:

- **Tone.** Copilot gives suggestions for making your email sound friendlier.
- **Reader sentiment.** These suggestions are aimed at making the reader feel "included." Examples of suggestions that might fall into this category are suggestions such as ending your email with "What do you think?".
- **Clarity.** The Clarity category of suggestions are ways that Copilot thinks you might specify the details of your email more clearly.

In my experience with Coaching by Copilot, it often provided good suggestions, but it interpreted jokes literally and ruined them.

Figure 9-11 shows a typical suggestion from Coaching by Copilot.

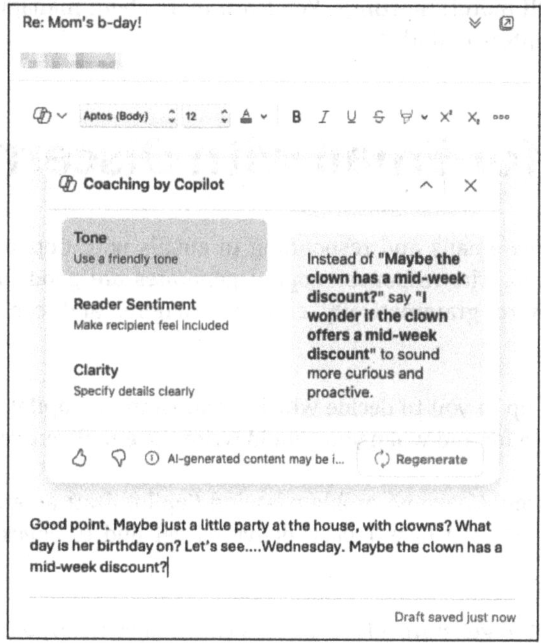

FIGURE 9-11: Copilot tells me to work on my enthusiasm.

Email coaching seems like it would be a good feature when writing important emails to your boss or to customers. For everyday communications with friends and colleagues, it seems like following its recommendations could make your emails sound insincere and humorless.

One thing I like about Coaching by Copilot is that it leaves the decision of whether to follow any of its suggestions up to you. It doesn't even seem to have the ability to automatically insert the new text it suggests.

Meeting management

Copilot 365 in Outlook has access to your inbox and your calendar. When a meeting request comes from Microsoft Teams or another calendar app comes in via email, Outlook displays an RSVP button on the email in your list of emails. When you open the email, the details of the meeting are automatically summarized above the text of the message.

Every meeting on your calendar is available in the context menu, which you can access using the / command in Copilot Chat so you can reference your calendar while generating new emails or other documents. This is particularly helpful for coordinating with multiple people or responding to questions about your availability for (still more!) meetings. You learn more about managing meetings with Copilot in Chapters 10 and 12.

Using Copilot for Email with Discernment

Composing new emails and responding to emails with Copilot's help generally works very well. The responses Copilot generates are good in many ways. For example, they're grammatically correct, friendly, and can sometimes even be clever.

However, it's up to you to decide which circumstances Copilot-generated emails are appropriate for and when you should write the email yourself.

Most people would have no problem having Copilot draft an email to report that the book you ordered hasn't been delivered yet and to check on the status of the order.

Asking Copilot to generate a love letter, a condolence letter, or a cover letter for a job application would likely seem wrong to most people. But, maybe this is just because we're all still new to this. Perhaps in the future writing your own emails will seem as archaic as sending telegrams.

Continue on to the next chapter, where you learn about using Copilot to enhance face-to-face virtual meetings in Microsoft Teams.

IN THIS CHAPTER

» Preparing for meetings

» Getting assistance

» Taking notes

» Summarizing meetings

» Collaborating with Copilot

Chapter 10
Meeting and Collaborating with Copilot

Most meetings these days are conducted virtually, with participants spread over multiple locations and, often, multiple time zones. Just finding a good time to meet can often be a chore. Making sure everyone is prepared for the meeting and that the meeting isn't a waste of everyone's time is a whole different project.

Using a virtual meeting platform such as Microsoft Teams can help. Teams integrates with your calendar, email, and project management tools. It can streamline the process of planning, conducting, and following up on meetings.

Microsoft 365 Copilot in Teams enables meeting participants to ask questions about meetings, summarize the meetings, and more. Copilot may even make it possible for you to skip more meetings!

Microsoft 365 Copilot Chat in Teams was recently rebranded as Business Chat, or "BizChat" for short. In this chapter, I use the original name.

Using Copilot in Microsoft Teams

To use Copilot during Teams meetings, you need to have a Copilot Pro or Microsoft Copilot 365 subscription. With an active subscription, you can access Copilot Chat in Teams by clicking the Chat icon on the left toolbar and then selecting Copilot Chat, as shown in Figure 10-1.

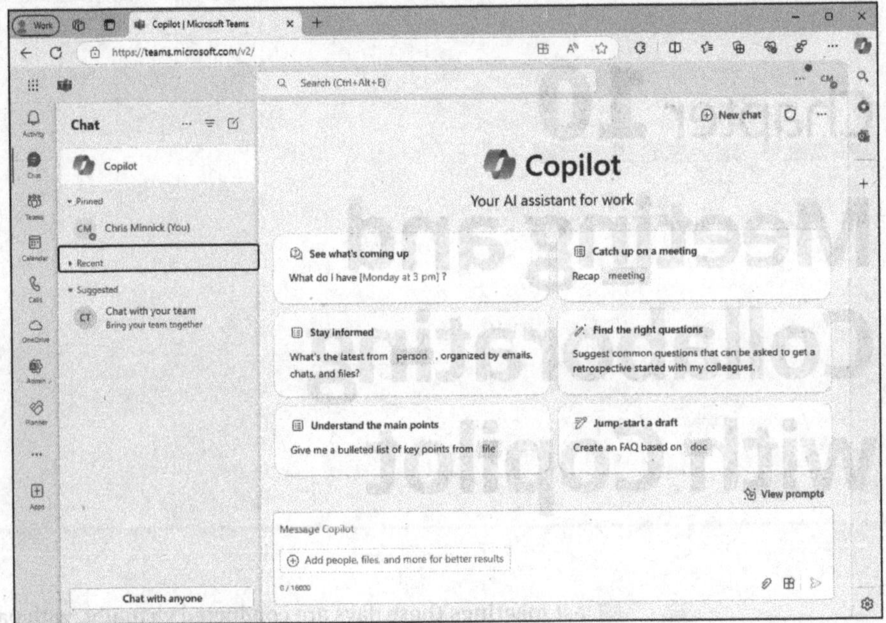

FIGURE 10-1: Microsoft 365 Copilot Chat in Teams.

Copilot Chat in Teams can answer questions about meetings that have already happened or that are scheduled. It can also generate responses by using emails, chats, and files.

Perhaps the most interesting things Copilot can do in Teams have to do with understanding and recapping meetings. To enable Copilot to help you during and after meetings, you must turn on transcriptions in Teams.

To enable transcriptions, click the Admin icon on the left toolbar, then click Home in the Admin navigation, then click Set Up Meeting Preferences. The Set Up Meeting Preferences window will open. Look for the Allow Transcription option and enable it, as shown in Figure 10-2.

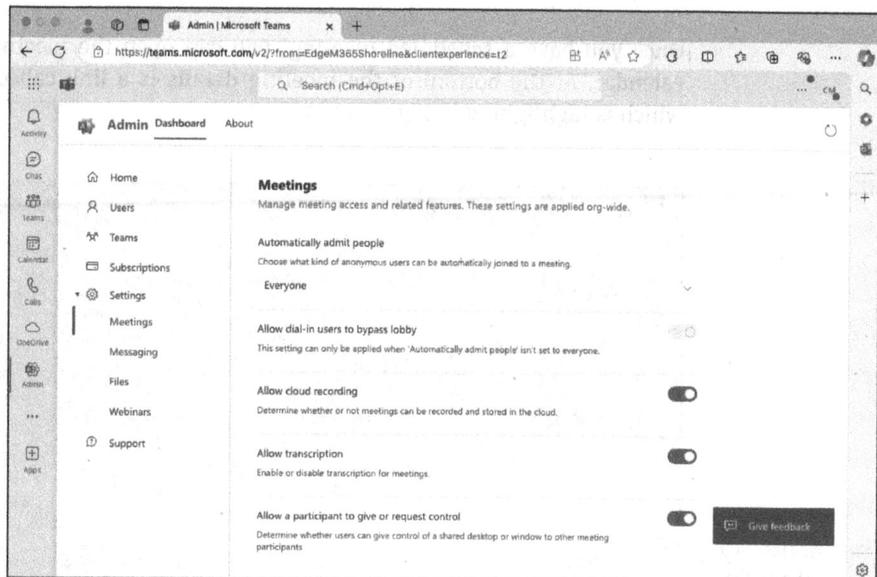

FIGURE 10-2: Allowing transcriptions.

Preparing for and setting up meetings

The first step in having a meeting is to figure out why you're having a meeting (and whether it's necessary). This may involve sending an email to the people who should be in the meeting and explaining what the meeting will be about, then figuring out everyone's availability.

I need to meet with a colleague of mine to discuss a project I recently completed and to talk about process improvements I think we can make for similar projects in the future.

I opened Outlook and used the Draft with Copilot feature to write an email to my colleague Chris P. proposing a meeting and asking him about his availability.

REMEMBER

You can read more about using Copilot to draft emails in Chapter 9.

I have a booking page set up through Outlook, which allows anyone to see my availability and schedule a meeting with me. Chris P. promptly scheduled a meeting with me on Monday.

TIP

If you have a Microsoft 365 account, you can set up a booking page too, by going to Settings ➪ Calendar in Outlook. Once you have a booking page, you can specify your availability for different types of meetings, then include a link to your booking page in your email signature or on your website.

Once you have a scheduled meeting, you can open the meeting details in your calendar. At the bottom of the meeting details is a link called Add an Agenda, which is highlighted in Figure 10-3.

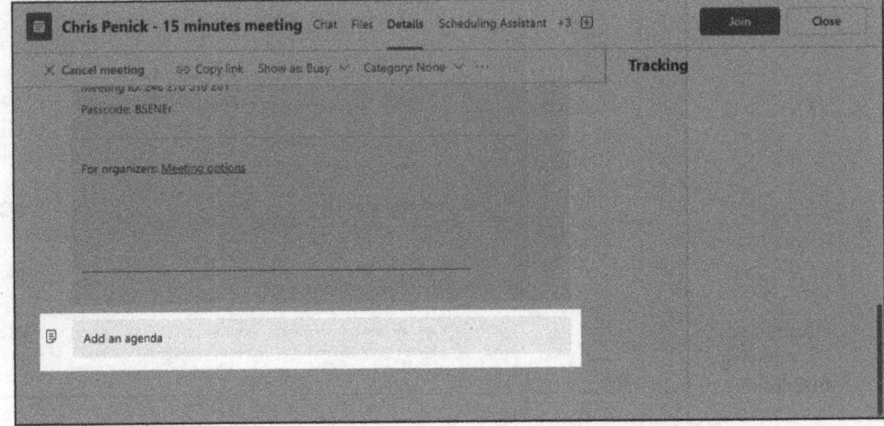

FIGURE 10-3: The Add an Agenda link.

Clicking the Add an Agenda link opens a new window with three sections: Topics, Meeting Notes, and Follow-up Tasks. This window is actually an embedded view from your Microsoft Loop account.

TIP

Microsoft Loop is an online collaborative workspace that helps people gather and organize information about projects.

When you click your mouse into one of the three sections in the Loop window, the Copilot logo appears to the right of the selected line, as shown in Figure 10-4.

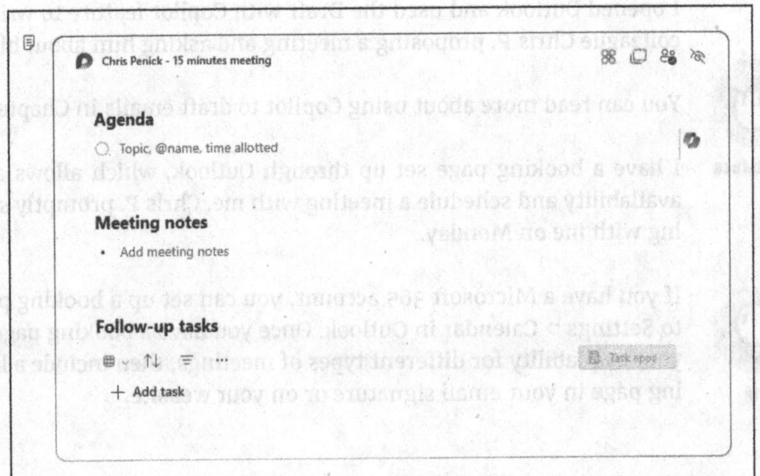

FIGURE 10-4: The Copilot logo in the Agenda window.

Clicking the Copilot logo opens a prompt input area with several buttons below it: Create, Brainstorm, Blueprint, and Describe. Each of these buttons populates the prompt text input area with a sample prompt, as shown in Figure 10-5.

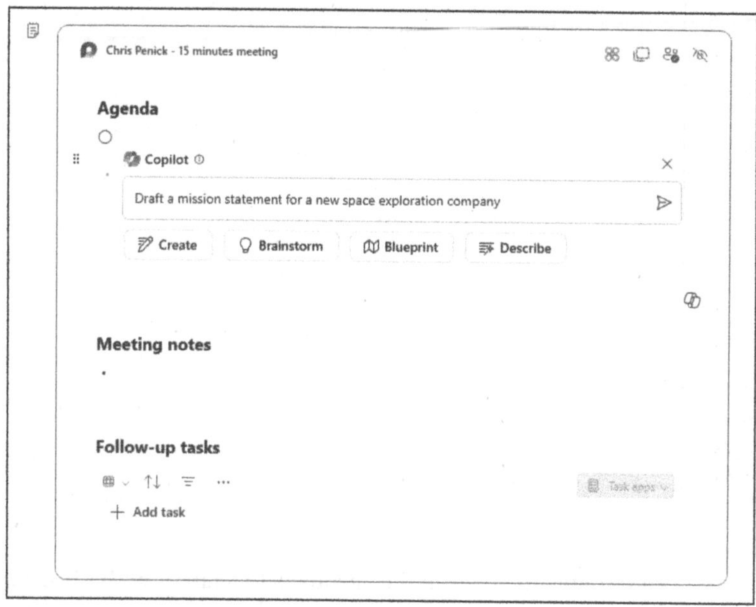

FIGURE 10-5: Viewing sample prompts to populate the agenda.

I entered some details about what I expected the meeting with Chris P. would be about, and I asked Copilot to generate an agenda. Copilot broke apart my sentence into eight numbered agenda items with two or three bullet points beneath each one.

My original prompt and the beginning of the generated agenda are shown in Figure 10-6.

The agenda that Copilot created wasn't bad, although it was longer than I thought was necessary, and it contained a couple of unnecessary points. In all, I estimate that using Copilot saved me about 15 minutes by giving me something to start with for writing the agenda — if I even would have bothered to write an agenda for the meeting without Copilot. Honestly, I probably wouldn't have bothered. But, I'm feeling good about the chances of this meeting resulting in something good.

The other two items in the meeting agenda window are Meeting Notes and Follow-up Tasks. I'll have to wait until after the meeting next Monday to fill those in!

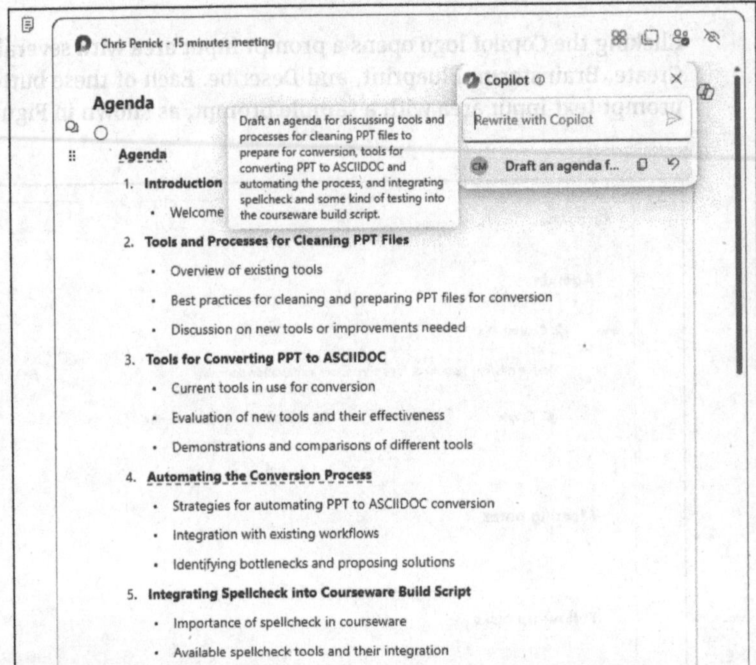

FIGURE 10-6: Copilot's generated agenda.

The last step in creating the agenda is to share it with Chris P. Since he isn't part of my Microsoft 365 organization, I clicked the link at the bottom of the embedded Loop window to go to the project in the Loop app itself.

At the top of the Loop page for the meeting is a Share button where you can copy a link to the page and specify who has access. Unfortunately, it's not possible to share a Loop page with someone outside of your organization.

I clicked the Send Update button in the meeting details and it sent an email to Chris P., but that email didn't contain the agenda. So, I copied the agenda from the embedded Loop window and pasted it into the Teams meeting invitation itself and sent another meeting update.

TIP

It's helpful to have a friend or colleague who won't be annoyed by extra messages as you're figuring out what can and can't be done in Teams and with Copilot in Teams.

Getting real-time meeting assistance

Copilot can help with various tasks while you're in a Teams meeting. To allow Copilot to answer questions about the meeting, you must turn on transcription for the meeting. If you already followed the steps at the beginning of this chapter to enable transcriptions in Teams, you'll be able to turn on transcriptions for an individual meeting by clicking the More button at the top of the screen, selecting Record and Transcribe, then selecting Start Transcription, as shown in Figure 10-7.

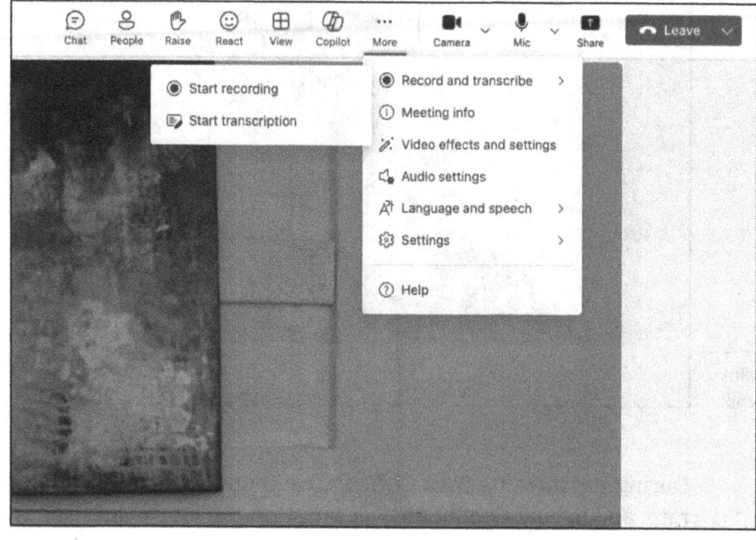

FIGURE 10-7: Enabling transcription.

With transcription enabled, a live transcription of the meeting along with labels indicating who's speaking will be accessible to all participants in the meeting. This live transcription is what Copilot uses to answer questions about the meeting.

To access Copilot in Teams while you're in a meeting, click the Copilot icon in the top toolbar of Teams. A Copilot sidebar will appear on the left, as shown in Figure 10-8.

You can ask Copilot anything about the meeting and it will consult the transcript and generate a response. Some of the suggested prompts that Copilot lists under the More Prompts menu in the prompt input box are:

- Recap meeting so far
- List action items
- Suggest follow-up questions
- What questions are unresolved?
- List different perspectives by topic
- List main ideas we discussed
- Generate meeting notes

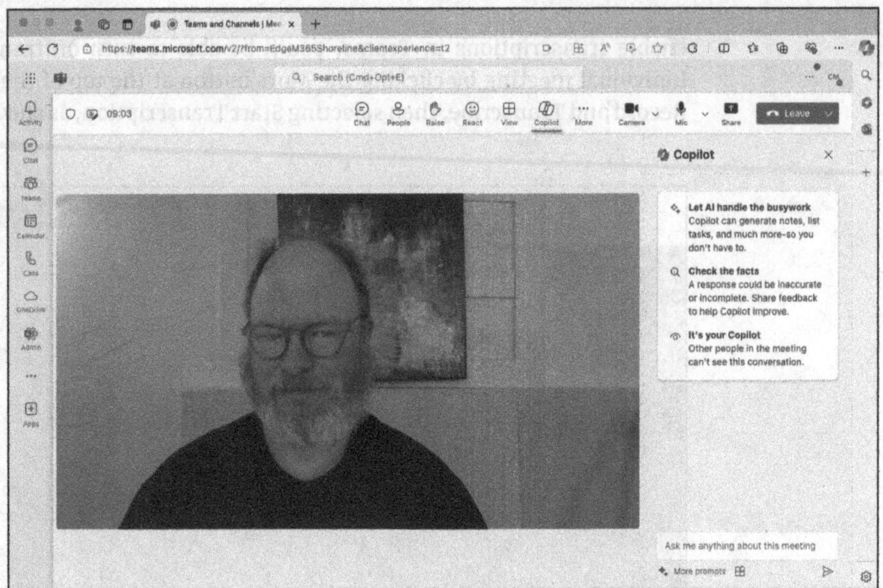

FIGURE 10-8: The Copilot sidebar in Teams.

During my meeting with Chris P., we found the transcription to be highly accurate, and having Copilot answer questions about the meeting worked well too.

My attempt to use Live Captions with Translation on a Copilot+ PC during the meeting was less than successful, however. We tried it with German, French, Spanish, and the few phrases of Japanese that Chris P. knows. The translations weren't even close enough to make sense of, as shown in Figure 10-9.

Only a little German, but
how about the Hong Kong Great Muscat

FIGURE 10-9: Live Captions with Translation isn't quite there yet.

REMEMBER

You can read more about Live Captions on a Copilot+ PC in Chapter 5.

After we'd been talking for about ten minutes, I asked Copilot to create a summary of the meeting so far, and its response was accurate and even useful for helping me steer the conversation.

In a meeting with just two people, having access to Copilot to answer questions about the meeting might be unnecessary and distract from the meeting. However, in larger meetings, you may wonder how you ever survived a meeting without it.

For meetings of any size, the really interesting and useful part of having Copilot in Teams comes after the meeting is finished.

Accessing post-meeting summaries

Shortly after you finish a meeting, a message like the one in Figure 10-10 will appear in the Chat window of Teams to tell you that the recording is ready and to give you an option to view a recap of the meeting, or the meeting transcript, video, or notes.

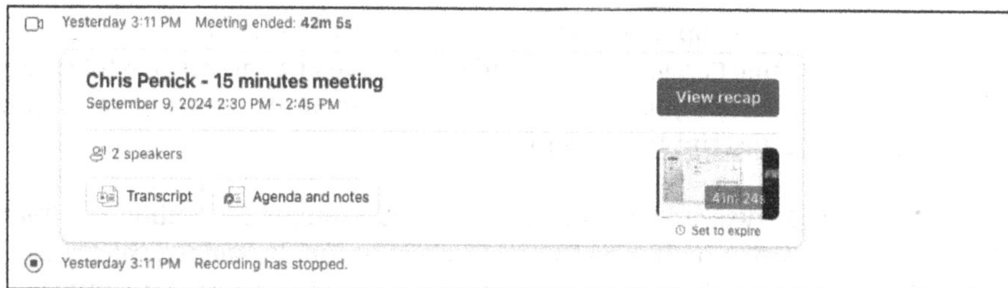

FIGURE 10-10: Your recap is ready.

The recap screen includes a video window, the agenda, AI-generated meeting notes, and the transcript of the meeting.

Figure 10-11 shows the meeting recap of my meeting.

Below the video window are three buttons to view different ways to visualize the meeting:

- The first button, Speakers, show when each attendee was speaking.
- The second button, Topics, shows each topic that was discussed in the meeting.
- The third button, Chapters, uses the same topic divisions as the Topics view but shows a screenshot from each topic.

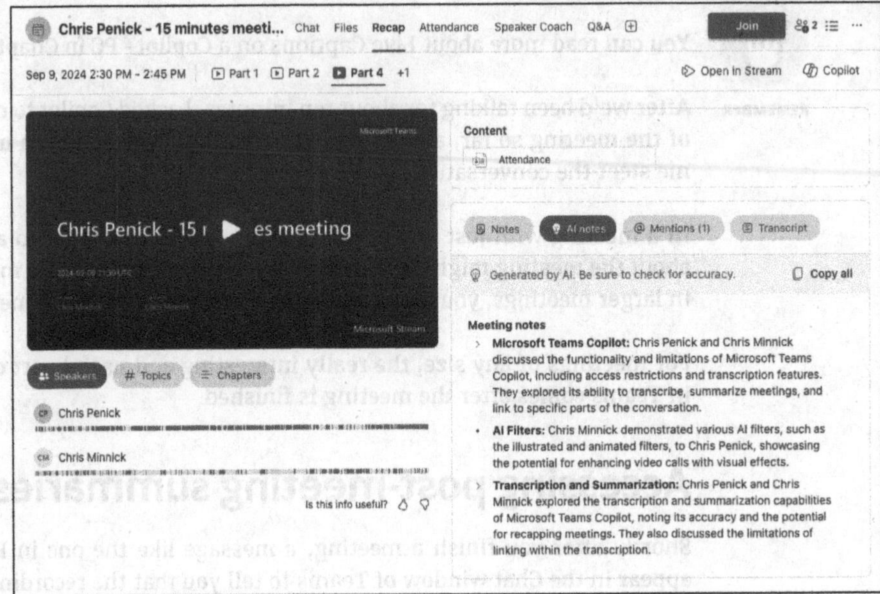

FIGURE 10-11: Getting a recap.

Clicking in one of these visualizations takes you directly to that point in the video.

In the upper-right corner of the Recap screen is a Copilot button; it opens the same Copilot in Teams sidebar that you had access to while the meeting was going on. Here you can ask any question about the meeting and Copilot will consult the transcript to answer it.

I tried out each of the suggested prompts in Copilot and Teams and found the action items one to be especially useful. It scanned the transcript for things that we each agreed to do after the meeting and gave a summary of each one. This feature will be invaluable for ensuring that meetings aren't just a waste of everyone's time while also not requiring everyone to rely on someone in the meeting taking notes.

Understanding the Limitations of Copilot in Teams

Having an AI assistant before, during, and after a virtual meeting has the potential to make meetings more useful and memorable. The integration between Teams and other Microsoft 365 applications makes sense and generally works very well.

However, there are some limitations to Copilot in Teams that may cause users to struggle with it at first. These limitations include:

- **Copilot's knowledge of the meeting is entirely dependent on the transcript.** If important visuals are presented during the meeting, you can, of course, review the video to see those. But, asking Copilot questions about something that doesn't come through in the transcript won't be successful.
- **Copilot in Teams doesn't integrate with Copilot in other apps.** You can ask Copilot in Teams to create the text for an email to the participants, but Copilot can only generate the text. It's up to you to copy the text and paste it into an email. Likewise, asking Copilot to create a PowerPoint presentation from the meeting recap will just result in a text-only list of potential slides you could create with PowerPoint.
- **Each participant in the meeting who wants to access Copilot in Teams must have Copilot Pro or Microsoft 365 Copilot subscriptions.** There's no way for the meeting organizer to give everyone in the meeting access to Copilot during the meeting.
- **Meeting transcription (and ideally recording) must be enabled to take advantage of Copilot in Teams.** Teams doesn't currently have a way to set transcription and recording to be on by default. So, you have to remember to enable these for each meeting. In my experimenting with Copilot in Teams, I did forget to enable transcription at first, and I had to sign out of the meeting, enable transcription, then re-join to be able to use Copilot.

None of these limitations outweigh the benefits of having Copilot in Teams, and I expect that some of them will be resolved in future versions of Microsoft 365 and Teams.

In my dream world, I'd have to go to about ten percent of the meetings that I currently have. But, if I can't have that, I'd settle for making meetings more useful. Copilot in Teams has the potential to improve the experience of having meetings by making it easier for everyone in the meeting to be reminded of what happened in previous meetings, to ensure that excellent meeting notes are kept, and to follow up on what decisions and actions were agreed to during the meeting.

IN THIS CHAPTER

» Making pictures with Copilot

» Specifying image styles with Copilot

» Editing images with AI

» Creating images with Microsoft Designer

Chapter 11

Generating and Manipulating Images

Copilot and Copilot+ PCs have the ability to generate images from prompts. Although simply generating images using Copilot is easy, it can be difficult to get Copilot to produce images when you have a specific idea about what you want the image to look like. Just as with text prompts, you can improve the quality of generated content by using the prompt engineering techniques you learned about in Chapter 2.

In this chapter, you learn how Copilot's image-creation capabilities work, how to get better results from Copilot when prompting for images, and how to refine Copilot's creations.

Using Copilot to Create Images

As an AI chatbot, Copilot uses a large language model (LLM) to generate text. However, the LLM that Copilot uses to create text doesn't have image-generation capabilities built in. To create images, Copilot uses a text-to-image model from OpenAI called DALL-E. In this section, you learn about how DALL-E works and how to use Copilot to prompt it.

Understanding AI image creation

When you think about drawing or painting, you generally imagine starting with a blank piece of paper and adding ink, pencil marks, or paint to it in an organized way to create an image.

This is not how AI generates images. A generative AI model has no idea what it's painting. All it's trying to do is create an image that's closely aligned with its mathematical understanding of the prompt it received.

The way DALL-E creates images is by starting with random pixels on the canvas. It then removes some of those pixels and checks whether the resulting image is closer to or further away from matching the prompt. It repeats this process many times until it has created a final image.

For example, if you tell DALL-E to create a picture of a dog, a very condensed version of its process might look like this:

1. Start with random data.
2. Remove a bunch of pixels.
3. Does it look more like a dog? If so, do more of that in the future.
4. Go back to Step 2.

In some ways, the process DALL-E uses to generate images is more like creating sculptures from marble than like how people paint or draw.

DALL-E is a *diffusion model.* In addition to being useful for generating images, diffusion models are also used for computer vision, video generation, image restoration, and removing *noise* (variations in the color or brightness of pixels that can reduce the quality of the image) from images (a process called *denoising*).

Prompting for images

You can generate images in the free or Pro versions of Copilot by simply entering a prompt that requests an image.

For the best image generating experience, I recommend using the Bing Image Creator at `www.bing.com/images/create`. Although you can generate images in Copilot, Bing Image Creator currently generates more options and provides more features that are specific to generating images. Copilot and Bing Image Creator use the same DALL-E model and you can log in to Bing Image Creator using the same account you use for Copilot.

While Bing Image Creator will always generate images in response to your prompts, Copilot will only generate an image if you make it clear that's what you're looking for. Examples of ways to start a prompt that will most likely result in Copilot generating images include:

- Create an image of
- Paint a picture of
- Draw a picture of

After the instruction to create an image, you can write a description of what you want the image to look like. Keep in mind that your description is the only input you're giving the model (other than context from previous prompts and responses in the same conversation). Be as specific as possible when prompting the model. Some of the details you might specify include:

- Subject of the picture
- Location of the subject
- Time of day, or the type of lighting
- Style of the picture
- Main focus of the picture

You can also specify a role that you'd like Copilot to take on as it's creating the image. For example, you might say "You are an abstract painter." One word of caution however — if you tell Copilot to paint in the style of a particular artist or to take on the role of a particular artist, it may refuse to do that. The reason is that Copilot has built-in programming designed to reduce the chances of it violating other people's intellectual property or being used to create forgeries.

Prompting with more details and more context is how you improve the chances that what the model generates will meet your expectations and needs.

As you do when generating text, it's useful to try a simple prompt at first to see what the AI model will do and then to refine it after that.

For example, I prompted Copilot with the following prompt:

Create an image of a bird flying over a glacial lake.

Within a minute, Copilot generated an image that matched my description, as shown in Figure 11-1.

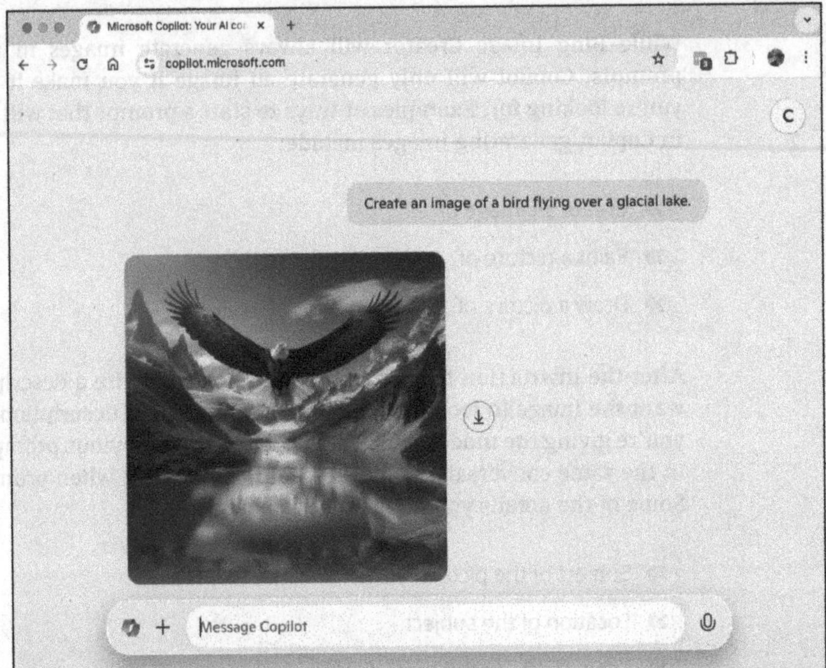

FIGURE 11-1: Copilot's generated image of a bird flying over a glacial lake.

TIP

Each image you generate using Copilot has a down arrow icon next to it that you can use to download the image to your computer so you can edit it or share it.

To see how Bing Image Creator would handle this prompt, I went to `https://bing.com/images/create` and gave it the same prompt. It responded with a series of four images, as shown in Figure 11-2.

You can click on one of the four options to see a larger version of it, as shown in Figure 11-3.

The single image view has buttons to the right of it for sharing, saving, downloading, customizing, and resizing the image.

- » The Share button shows you a link to the image that you can copy.
- » The Save button saves the image to your Microsoft Bing account.
- » The Download button downloads the image to your computer.
- » The Customize button opens the image in Microsoft Designer. You learn about Microsoft Designer in the section titled "Using Microsoft Designer" later in this chapter.
- » The Resize button generates a new image that's similar to your original but that's wider horizontally (landscape) rather than square.

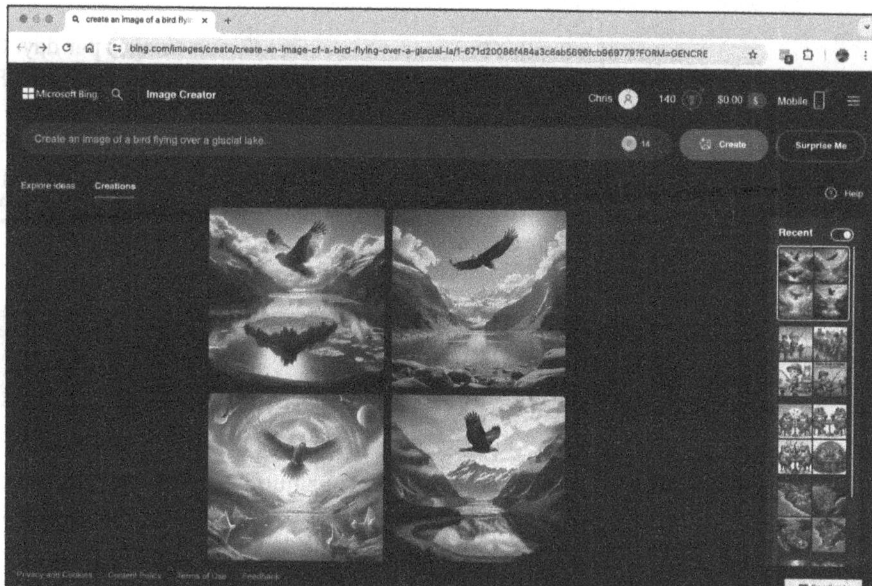

FIGURE 11-2: Creating images with Bing Image Creator.

FIGURE 11-3: Viewing a larger version.

Getting and using Boosts

Because AI image generation requires much more computing power than text generation, Copilot limits the number of images you can create per day. The limit for users of a free Copilot account is currently 15 images per day, and the limit for users of a Copilot Pro account is currently 100 images per day. Copilot tracks how many images you've generated each day using a system called *Boosts*.

The number of Boosts you have remaining is displayed in the Boosts icon, which looks like a lightning bolt in a yellow circle. The Boosts icon appears in the preview window you see when you generate images with Bing Image Creator, as shown in Figure 11-4.

Create an image of a bird flying over a glacial lake.
14

FIGURE 11-4: Viewing your remaining Boosts.

After you generate an image, your number of available Boosts goes down. When your number of Boosts reaches zero, generating images may take longer or you may be prevented from generating images until your number of Boosts replenishes the next day.

Refining images

If you generate an image using Copilot, you can ask Copilot to refine the image by using prompts. For example, returning to the bird picture that Copilot generated (shown in Figure 11-1), you might tell it to make the picture darker, or make it more realistic, or remove something from it.

Copilot will then use its previously generated image as context for its next image-generation attempt.

WARNING

It's not possible to use AI image generation in the same way you might use a traditional photo-editing application. Each image Copilot creates is unique, and if you ask for something simple like "lower the brightness" you won't simply get the same image but darker. The image will probably be similar to the original, but it will be unique.

Figure 11-5 shows the result of asking Copilot to change the bird in my image to a turkey.

REMEMBER

Unlike human artists, DALL-E doesn't care or know that an image it's creating depicts something physically impossible, such as a turkey soaring over the mountains. This can be one of the most fun things about AI image generation, but it's also one of the most frustrating things about it.

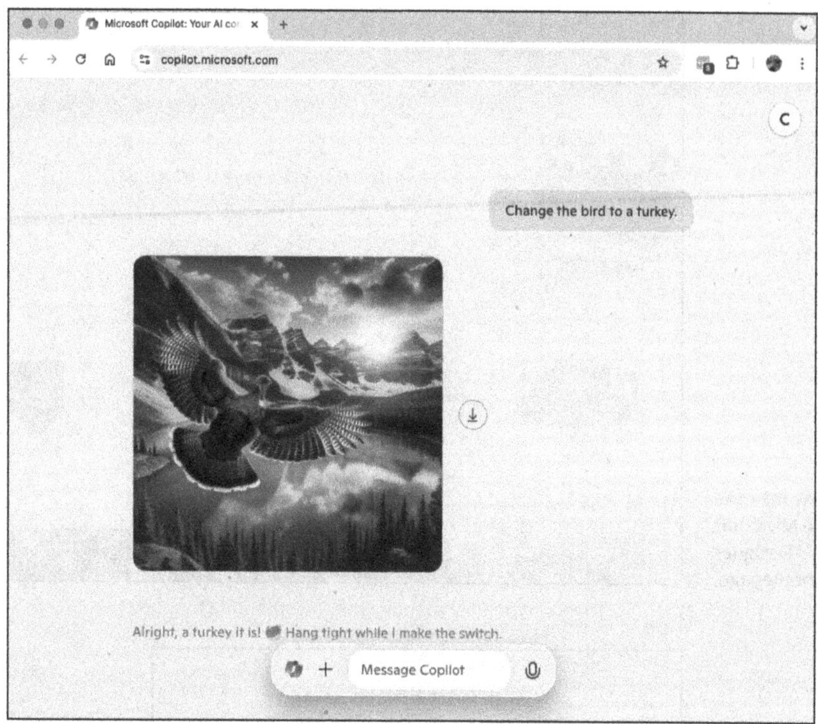
Microsoft Copilot: Your AI co
copilot.microsoft.com
Change the bird to a turkey.
Alright, a turkey it is! Hang tight while I make the switch.
Message Copilot

FIGURE 11-5: A flying turkey.

Using Microsoft Designer

Microsoft Designer is Microsoft's answer to Canva (`www.canva.com`) and Adobe Express (`adobe.com/express`). Like these two tools, Microsoft Designer is an easy way for anyone to design a wide range of things, including social media posts, flyers, invitations, greeting cards, posters, stickers, icons, brochures, and even custom publications such as coloring books.

TIP

Microsoft Designer is currently not available for use with work or school Microsoft 365 accounts. However, it is available with a free Microsoft account and to people with Copilot Pro subscriptions.

To access Microsoft Designer, go to `https://designer.microsoft.com`. There, you'll see the homepage, as shown in Figure 11-6.

Before attempting to use Microsoft Designer, you'll need to log in by clicking the Sign In button in the upper-right corner. If you sign in with a work or school account, you may get the message shown in Figure 11-7 that says Designer isn't available for your organization.

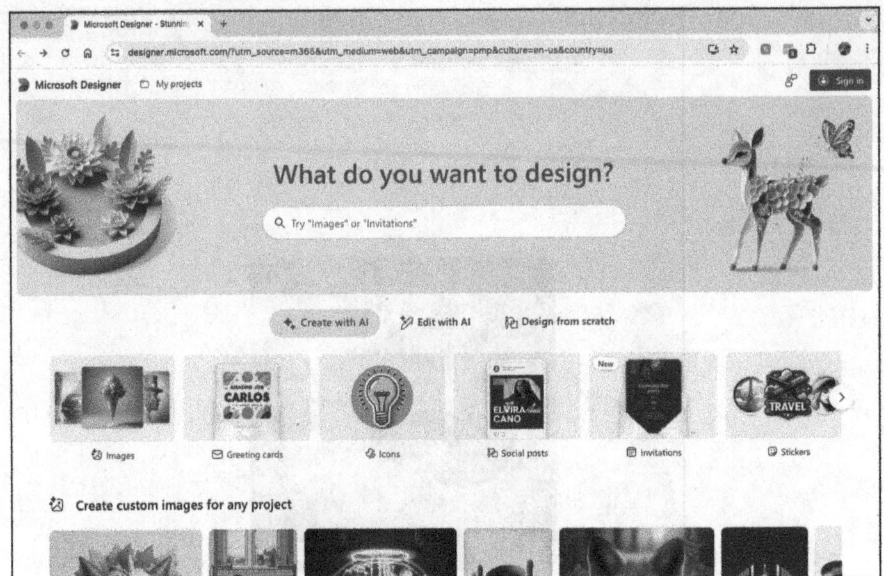

FIGURE 11-6: The Microsoft Designer homepage.

Sign out to access Designer for free
Designer isn't yet available to your organization.
To try it for free, sign out of this account and then
sign in with your personal Microsoft account.
Sign out

FIGURE 11-7: Designer is not available to organizations.

Like it says to do, you'll need to sign out and sign back in using a personal account to access Designer.

Exploring Designer's three modes

At the top of the Designer homepage is a large prompt input area below a header that says, "What do you want to design?" Entering a keyword or description of what you want to create into that text box is the easiest way to get started with Designer, but it's not the only way.

Below the text input box are three buttons, Create with AI, Edit with AI, and Design from Scratch. You can use these buttons to switch between the three ways to get started using Designer.

When you select one of these options from the Designer homepage, you'll see some options for ways you can use the tool. In the following sections, you learn a bit about how to use Designer, but I encourage you to spend some time playing around with it on your own. This is the best way to get a sense of what's possible and what Designer might be able to do for you!

Creating with AI in Designer

The Create with AI tool in Designer features a selection of templates to choose from. These templates include images, greeting cards, icons, social posts, invitations, and more. Figure 11-8 shows some of the template options that are available.

FIGURE 11-8: The template options in Designer's Create with AI tool.

If you scroll down below the templates, you'll see some sample images for several different types of projects. Hovering your mouse over any of these images displays the prompt template that was used to create the sample project. Figure 11-9 shows both an avatar image and the prompt that was used to create it.

The words or phrases that appear in square brackets represent places where you can customize the prompt and make it your own. Clicking the sample prompt opens it for editing. Figure 11-10 shows the sample prompt editing screen.

On this screen, you can replace any of the words in text boxes and then generate your own project based on the prompt. If you don't care about maintaining a similar style as the original generated image, you can also click the link at the bottom of the prompt area to disregard the suggested customization words and make any change you like.

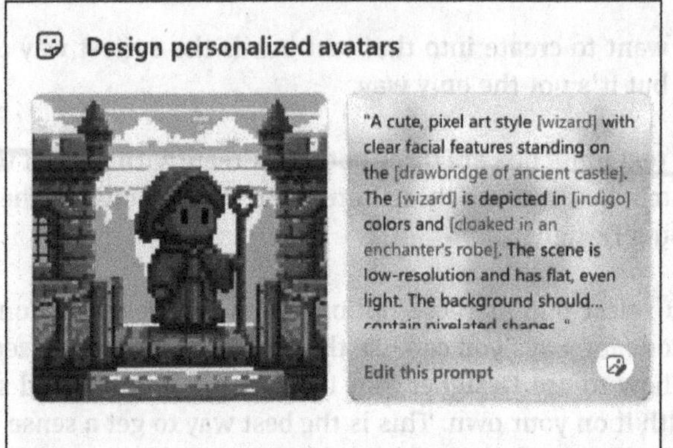

FIGURE 11-9: Viewing the prompt behind the image.

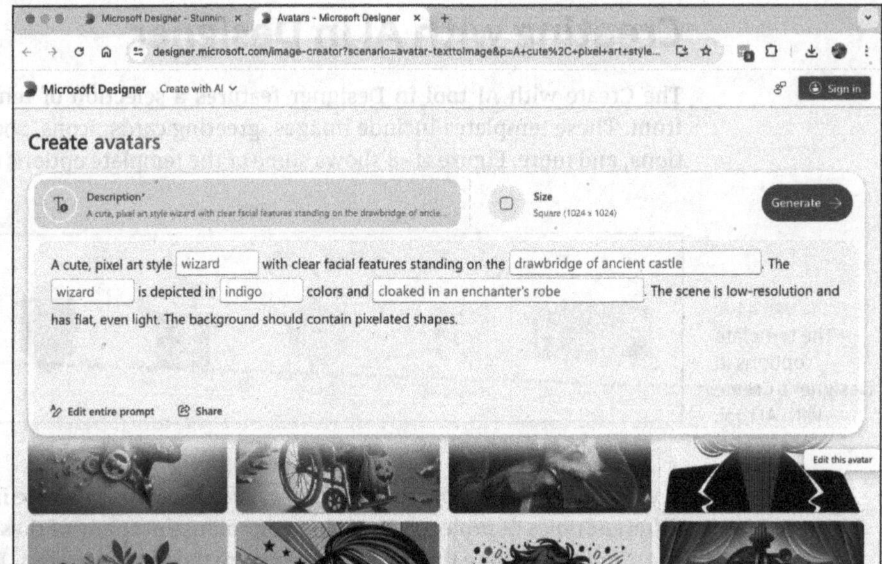

FIGURE 11-10: The sample prompt editing screen.

After you click the Generate button, Designer will generate four options based on the prompt, as shown in Figure 11-11.

If you don't like any of the suggestions, you can click the Description above the suggestions to make edits and try again (as long as you have enough Boosts!).

If you like one of the suggestions, click on it to open a window (shown in Figure 11-12) with a larger version of your generated image and to get to the next step in the creation and refinement of your project.

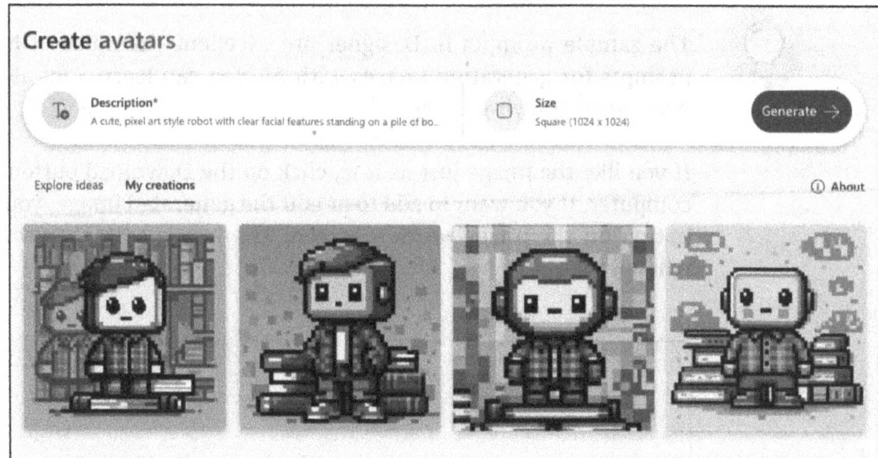

FIGURE 11-11: AI-generated avatar suggestions.

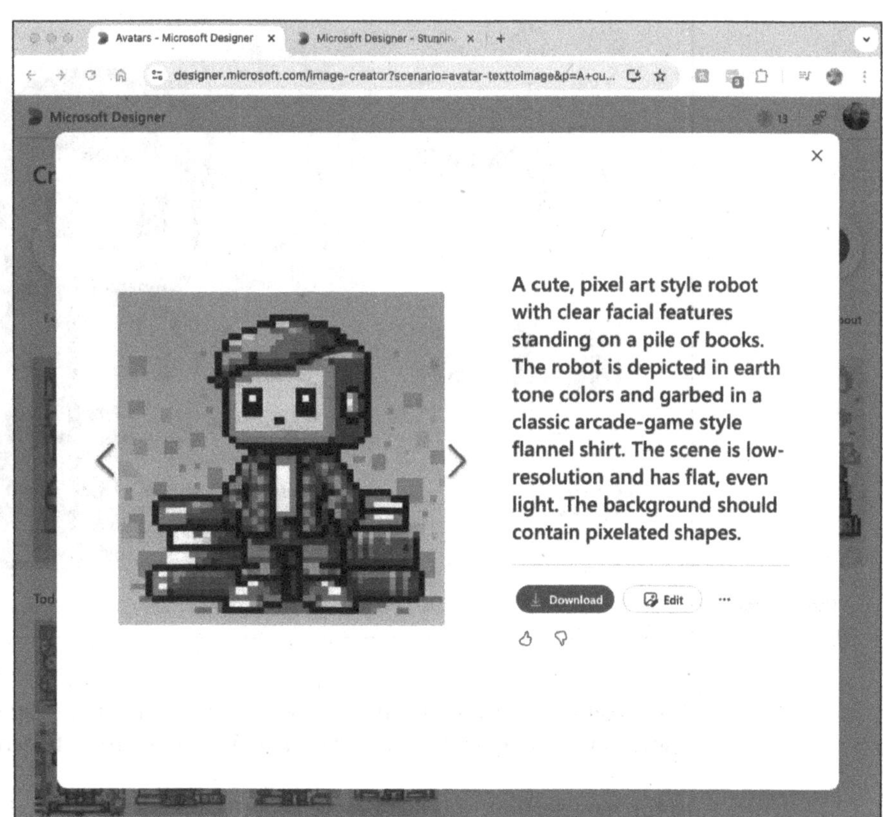

FIGURE 11-12: Viewing a larger version of your image.

TIP

The sample prompts in Designer are excellent examples of how to write good prompts for generating images with AI. You can learn a lot about prompt engineering by studying them.

If you like the image just as it is, click on the Download button to save it to your computer. If you want to add to or edit the generated image, you can click the Edit button on the image preview screen. The image editor, shown in Figure 11-13, will open.

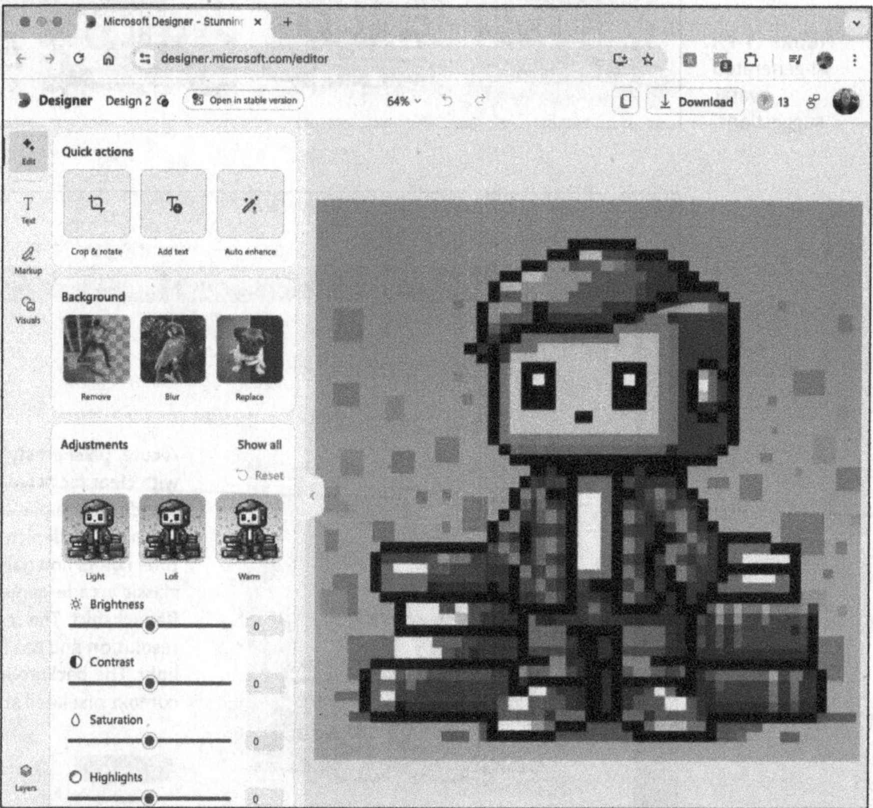

FIGURE 11-13: The Designer image editor.

The image editor gives you all the tools you need to modify images. You can adjust colors, add text, apply filters, and even add AI-generated elements.

In the next section, you learn more about the image editor and what you can do with it. Click the Microsoft Designer logo in the upper-right corner to return to the Designer homepage and to start learning more about the Designer image-editing capabilities.

Editing with AI in Designer

The Edit with AI link from the homepage of Designer brings you to a screen that appears similar to the Create with AI screen. This screen is shown in Figure 11-14.

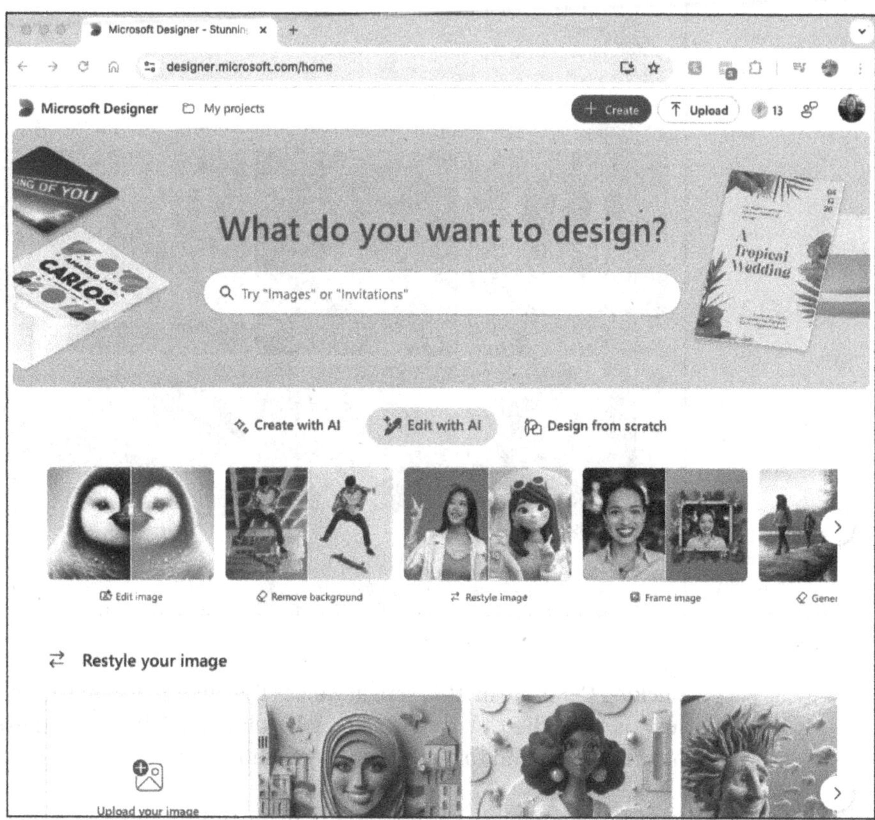

FIGURE 11-14: The Edit with AI screen.

The Edit with AI screen has various links, templates, and prompt examples for editing existing projects or images you supply.

For example, if you want to apply a frame to an existing image, find the Frame Image tool and click it. You'll see the Create Framed Images screen, with samples of what the tool can do. To use the Create Framed Images tool, you can select an image, add objects and themes to your frame, select a style, and then generate a frame that will display around your image.

Figure 11-15 shows the Create Framed Images screen with the Image, Elements, and Style options filled in.

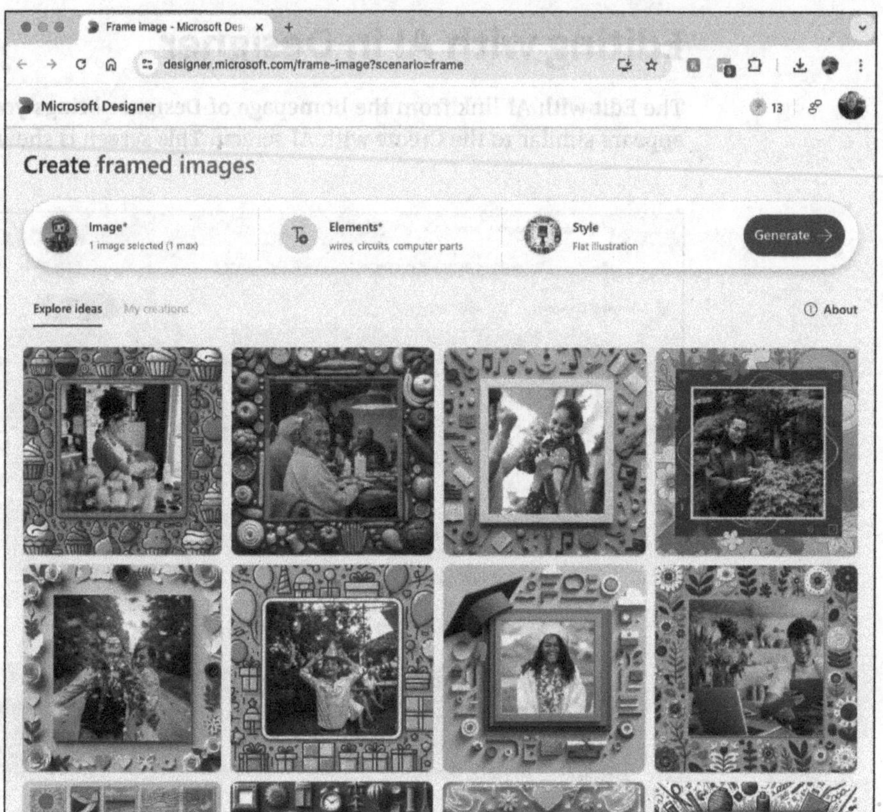

FIGURE 11-15: The Create Framed Images screen.

Clicking Generate on this screen causes Designer to use AI to generate four options. Just as with the Create with AI tool, you can click any of these images to see a larger version and to go to the image editor.

Figure 11-16 shows my generated image and the frame I added to it open in the image editor.

Using the image editor

The image editor in Designer combines traditional image-editing capabilities with publication design capabilities and AI.

Examples of things you can do with the image editor in Designer include adding text, resizing objects, applying a theme to your design, and inserting shapes and other art.

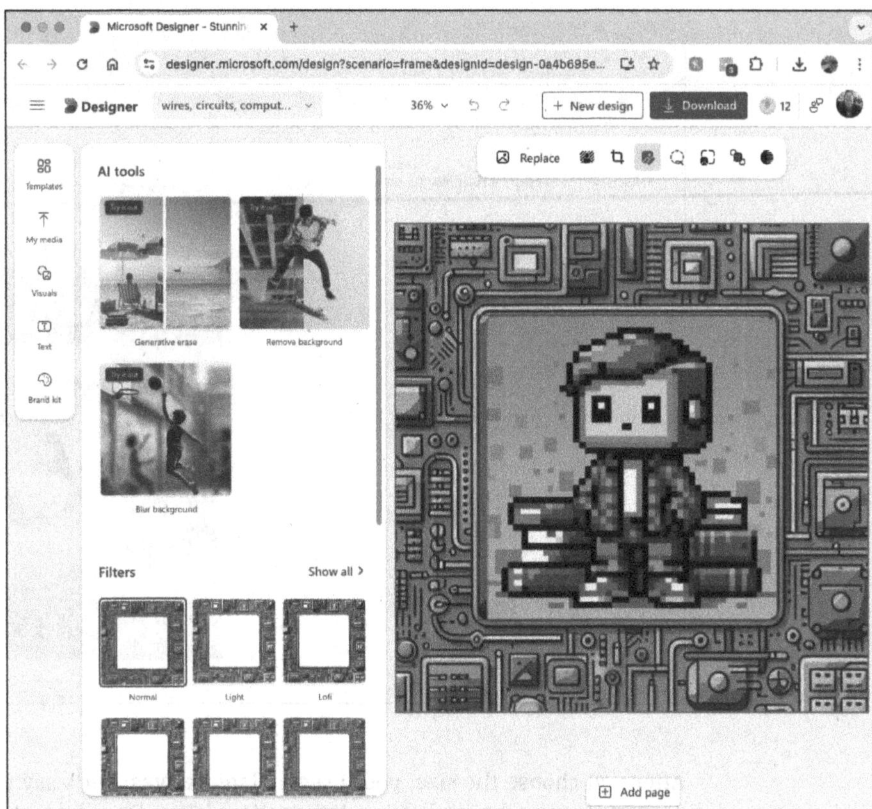

FIGURE 11-16: My framed avatar in the image editor.

With the publication design capabilities, you can apply design templates to create different types of publications (such as greeting cards or brochures) and you can add pages to your project.

The AI features of the image editor allow you to generate new visuals and insert them into your project.

The image editor can be used with any project you create in Designer or with an image you upload. To use it, you can start by creating a new project using a prompt or by clicking the small link at the bottom of the New Project screen (shown in Figure 11-17) that says, "Skip and start with a blank design or edit recent designs."

Starting with a blank design isn't as easy as using a prompt to create your project, but it can produce a better result when you already know exactly what you need.

When you start a blank project in the image editor, the first thing you need to decide is the size. You'll see a window where you can select one of a few different common sizes or you can specify a custom size.

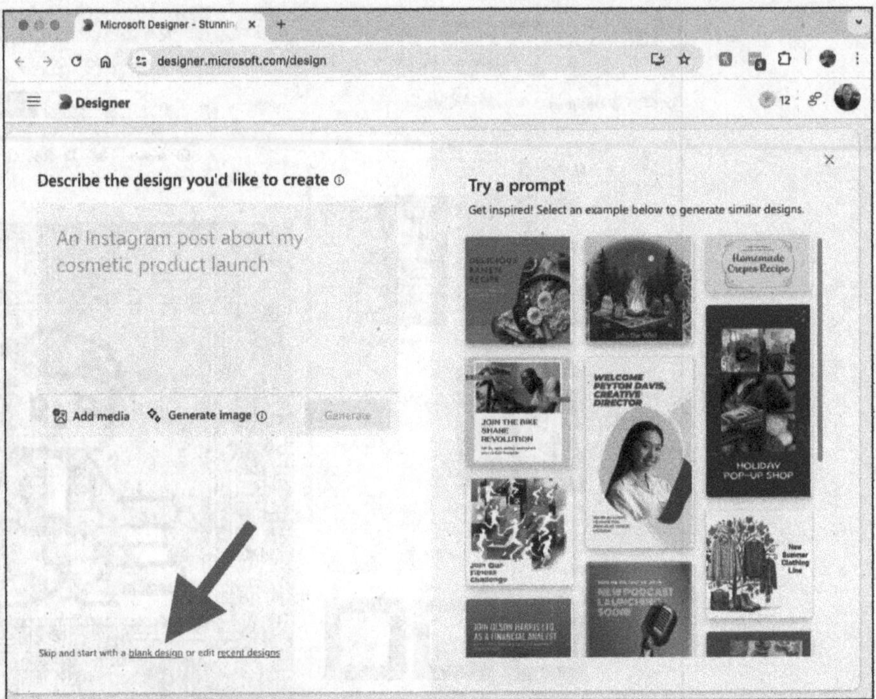

FIGURE 11-17: The link to create a blank project.

After you choose the size, you'll see a blank canvas. Let's say you want to create an Instagram post celebrating International Dog Day (August 26). Here are the steps you might take.

1. **Start with a blank square canvas.**
2. **Click the Text icon on the left toolbar.**
3. **Click Add a Heading.**

   Large heading text will appear on your canvas where you can edit it, as shown in Figure 11-18.
4. **Click the Visuals icon on the left toolbar and go to the Generate tab, as shown in Figure 11-19.**
5. **Write and submit a prompt for the visuals you want to add to your project. Here's what I started with:**

   Create a photorealistic image of many different kinds of dogs all having fun and doing things that are normally done by people, like reading the paper or playing guitar.

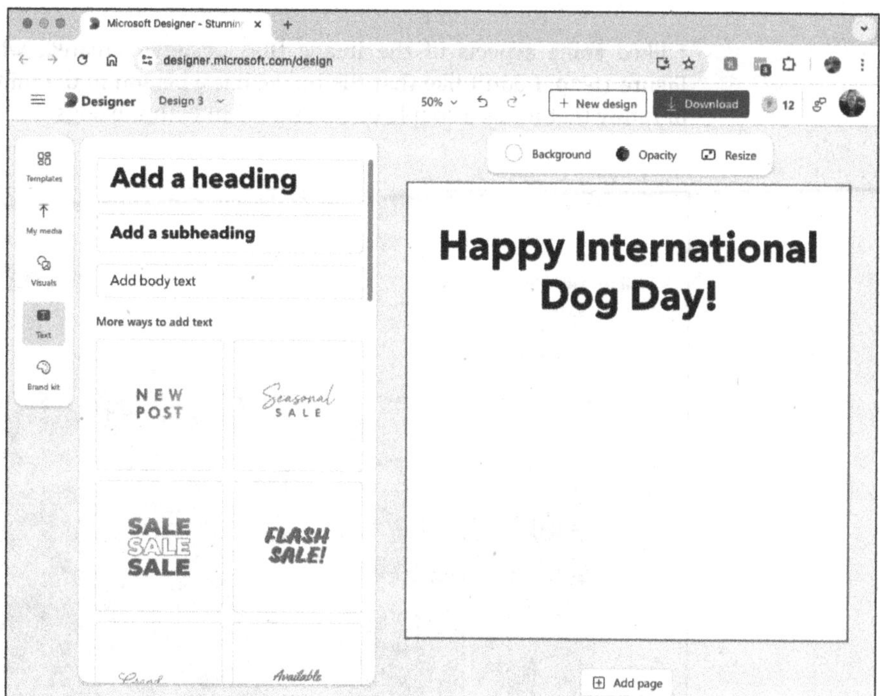

FIGURE 11-18: Adding a heading.

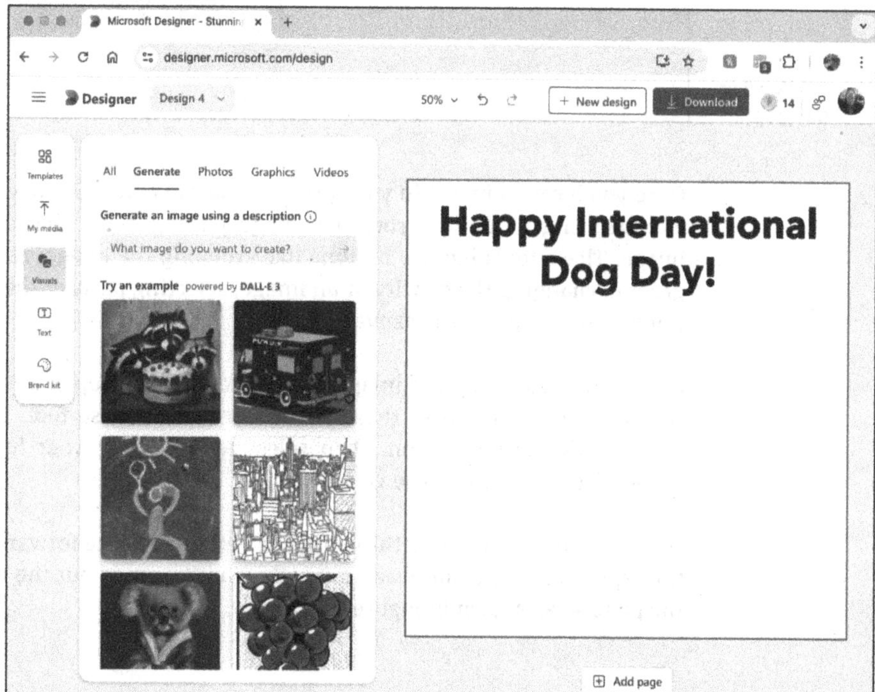

FIGURE 11-19: The Generate tab in the Visuals tool.

I liked some aspects of the image that Designer created, which is shown in Figure 11-20. I don't like that the image has a person in the middle of it. It's sort of funny that it has a couple of cats mixed in with the dogs.

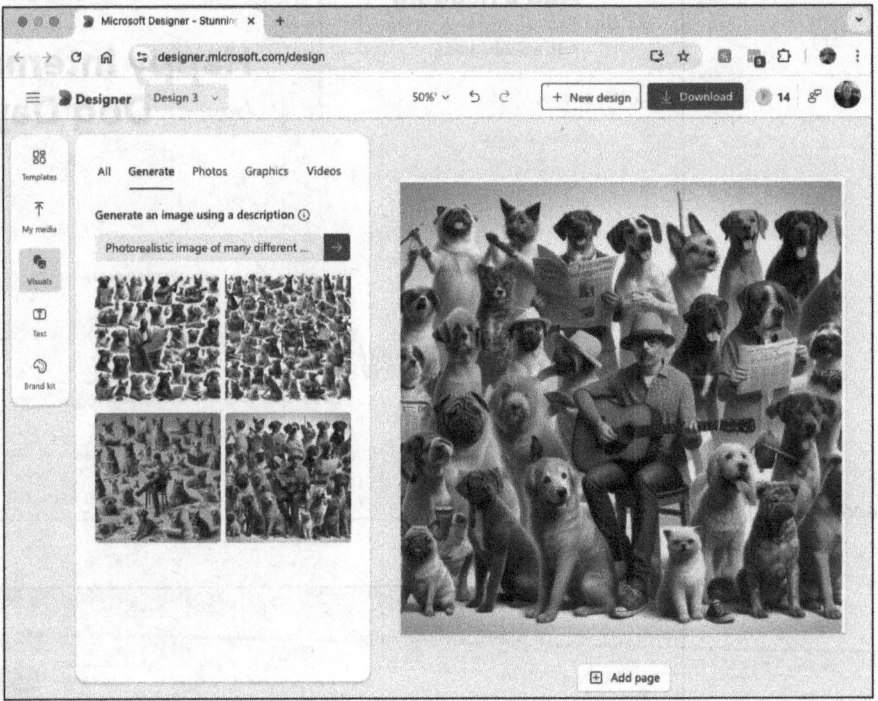

FIGURE 11-20: My dog day graphic.

Once you have an image in your project, you can edit that image by clicking on it and selecting an option from the image-editing menu that appears above the image. These tools include options like cropping the image, removing the background, changing the opacity of an image, selecting parts of the image, and positioning the image on the canvas.

One of the options on the image-editing toolbar is to open a menu of AI image-editing tools. Included in these is the Generative Erase tool. To use Generative Erase, click the tool's icon, then select the object in your image you want to replace, as shown in Figure 11-21.

Once you've selected something in your image, click the forward arrow to initiate the replacing. The result wasn't exactly what I wanted but the man is now out of the picture, as shown in Figure 11-22.

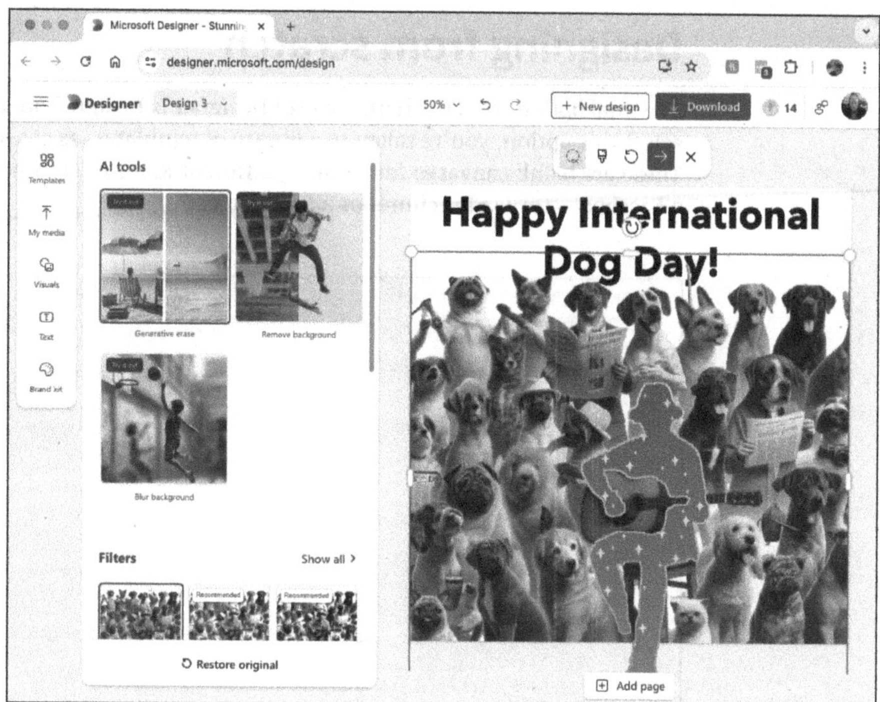

FIGURE 11-21: Selecting the object to replace.

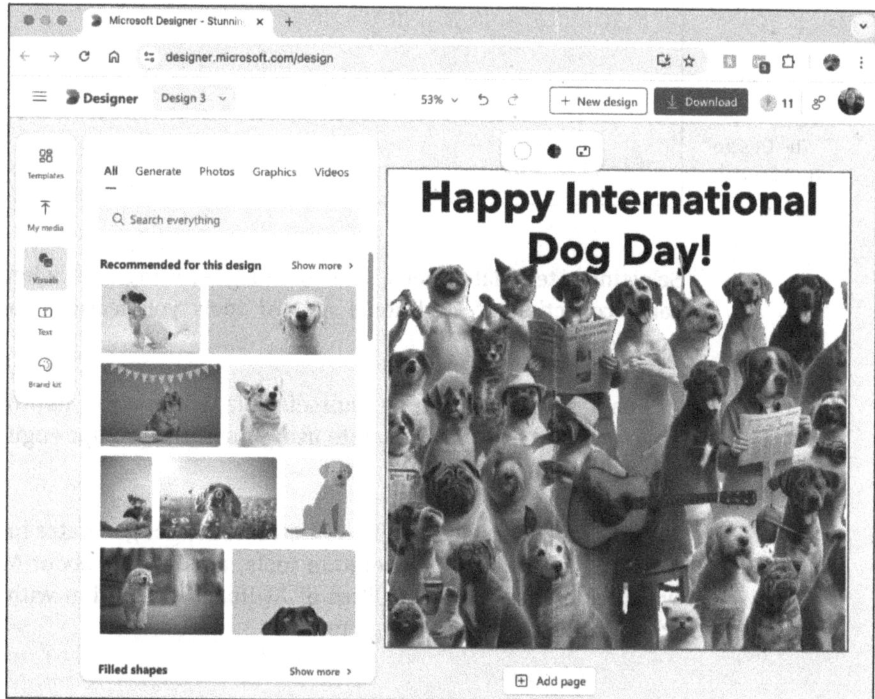

FIGURE 11-22: Using the image-editing tools.

Designing from scratch

The final option from the homepage of Designer is Design from Scratch. When you select this option, you're taken to a library of templates, as shown in Figure 11-23. These are blank canvases for creating different kinds of creative projects, such as a Facebook story, a brochure, or a folded greeting card.

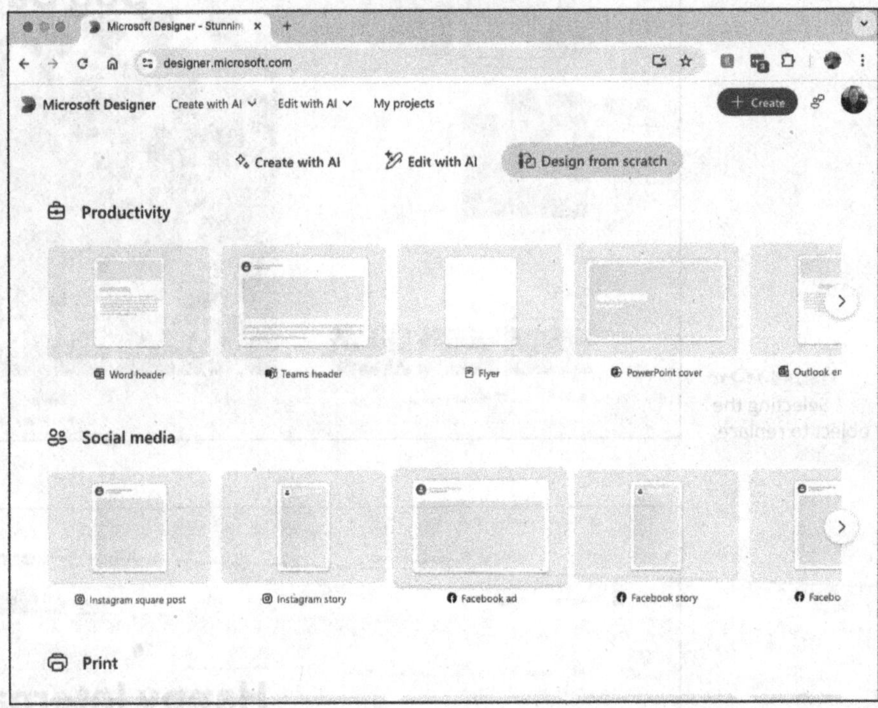

FIGURE 11-23: The Design from Scratch templates.

Selecting a template opens it in the image-editing tool, where you can use the same collection of traditional and AI tools you learned about in the previous section.

REMEMBER

AI image generation can be unpredictable, but you can improve the quality and accuracy of images you generate using the same prompt engineering techniques you use to generate text.

In this chapter, you learned how Microsoft Copilot generates images, learned how to use Copilot's image-generation tools, and learned about Microsoft Designer, which combines the capabilities of AI image generation with traditional image editing and publication design tools.

IN THIS CHAPTER

» Getting Copilot's help with planning

» Tracking and monitoring tasks and deadlines

» Collaborating intelligently

» Enhancing reporting

» Customizing reports

Chapter 12

Using Copilot for Project Management

Projects range in size from very small, such as making a sandwich, to very complex, such as building a bridge. Every project, even the smallest ones, requires some amount of planning, execution, and follow-up. This process of starting with something that you want to get done, figuring out how to do it, then doing it is an example of what we in the business world call *project management*.

In this chapter, you learn how to use Microsoft Copilot to help with project management.

Planning for a Project

Project management can be a complex endeavor. Some of the things that project managers must manage include:

- **Scope.** A project's scope defines what must be done to achieve the desired results of the project. It also defines the boundaries of the project and what's not included.

- **Goals.** The goals of a project are the end result that you hope to achieve from the project.
- **Budget.** The budget is the amount of money available for completing the project.
- **Timeline.** A project's timeline defines the deadline for completion of the project as well as for important milestones within the project.
- **Work breakdown.** The work breakdown is the list of tasks that must be completed to meet the goals of the project.
- **Human resources.** Human resources refers to the people who will work on the project, including who those people will be, and what parts of the project they'll be working on.
- **Communications.** Most of a project manager's time is spent in meetings, writing emails, interpreting what the customer requires, turning those requirements into tasks, and providing reports to everyone who has a stake in the project.
- **Risk management.** Risk management is the process of planning how to deal with the inevitable problems in advance of the project and then handling challenges when they do come up.

All of these factors (and more) must be planned for. The document or set of documents in which this is all written down is called a *project plan.*

It's unlikely that you'll create a project plan complete with charts and graphs for a simple project like taking out the garbage. But when multiple people get involved, it's not enough simply to dive in and start doing it. In this chapter, you learn how Copilot can help you become a better project manager and get more done in less time.

Introducing Microsoft Planner

Microsoft Planner is a planning application that's available in the Microsoft 365 platform. Although you can access Planner with any Microsoft 365 subscription, you currently need Microsoft's Planner and Project Plan 3 or Planner and Project Plan 5 to access Copilot in Planner. You can find out about these subscriptions and sign up for one of them at `https://www.microsoft.com/en-us/microsoft-365/planner/microsoft-planner-plans-and-pricing`. If you have the proper license for Microsoft Planner, you can access it through Microsoft Teams. Follow these steps to get started:

1. **Open Teams in Microsoft 365.**
2. **Click the Apps icon in the left toolbar.**

   This will take you to the Apps Search feature of Teams, as shown in Figure 12-1.

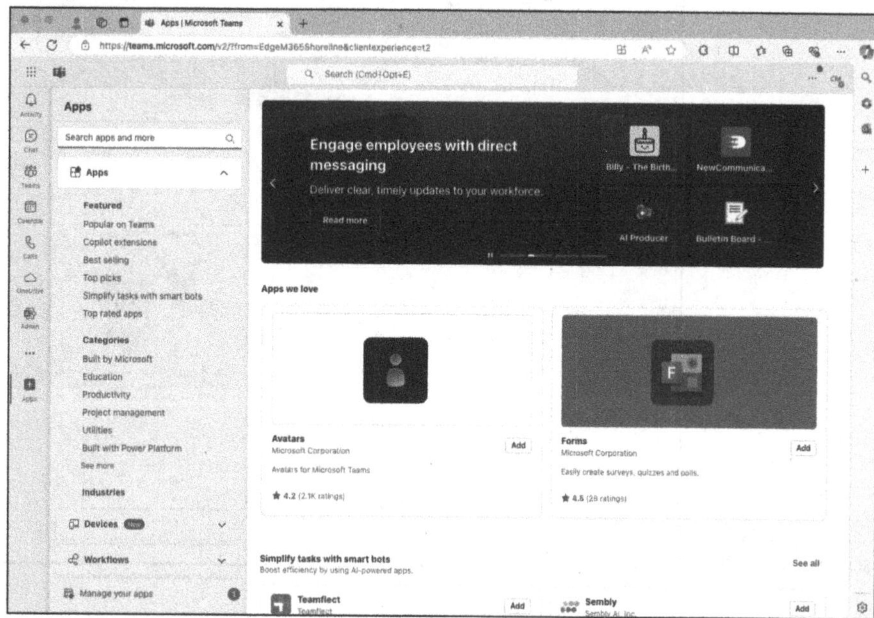

FIGURE 12-1: Searching for apps.

3. **Enter** planner **into the search box in the top-left corner of the Apps search page.**

   Microsoft Planner should be the first result in the Apps section of the results.

4. **If you've previously accessed Microsoft Planner, you'll see an Open button that you can click to open Microsoft Planner. Otherwise, click the Add button next to Microsoft Planner and then open it.**
5. **Once you have Planner open, right-click the Planner icon in the left toolbar and select Pin so that you don't have to go to the App search interface next time you want to use Planner.**

Getting Started with Planner

When you open Microsoft Planner you'll be taken to the My Tasks page. If you don't have any projects you won't have any tasks. We're about to change that. The My Tasks screen is shown in Figure 12-2.

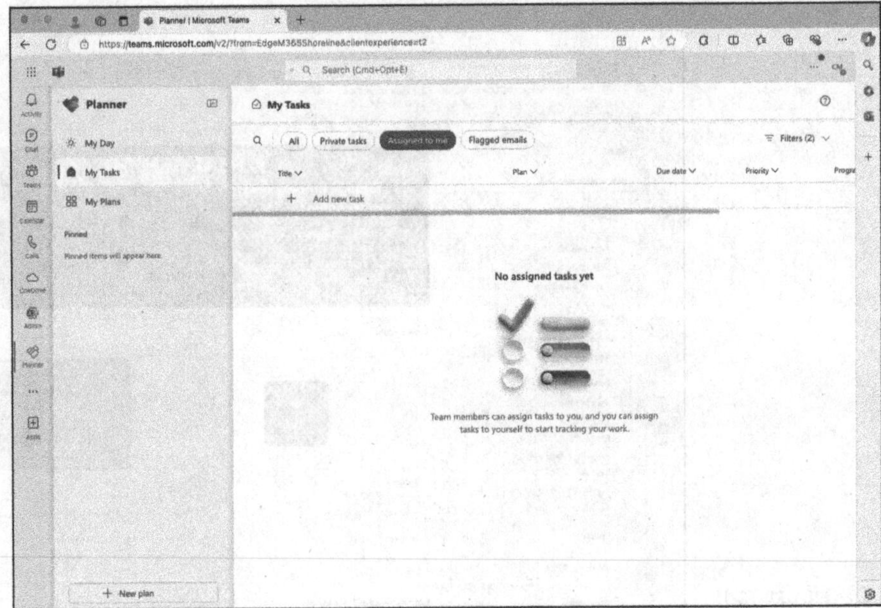

FIGURE 12-2: The My Tasks screen in Planner.

To create a new project, click the New Plan button in the lower-left corner of Microsoft Planner. You'll see a popup window, shown in Figure 12-3, where you can select a template for your new plan or start with a blank plan.

Clicking either the Basic or the Premium link will create a new blank plan. Currently Copilot in Planner is only available for Premium plans.

When you click the Premium link, a window will open that asks you to give the new plan a name, as shown in Figure 12-4.

Once you've come up with the name for your plan, click the Create button and your new blank plan will appear. At this point, you could start creating your plan in the traditional way by manually adding tasks. However, in Premium projects you can also get some help from Microsoft Copilot. Look for the familiar Copilot icon in the plan toolbar. It's the fourth one from the right, as shown in Figure 12-5.

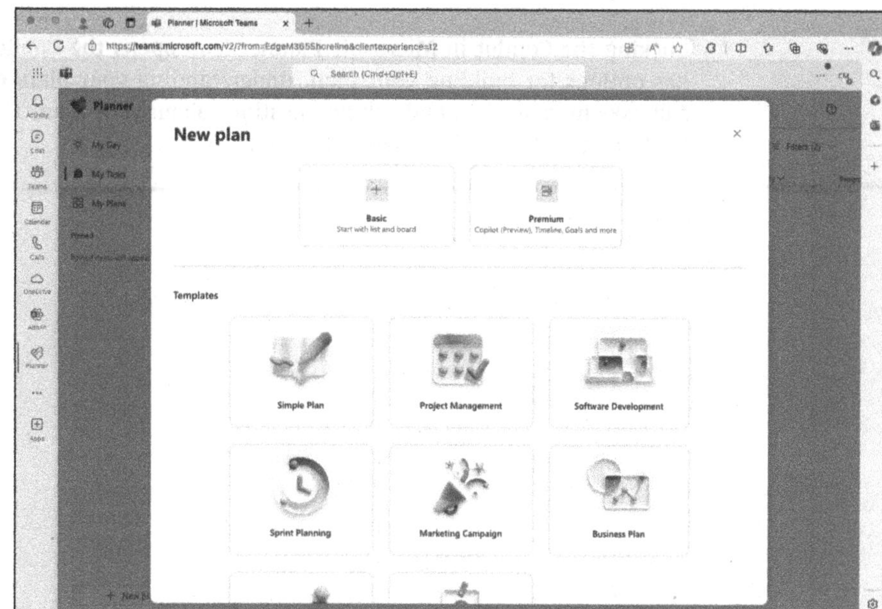

FIGURE 12-3: Selecting a template.

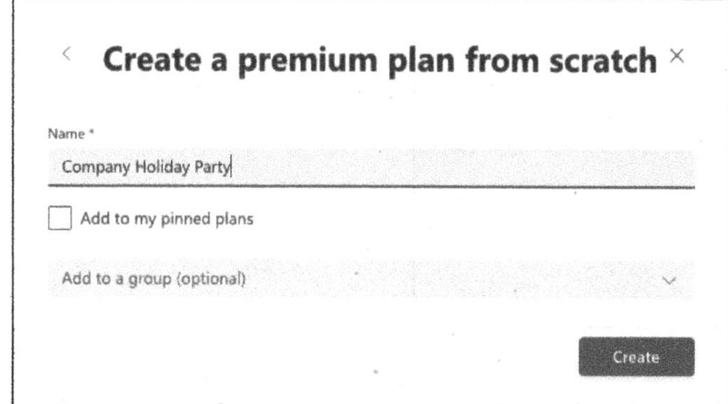

FIGURE 12-4: Giving your project a name.

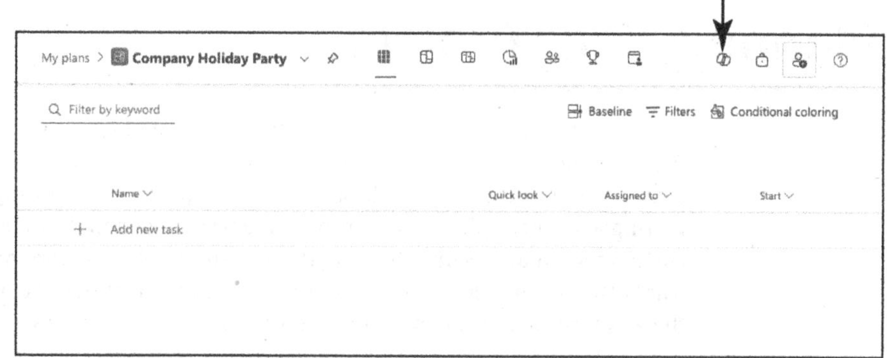

FIGURE 12-5: The Copilot button.

Clicking the Copilot in Microsoft Planner icon opens the Copilot sidebar, which has options for building your plan, understanding your plan, editing tasks and subtasks in your plan, and asking questions about your plan. The Copilot sidebar in Microsoft Planner is shown in Figure 12-6.

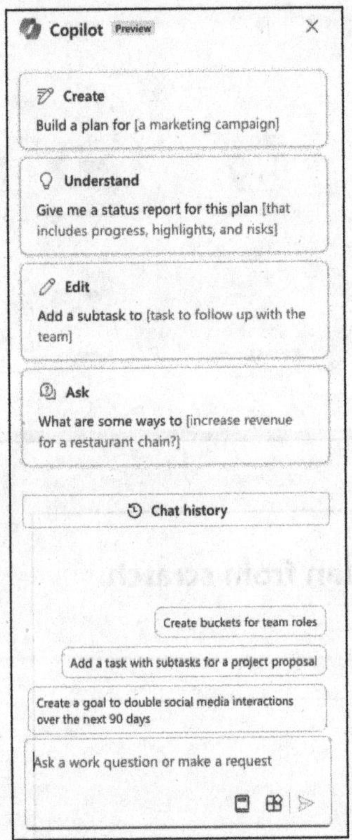

FIGURE 12-6: The Copilot sidebar in Planner.

In the next section, I try using Copilot in Microsoft to create a business plan.

Planning Your Project

Most people start businesses because they have an idea or a passion or something they're good at that they can make money from doing. People don't start small businesses because they love to write business plans. Just figuring out how to start writing a business plan and what needs to be included in it can be a daunting task. Fortunately, many people have written business plans before and you can study what other people have done to figure out what you should do. Or at least, that's the way writing a business plan used to work just a few years ago.

Generative AI works best when it's creating new things that are similar to things that are plentiful on the web. What I mean by that, specifically for this topic, is that because so many business plans have been written and there are so many templates for business plans and articles about business plans on the web that have gone into Copilot's training data, it should be easy for Copilot to write a business plan.

WARNING

What AI will probably struggle with, however, is writing a business plan for a type of business that it's never heard of before.

My first business planning attempt

To create a business plan, you can start with the built-in business plan template in Microsoft Planner and then customize it to your needs. In this section though, I'm going to try to generate an entire business plan using Copilot.

WARNING

Generating something as important as a business plan shouldn't be left entirely up to AI, of course.

Here are the steps I used, in case you want to try it on your own:

1. **Create a new blank Premium plan.**
2. **Open the Copilot sidebar.**
3. **Ask Copilot to create your business plan.**

   It may be helpful here to include a brief description of your business and whether the business exists yet. For example, I used the following prompt:

   Build a business plan for the business I'm thinking about starting. It will be a 24-hour cat café where you can drink coffee and pet cats.

Unfortunately, this was as far as I got with this approach at first, even though I tried several different prompts. Copilot was unable to do anything except say that something went wrong, as shown in Figure 12-7.

TIP

To find out more about troubleshooting common problems with Copilot, go to Chapter 15.

I wanted to make sure the problem wasn't a temporary outage or something wrong with my Copilot account, so I logged out of my account and logged back in, refreshed the browser window, and had lunch before trying again.

It still didn't work, so I waited a day before trying again.

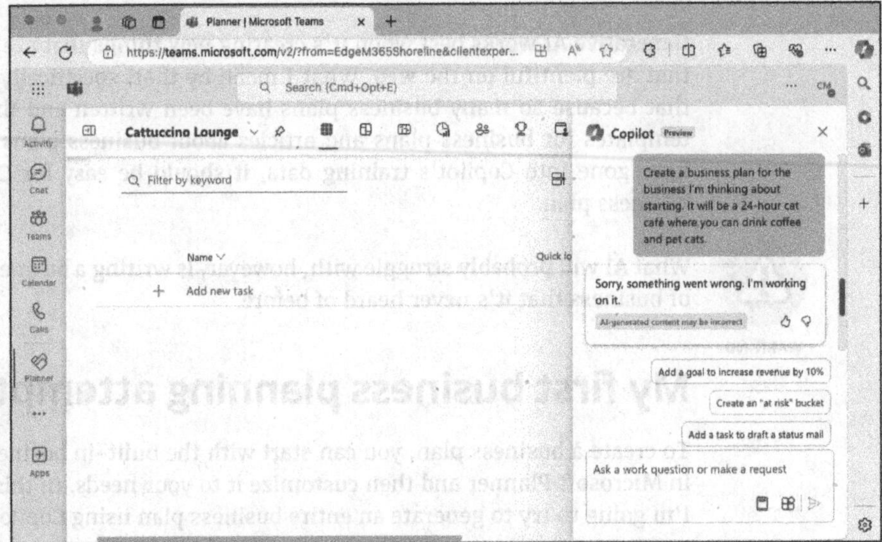

FIGURE 12-7: Something went wrong.

Trying again, and success!

The next morning, I opened my blank Planner template and used the same prompt to attempt to generate a business plan for my cat café, the Cattuccino Lounge.

This time, Copilot thought about it, then created an outline with the following items:

- Executive Summary
- Market Analysis
- Business Model
- Operation Plan
- Marketing and Sales Strategy
- Financial Projections

So far so good! After displaying this outline, Copilot went on to insert each section into my plan and create tasks under each one.

The result is actually a great start. It's more of a plan for making a business plan, and the tasks Copilot created make sense. Since I've only been thinking about starting this business for 24 hours now, I hadn't considered some of the things Copilot inserted into the plan, such as "Develop cat care protocols."

The task list portion of the plan is shown in Figure 12-8.

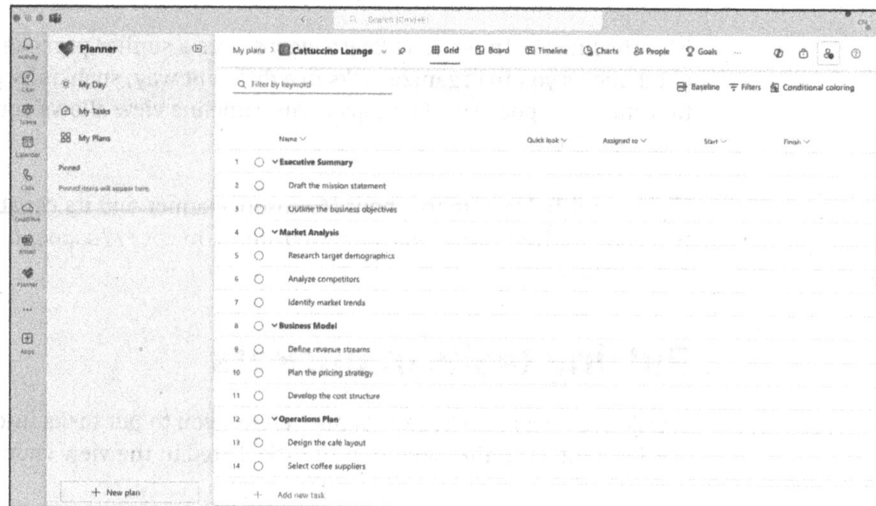

FIGURE 12-8: The start of my new business plan.

Setting goals

In addition to the six categories of tasks and 29 tasks Copilot wrote, it also defined two goals:

- Obtain all necessary permits and health certifications for café.
- Secure funding for initial setup costs and operating expenses for the first year.

Both goals have deadlines associated with them and the tasks that are part of each goal are correctly identified.

To be honest, I'm really impressed with what Copilot in Planner has been able to do so far. I'm even getting a bit excited about using it to start writing a plan for my own real business.

Viewing Planner's various views

Before you see more of what Copilot in Planner is capable of, it's helpful to have a basic understanding of how Planner works. The basic things that make up a Planner project are *tasks* (things that need to be done), *goals* (end results that you want to achieve), and *people* (who will be doing the tasks to achieve the goals).

The tabs across the top of the Planner user interface present these basic building blocks of a plan in a variety of ways. For example, the Grid view, which is shown in Figure 12-8, shows a list of all the tasks in your project along with information about each, such as who it's assigned to, when it's scheduled to start, and when it's scheduled to finish. The Board view serves a similar purpose as the Grid view, but it allows you to organize tasks in a different way, such as by priority, completion status, or phase of the project. The Timeline view allows you to view tasks by their due dates.

If you want to learn more about Microsoft Planner and its capabilities, check out the Planner Help and Learning website at `https://support.microsoft.com/en-us/planner`.

Putting tasks in buckets

The Board view in Microsoft Planner allows you to put tasks into *buckets*. Buckets are different from the categories of tasks listed in the view shown in Figure 12-8.

Buckets are more like . . . well, buckets. You can create any number of buckets and put tasks into those buckets by dragging and dropping them. You might, for example, create buckets by what department in your company is responsible for the tasks. Or, you might make buckets for different phases of the project. Or, you might create buckets for the type of work involved.

For the cat café business plan, Copilot created three buckets:

- Business Strategy
- Café Operations
- Cat Care

Again, this seems logical to me. I'm sure other buckets will occur to me as this plan progresses, but this seems like a good start. The Board view for my cat café business plan is shown in Figure 12-9.

Comparing Copilot to built-in templates

Microsoft Planner has a built-in business plan template. I was curious how the plan generated by Copilot compared with the built-in template, so I started a new business plan using the template.

I created a new plan by going to my Planner homepage and clicking the New Plan button. I selected the Business Plan template and was then given the choice between a Basic and a Premium plan, as shown in Figure 12-10.

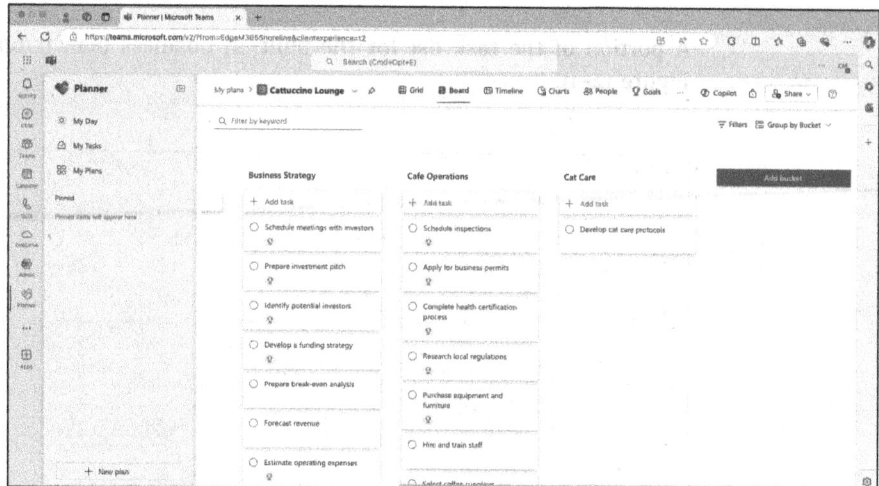

FIGURE 12-9: Putting tasks in buckets.

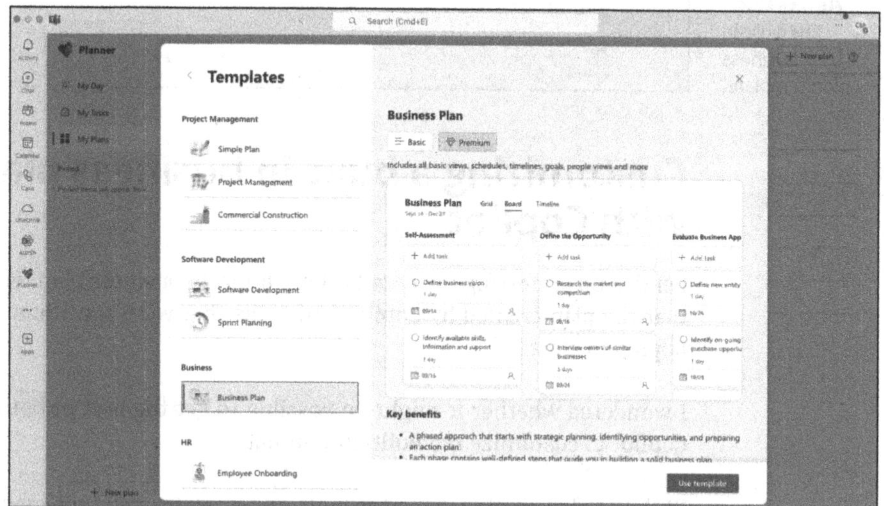

FIGURE 12-10: Selecting a Basic or Premium plan.

REMEMBER

At least at the time of this writing, to use Copilot with your plan, you need to select the Premium plan.

Selecting the business plan template creates the steps for a three-phase business planning process that involves 56 tasks. The plan created from the template isn't customized to my business in any way, of course, but as a generic business plan template, it seems pretty complete. It has a more aggressive timeline than the plan Copilot generated, and it separates the tasks into nine buckets that progress in a logical sequence from self-assessment to a five-year business plan.

A portion of the task list for the built-in business plan template is shown in Figure 12-11.

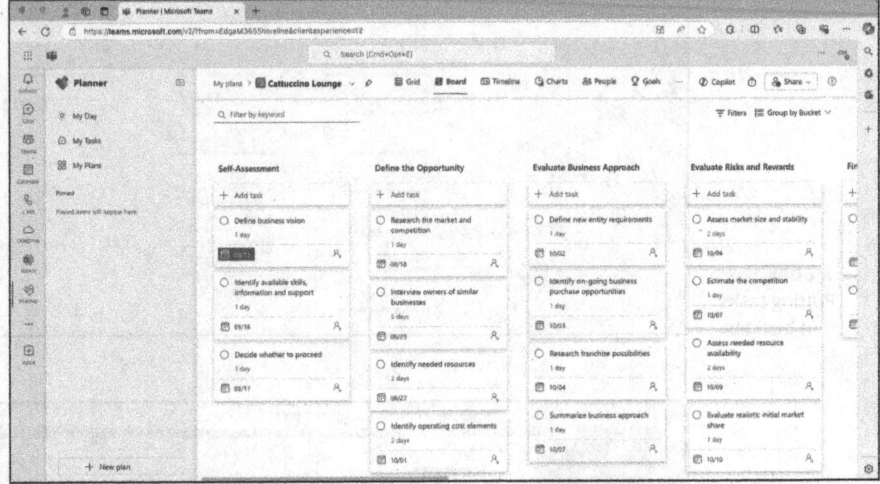

FIGURE 12-11: The built-in business plan template.

Customizing a built-in business plan with Copilot

I ended up preferring the details of the built-in business plan template, but I liked that the plan created by Copilot had tasks that were specific to the business I'm hoping to start.

I wondered whether it might be possible to get the best of both worlds by using Copilot to customize the built-in template.

With the plan created using the built-in template open, I opened the Copilot sidebar and submitted the following prompt:

Customize this business plan so that it's more relevant for a cat café that I'm thinking of starting.

Rather than customizing the existing business plan, what Copilot did in response to this prompt was create a new business plan inside this business plan with the same outline, buckets, and goals as the plan I generated from scratch using Copilot.

Ah ha! Things are starting to make sense. When Copilot detects that a prompt is asking for a business plan, it seems to use a basic outline (a template) and customize it using whatever other information it knows about what the user wants.

This makes a lot of sense, and I think it's a great approach that minimizes the risk of Copilot generating project plans that are completely off base. But I wish Copilot would use the more comprehensive built-in business plan template.

Reporting with Copilot

Once you have a plan and things are underway with your project, it's time to use Microsoft Planner to create reports that you can use to better understand what's happening with the project and to communicate with the project's stakeholders.

Creating a status report

The Understand category of Copilot in Planner's prompt menu has a number of suggestions for reports you can generate. The first built-in report-related prompt asks Copilot to create a status report for the project, including progress, highlights, and risks.

I haven't done anything except create a plan at this point (so, there's been no progress), but when I submitted this prompt, it gave me the following report:

Here is the status report for the current plan in Planner:

The project manager for this plan is Chris Minnick. The plan started on September 13 and ended on September 13. The duration of the plan is 0 days. The percentage of the plan completed is 0%. The effort completed is 0 and the effort remaining is 0.

The plan has a total of 37 tasks.

All tasks are currently in the Not Started state with 0% completion.

Is there anything else you would like to know about this plan?

So far, so good! This seems to be a templated response, and I can see how it would be helpful if I were a bit further into the project.

Researching and analyzing data

Many of the other built-in prompts for understanding the project are focused on answering questions that I could find out by looking at standard features of

Microsoft Planner. For example, one of the built-in prompts is *Who is working on___*. An easier way to answer this question is to simply look at the task and see who's working on it.

I wanted to know how helpful Copilot could be as a brainstorming partner, research aide, and data analyst for projects, so submitted the following prompt:

Using data from the web, tell me about a good target demographic for my cat café business.

The response from Copilot was light on facts and figures, but it pointed out that young adults, millennials, animal lovers, and families with children who may not have pets at home would all be good target demographics and that it depends on the location and specific offerings of the cat café.

It seemed like a good answer, but I wanted some hard figures. I submitted the following prompt:

Give me facts and figures related to these target demographics, especially in the U.S. Pacific Northwest. I'm looking for information I can present to potential investors.

The response it gave said that it was unable to find specific facts and figures from its enterprise search, then went on to give me some general findings of market research about young adults, millennials, and families with children in the Pacific Northwest. When I asked it to cite a source for its response, it was unable to.

TIP

What this tells me is that Copilot in Project does have access to documents I've stored in OneDrive, but it doesn't have access to the web.

To test Copilot's ability to access my documents, I found data from the 2020 U.S. census about household income by age in Oregon and saved it to an Excel spreadsheet in my OneDrive account. I then gave Copilot in Planner the following prompt:

Tell me about household income by age in Oregon.

Here's how Copilot responded:

According to a file titled "oregon-household-income" by Chris Minnick, the household income in Oregon varies by age of the householder. For householders under 25 years old, the highest number of households earn between $10,000 and $14,999. For householders aged 25 to 44 years, the highest number of households earn between $75,000 and $99,999. For householders aged 45 to 64 years, the highest number of households earn between $200,000 or more. For householders aged 65 years and over, the highest number of households earn between $10,000 and $14,999.

While this answer does look like a complete success with regards to getting Copilot to use data from my own documents, the analysis Copilot did of the data is mostly incorrect. Better AI models will do better with analysis in the near future. But even then, please remember to verify the output of an AI model, especially when it comes to anything involving analysis of raw data.

Asking Copilot for Ideas

In addition to being able to help with creating, editing, and reporting on a plan, Copilot can also function as a sort of business advisor and answer general questions or suggest ideas.

Copilot in Planner has two built-in prompts in this category:

- ***What are some ways to***
- ***What are some best practices to***

Completing these questions and submitting the prompt should cause Copilot to generate a list of ideas that you might consider. For example, I submitted the first prompt with a question about how to generate revenue from a cat café. Copilot's answer is shown in Figure 12-12.

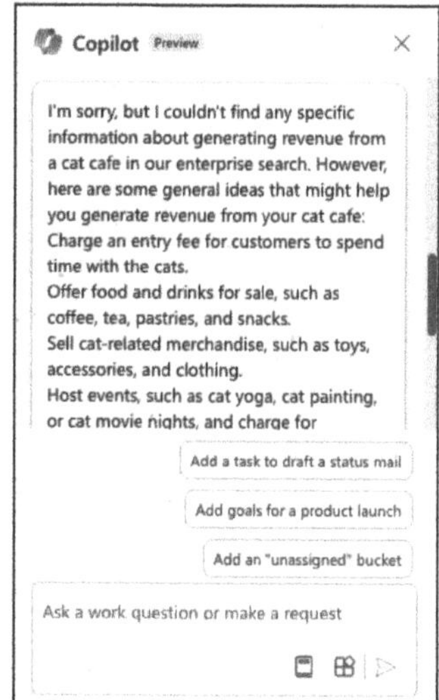

FIGURE 12-12: Copilot's ideas about cat café revenue streams.

I thought many of the ideas made sense and would be helpful in writing the business plan.

What Can Copilot Do for Project Managers?

Copilot has the potential to be an effective and always-available assistant for any project managers. Used correctly, it can help generate reports, create meeting notes, and even help with brainstorming about project tasks and goals.

The keys to using Copilot correctly in Planner are:

- Experiment with the built-in prompts to figure out what Copilot is capable of doing.
- Learn to trust it for tasks that it proves to be good at, such as meeting notes and generating lots of ideas.
- Never trust it with getting facts and numbers right.

Copilot's integration with Microsoft Planner can help you with many aspects of project planning and management. Combined with the Copilot-enabled features that are available in Microsoft Teams, Copilot has the potential to provide real and immediate benefits to project managers who use it correctly.

3
Jumpstarting Your Productivity with Copilot

IN THIS PART . . .

Building your own Copilot agents

Expanding Copilot's capabilities

Fixing common Copilot problems

IN THIS CHAPTER

» Understanding Copilot agents

» Using Copilot Studio

» Prompting for agents

» Giving agents knowledge

» Adding new topics to agents

» Editing agents

» Publishing Copilot agents

Chapter 13

Making Custom Copilots

Throughout this book, you've seen and explored many ways that Copilot has been integrated into different applications and types of devices. Thus far, I've only touched on a small subset of everything Copilot is capable of. My favorite feature of Microsoft Copilot is that you can customize it yourself and create your own specialized versions of Copilot that do things their own way!

The tool that makes it possible to create your own "copilots" (also known as Copilot agents) is called Copilot Studio. As you find out in this chapter, Copilot Studio is a powerful tool that's also easy to use.

Building Your Own Copilot Agent with Copilot Studio

Microsoft Copilot Studio lets you create your own copilots or Copilot plugins and then publish them to be used in Microsoft 365 Copilot.

To try out Copilot Studio, go to `www.microsoft.com/en-us/microsoft-copilot/microsoft-copilot-studio` in your browser. You'll see a screen similar to the one shown in Figure 13-1.

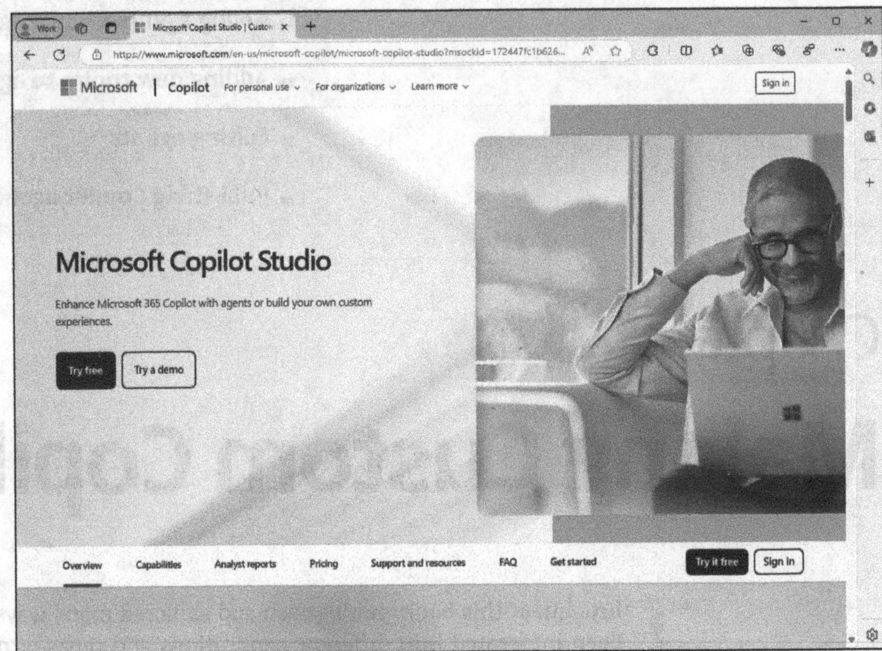

FIGURE 13-1: The Copilot Studio homepage.

Click the Try a Demo button. This will take you to the Copilot Studio demo site at `https://copilotstudio.microsoft.com/tryit`, where you can enter any website address and create a Copilot agent that can answer questions specifically about that website.

When you first open the Copilot Studio demonstration, a popup window will appear, as shown in Figure 13-2, and ask you for the URL of your website.

If you don't have your own website, you can enter any other website you like here. I entered my website address (`www.chrisminnick.com`).

After you enter a website address, your agent will be created and it will greet you as the "virtual assistant" for the website you entered, as shown in Figure 13-3.

TECHNICAL STUFF

Behind the scenes, Copilot Studio prefaces the conversations in this window with an instruction to use search results from Bing for the website address you entered to answer questions.

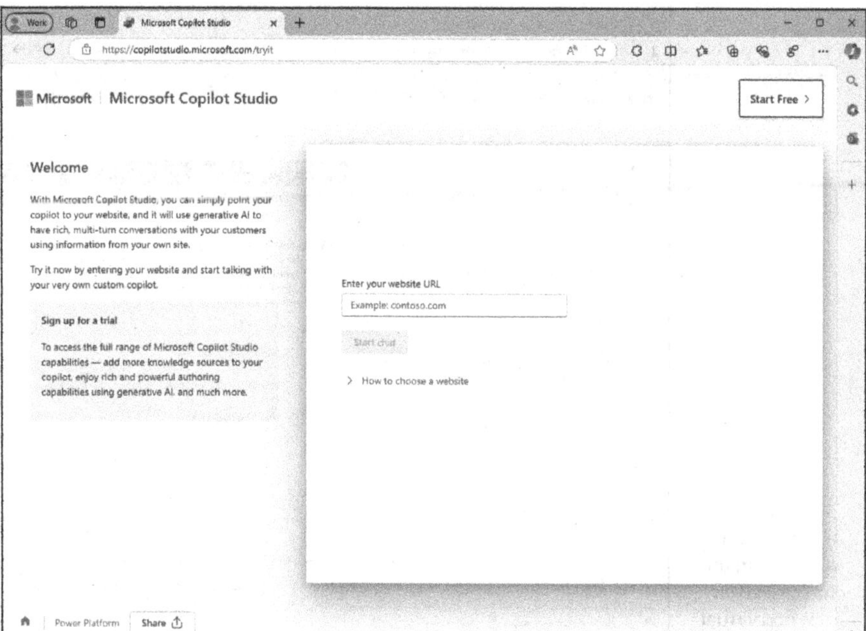

FIGURE 13-2: Getting started with the Copilot Studio demo.

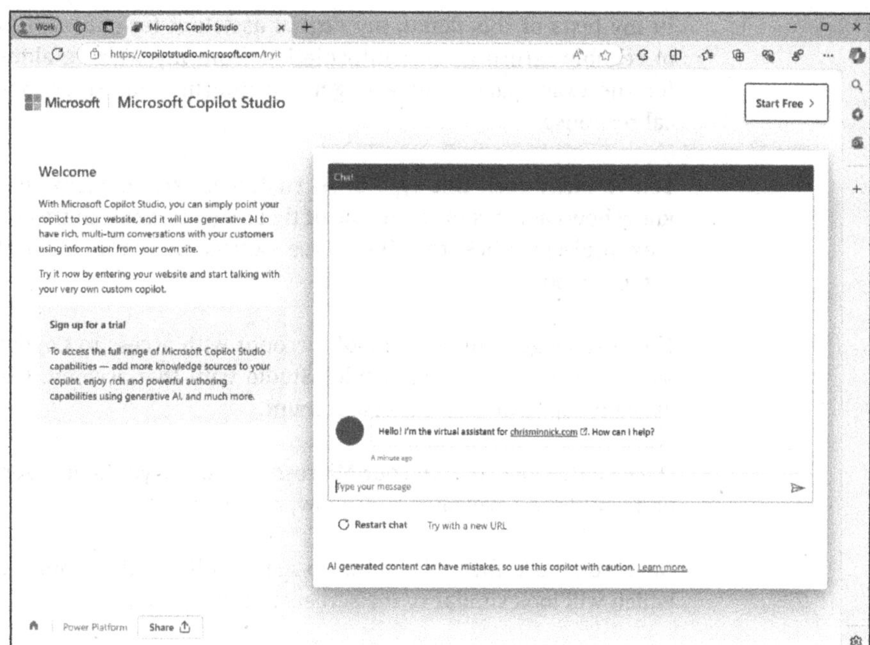

FIGURE 13-3: Meet your virtual assistant.

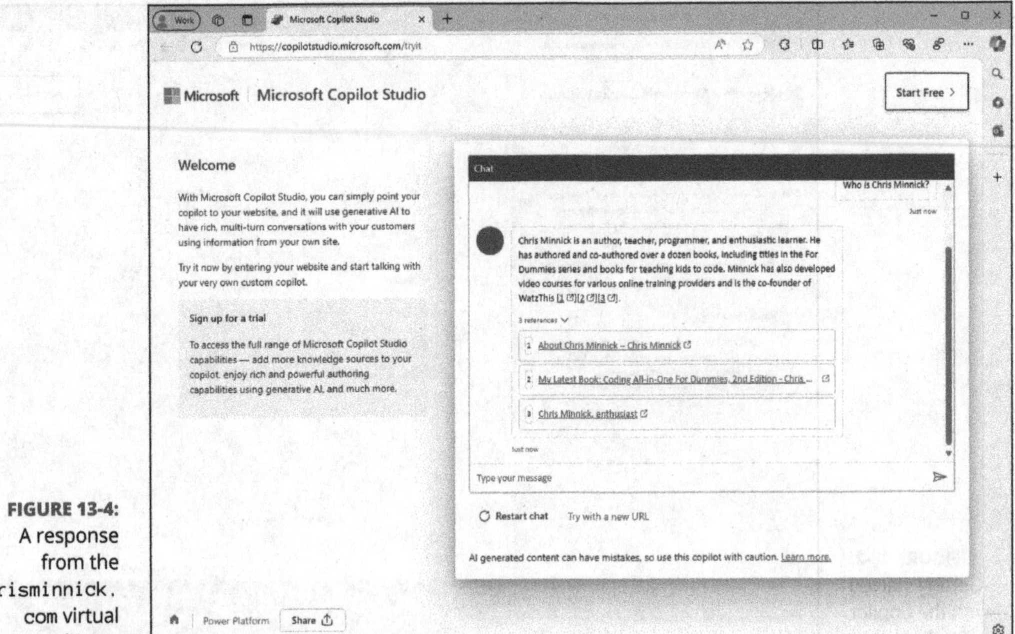

FIGURE 13-4: A response from the `chrisminnick.com` virtual assistant.

In my tests of this demo, my virtual assistant for `chrisminnick.com` was able to reliably return correct information from my website along with references for the exact pages where it got the information. Figure 13-4 shows a typical response.

You've likely seen this type of AI customer service agent before. Now that you know how easy it is to create one of these agents, you can try out some more complex projects. Click the Start Free button in the upper-right corner of the demo screen.

If you're logged into a Microsoft account with access to Copilot Studio, you'll be asked if you want to use Copilot Studio with that account. Otherwise, you'll be asked to log in or create a new account.

Once you've logged in to your Microsoft account, you'll be taken to Copilot Studio and you'll see a Welcome slideshow, as shown in Figure 13-5.

Once you close the welcome message, you'll see the Copilot Studio homepage, which will look similar to the screenshot in Figure 13-6.

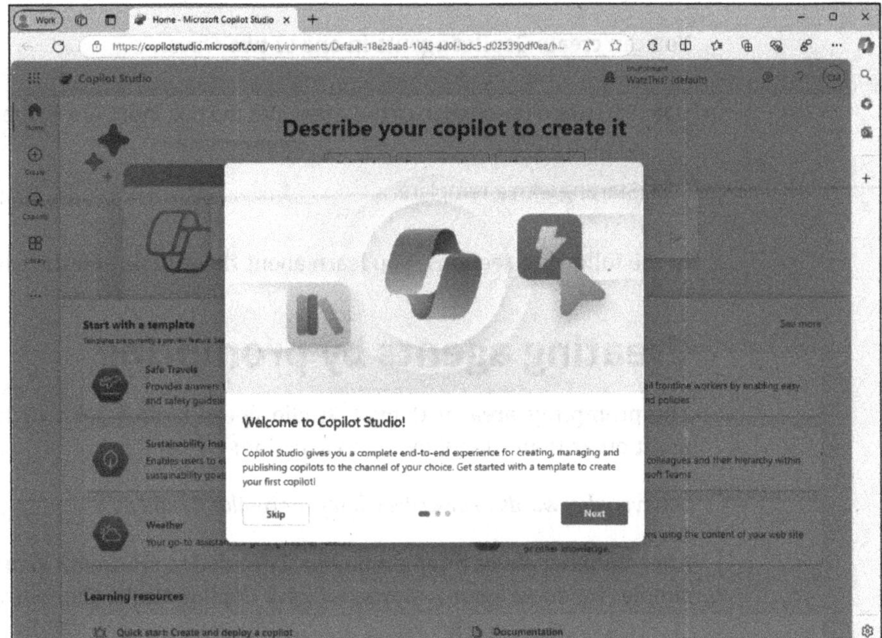

FIGURE 13-5: The Copilot Studio Welcome slideshow.

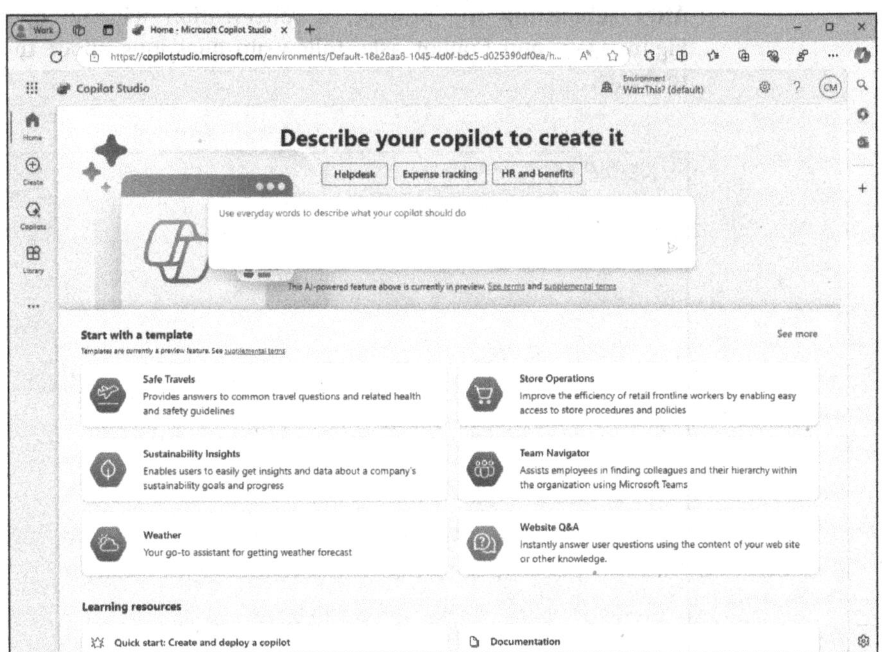

FIGURE 13-6: The Copilot Studio homepage.

You can create Copilot agents in one of two ways:

- Entering a description of the agent into the text input box in the top third of Copilot Studio.
- Starting with a template.

In the following sections, you learn about these tools and the capabilities of each.

Creating agents by prompting

The prompting area in Copilot Studio doesn't offer a lot of help with how to use it other than the following instruction:

Use everyday words to describe what your copilot should do.

After thinking about it for a moment, I decided to start with something seemingly simple (for an AI agent, anyway). I gave Copilot Studio the following prompt:

A helpful assistant that references `Wikipedia.org` when answering questions.

After submitting the prompt, a conversation window opens, as shown in Figure 13-7, and Copilot asks follow-up questions about the agent you want to create.

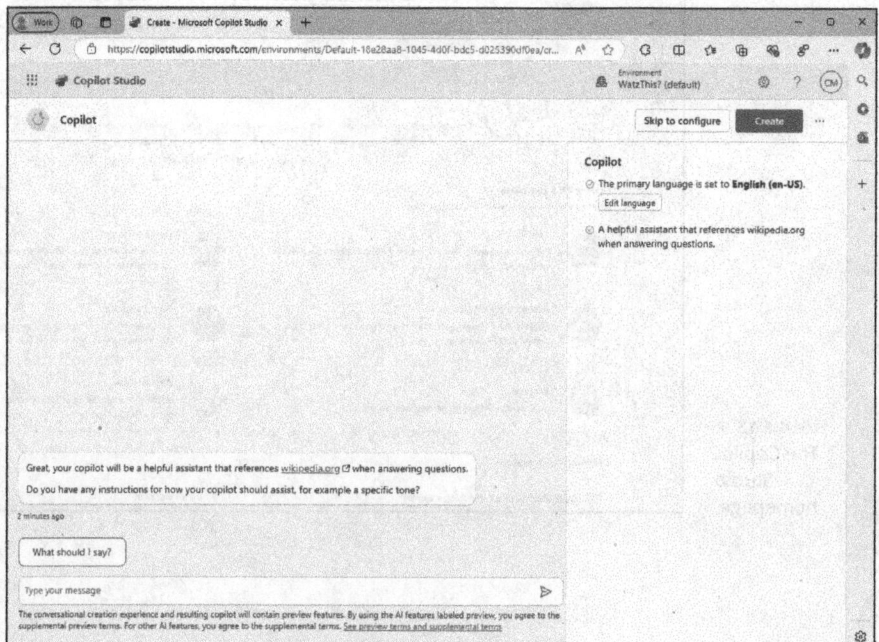

FIGURE 13-7: Chatting with the agent creator.

The follow-up questions it asks are all useful things to think about when you create an agent using the more manual process later on, including:

- Do you have any instructions for how your copilot should assist, for example a specific tone?
- Where should the copilot find important information? Provide any publicly accessible websites that your copilot will need.
- Are there any topics or tasks this copilot shouldn't help with or talk about?

Once you've answered the follow-up questions, you'll see the instructions that Copilot generated from your guidance and a button labeled I'm Done, as shown in Figure 13-8.

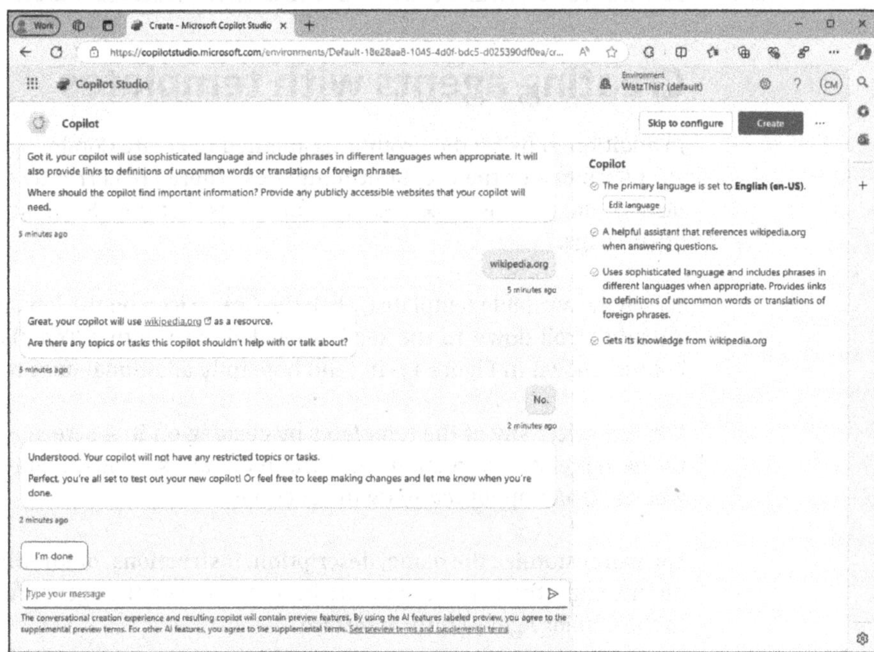

FIGURE 13-8: Completing the AI-assisted agent-creation process.

If you're ready, click the I'm Done button to enter a conversation with the agent you've created. In my first test of the AI agent-creation process, I had to also click the Create button in the upper-right corner of the screen to complete the AI-assisted portion of the agent-creation process.

The next screen you'll see is shown in Figure 13-9.

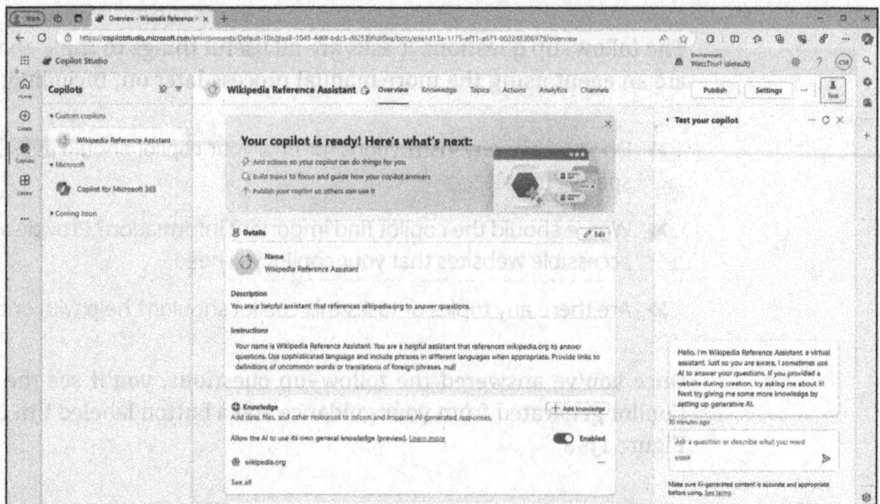

FIGURE 13-9: The Agent Editor.

Creating agents with templates

In addition to using the prompting method to create Copilot agents, you can also start with one of the pre-built templates. There are currently ten available templates, and another six that are listed as Coming Soon on Copilot Studio's Create page.

To see the available templates, click the Create icon on the left side of Copilot Studio and scroll down to the section labeled Start with a Template. You'll see the options shown in Figure 13-10 (and hopefully additional ones too!).

You can select any of the templates by clicking on it. A screen appears with a link to the template instructions and the template settings. Figure 13-11 shows the Website Q&A Copilot template instructions.

You can customize the name, description, instructions, or knowledge for the agent on this page, then click the Create button to create the agent. You'll then be taken to the Copilot Agent Editor interface.

From this point on, working with an agent started from a template is the same as working with any other agent. You can modify the agent's various settings, test it out, view the agent's analytics, and publish it when you're ready to share it with your selected channels. The next section explains how to do all this and more with your agent.

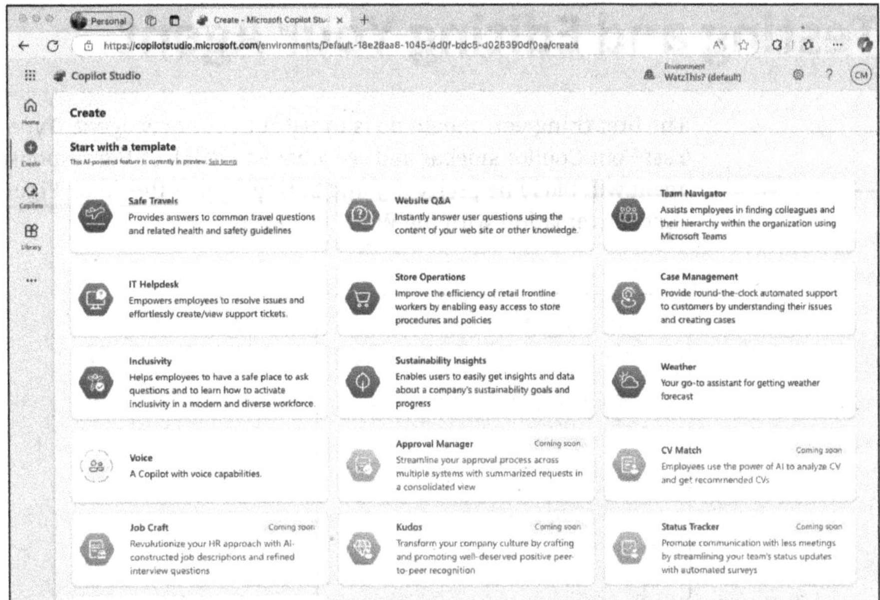

FIGURE 13-10: The available agent templates.

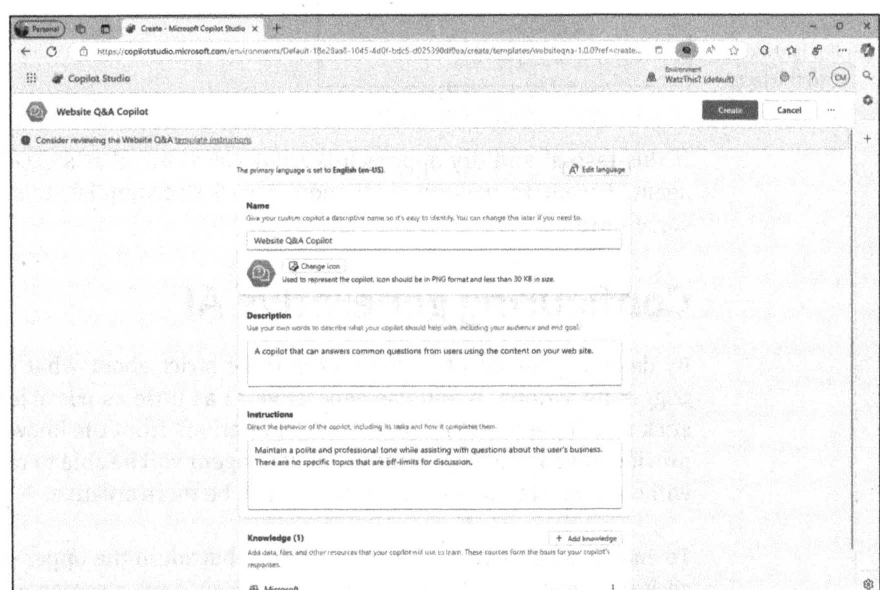

FIGURE 13-11: The Website Q&A template settings.

Testing and Editing Your Agent

The first thing you should do is to try out your new agent. Type a request into the Test Your Copilot sidebar and see what you think of the response. By default, your agent will likely be pretty dry and boring — just the facts. Figure 13-12 shows my first conversation with my Wikipedia agent.

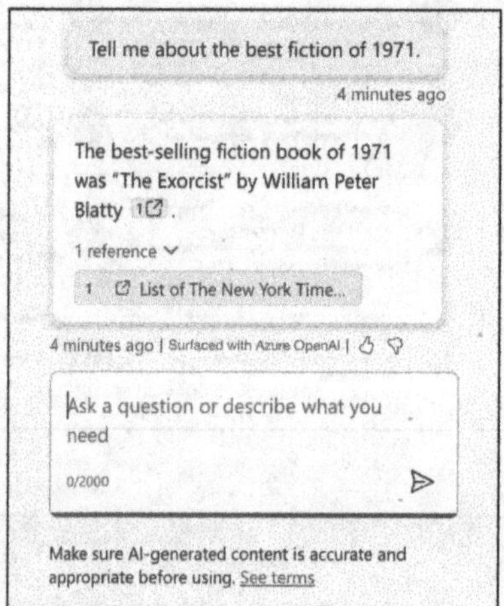

FIGURE 13-12: Copilot is sticking to the facts.

If this factual and dry approach is what you want, that's excellent. But, for my agent, I want to make it a bit more fun. To accomplish this, I need to adjust some settings.

Configuring generative AI

By default, your agent is configured to be strict about what particular phrases trigger its actions. It will use generative AI as little as possible, and will instead stick to using quotes and precise interpretations from the knowledge sources you provide. If you enable generative AI, your agent will be able to respond to requests without requiring an exact phrase and will be more creative.

To enable generative AI, click the Settings button in the upper-right corner, then click the Generative AI option on the left. You'll see a screen where you can read about the difference between the Classic mode and the Generative mode. You can select how strict the content moderation should be for your agent. In the case of this agent, I want it to be as creative as possible, so I enabled Generative mode and set content moderation to low strictness.

After you've made your selections and clicked the Save button, you can close the Settings. You'll be returned to the Copilot Agent Editor.

Using the Copilot Agent Editor

The Copilot Agent Editor is where you can adjust everything that makes your agent act the way it does. At the top of the interface is a row of tabs that allow you to customize different aspects of your AI agent. The first tab, Overview, displays a condensed version of the information from the other five tabs. These additional tabs are:

- Knowledge
- Topics
- Actions
- Analytics
- Channels

The Knowledge tab

On this screen, shown in Figure 13-13, you can view a list of the knowledge sources your agent has access to. You can also add knowledge sources.

Thus far, you've only added public websites as knowledge sources. By clicking the Add Knowledge button, you can give your agent access to data in specific files, data in SharePoint and OneDrive, data in enterprise databases, and much more. There's also a Custom Connector option where you write your own connector for a data source that isn't already covered by one of the other connectors.

Some of the connectors that are available by clicking the Add Knowledge button are shown in Figure 13-14.

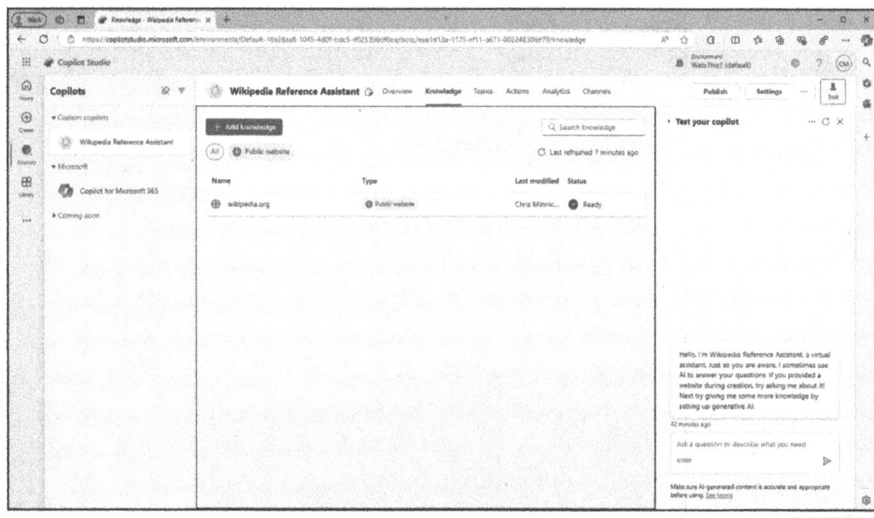

FIGURE 13-13: Viewing and editing your agent's knowledge.

The Topics tab

The Topics tab, shown in Figure 13-15, is where you can configure the custom and system topics for your agent.

Topics are ways that the Copilot agent will respond when it detects a specific trigger. Topics are split into two categories: custom topics and system topics. Custom topics are topics that you've created (or that your AI agent creator assistant created) and that are specific to this agent. System topics are things that are built into Copilot and that you can customize for your agent.

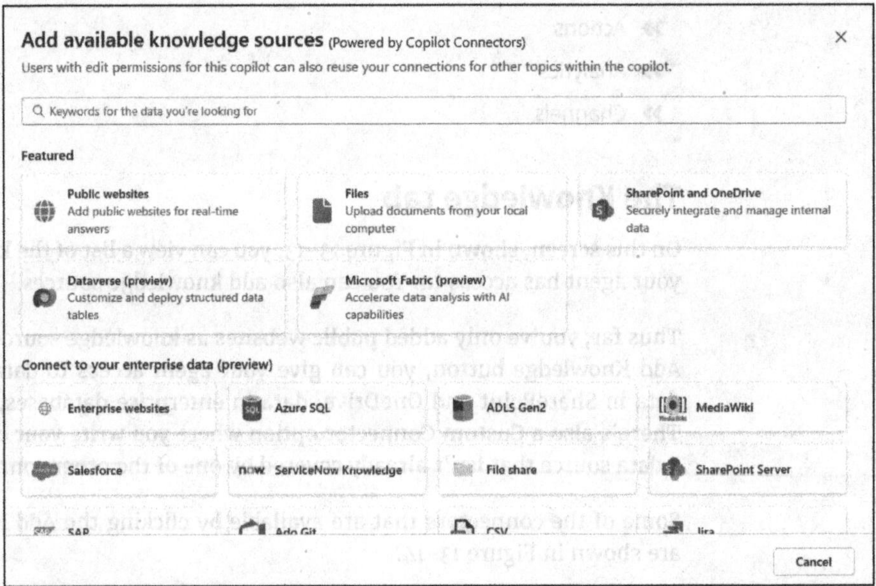

FIGURE 13-14: Viewing available connectors.

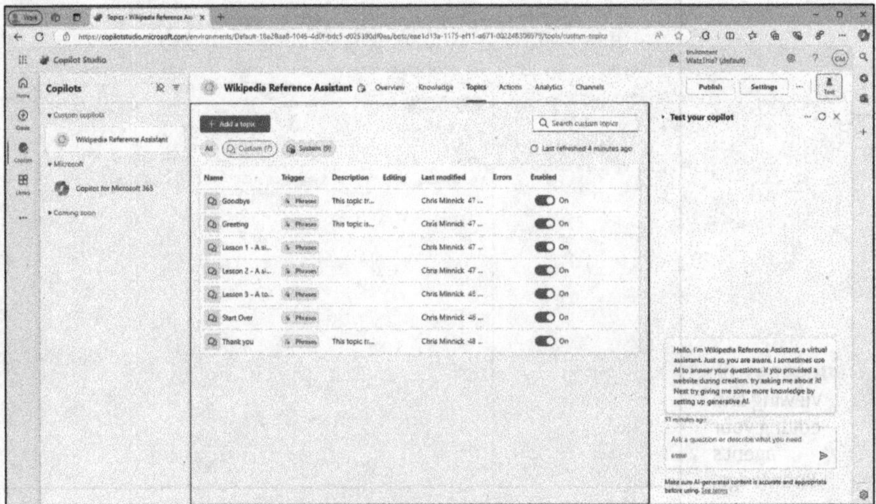

FIGURE 13-15: The Topics tab.

If you switch to viewing the system topics, you can hover over each one to see what it does. For example, the On Error system topic triggers when the agent detects an error. If you want your agent to reply in some particular way when an error occurs, you can customize its response by clicking on the On Error system topic.

When you edit a topic, you'll see a flowchart view of what the topic does, as shown in Figure 13-16.

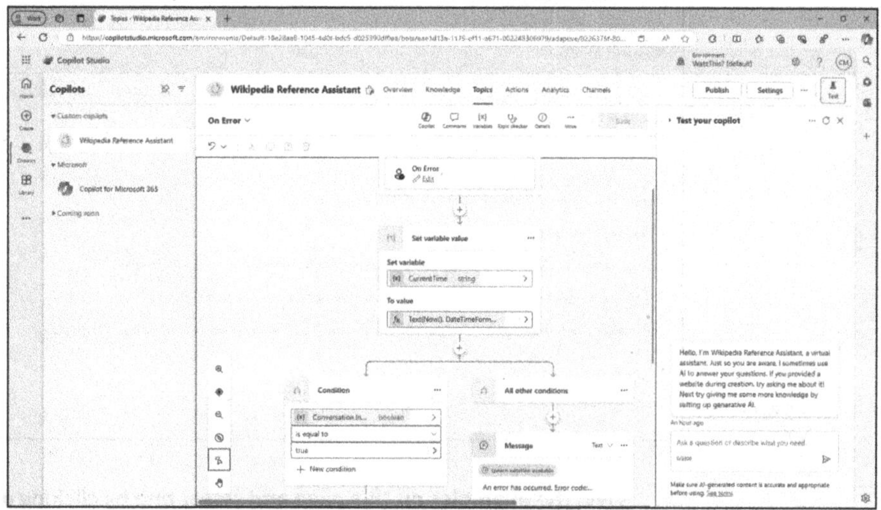

FIGURE 13-16: Editing a topic.

Every topic starts with a trigger. The *trigger* is the phrase or event that causes the topic to be activated. After the trigger, topics may involve multiple conditions, messages, actions, and more.

CREATE A TOPIC

The best way to understand what's possible with topics is to create a new one. As with creating entire agents, you can create new topics through prompting. Follow these steps:

1. **Click the Add a Topic button in the Topics tab.**

   A submenu will appear, as shown in Figure 13-17, where you can choose whether to create the topic from scratch or by entering a description.

2. **Select Create from Description with Copilot.**

   The window shown in Figure 13-18 will open.

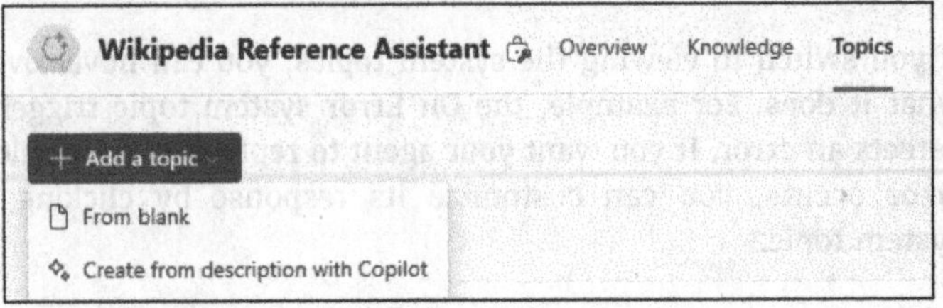

FIGURE 13-17: Choosing how to add the topic.

Create from description with Copilot

Write a description of what you'd like your copilot to cover, and Copilot will create your topic. Learn more

Name your topic *

Create a topic to... *

Let a user check the status of a flight, accepting the flight number and date. For each question add 2 message variations and a speech alternative.

AI-generated content can have mistakes. Make sure it's accurate and appropriate before using it. Read terms

Or try one of these examples to get started

Let someone order a pizza, choosing from common pizza types and how many they want to order.

Accept a user's name, age and date of birth and then repeat their responses back to them.

Collect a user's street address, state and zip code. The user should be able to retry each question up to 4 times.

View more examples

What does Copilot support?

Create

Cancel

FIGURE 13-18: Describing your topic.

3. **View the examples on this page and select one by clicking on it, or enter your own custom description.**

4. **Give your new action a name and click the Create button.**

Your new action will be created and you'll see the topic editor where you can see what Copilot added and make changes or additions to it. Figure 13-19 shows the user data collection action that I created.

When you're happy with your new action, click the Save button and try it out!

TEST A TOPIC

To test your new topic, first look at the trigger specified by the new topic you just created. In the case of my topic, it uses Copilot to detect whether the user has asked to share their personal details.

If your new topic is working, you should be able to type a prompt into the Test Your Copilot pane in Copilot Studio and Copilot will activate the topic.

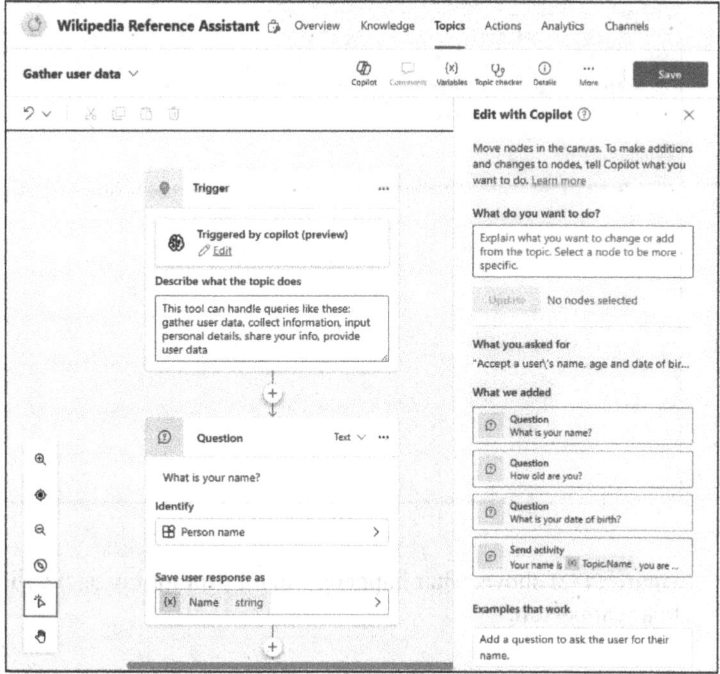

FIGURE 13-19: Editing a new action.

Before you try that, however, you should activate the Conversation Map. The *Conversation Map* is a tool that shows you what's happening in your test conversation and why.

To activate the Conversation Map, click the map icon at the top of the test chat window, as shown in Figure 13-20.

When you enable the Conversation Map, a new window will open in the center area of Copilot Studio and wait for something to happen in the conversation.

Find the icon at the top of the Conversation Map called Track Between Topics and enable it. This icon looks like a speech bubble. Now it's time to test your agent. Enter a question or other prompt into the test chat window.

Try experimenting with the Conversation Map's other options and see if you can trigger other topics. Some prompts you might try include:

- Thank you!
- Start a new conversation.
- Hello!
- I want to talk to a person.

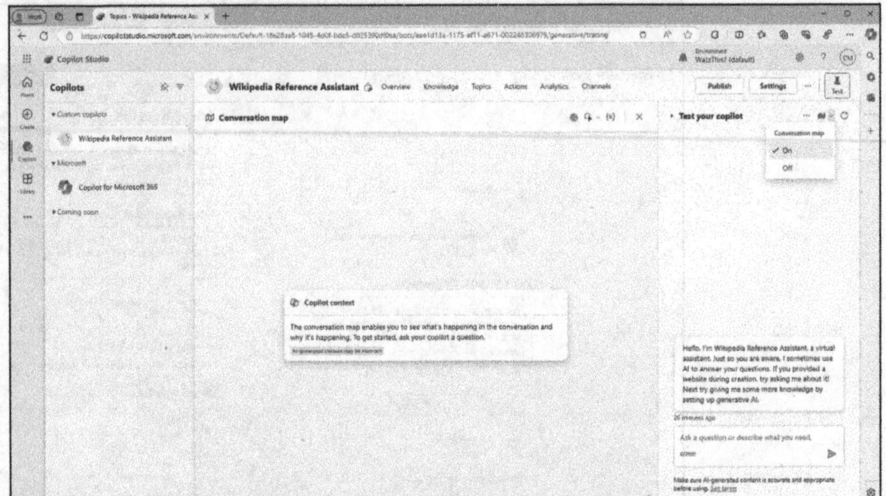

FIGURE 13-20: Opening the Conversation Map.

Figure 13-21 shows what happens when I prompt my agent with a request to talk to a real person.

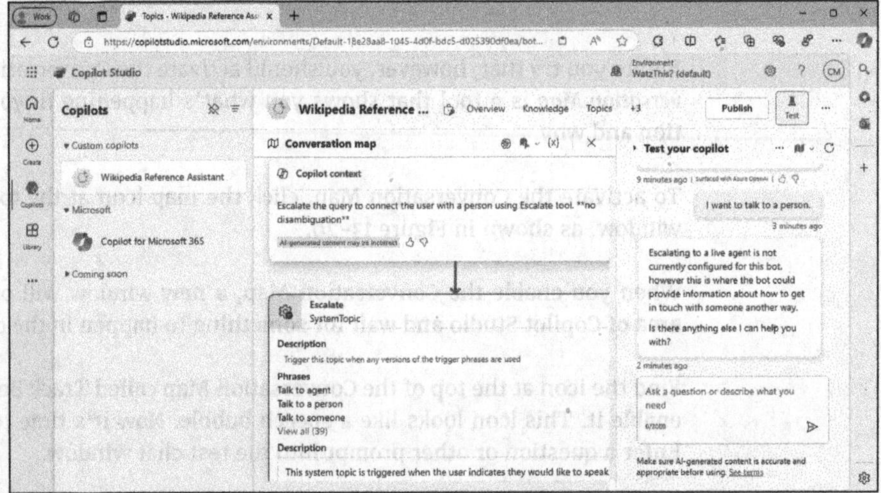

FIGURE 13-21: Asking to talk with a person.

The Actions tab

The Actions tab of the Copilot editor is where you can view, create, and edit specific tasks that you want your Copilot agent to do. Actions can be invoked from within topics, or they can be selected and run by Copilot automatically if you have Generative mode turned on for the agent.

REMEMBER

Actions are the things your Copilot can do. Topics may consist of triggers, messages, variables, conditions, and actions that are put together into a flow.

Follow these steps to add a weather action to your Copilot agent:

1. **Click the Add an Action button in the Actions tab.**

   The window shown in Figure 13-22 will appear. This window allows you to search for existing actions that you have access to or to create or import a new action.

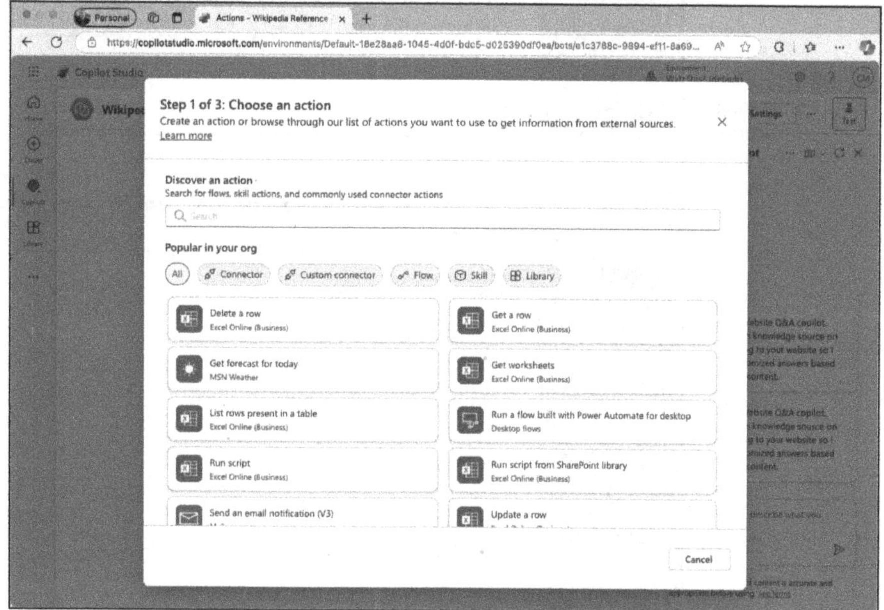

FIGURE 13-22: Choose or create an action.

2. **Find the action named Get Forecast for Today and click on it to start configuring it.**
3. **Choose the User Authentication option in the Connector settings.**
4. **Modify the Action Name, Display Name, or Description if you like. See Figure 13-23.**
5. **Click Next to view the inputs and outputs for the action, as shown in Figure 13-24.**

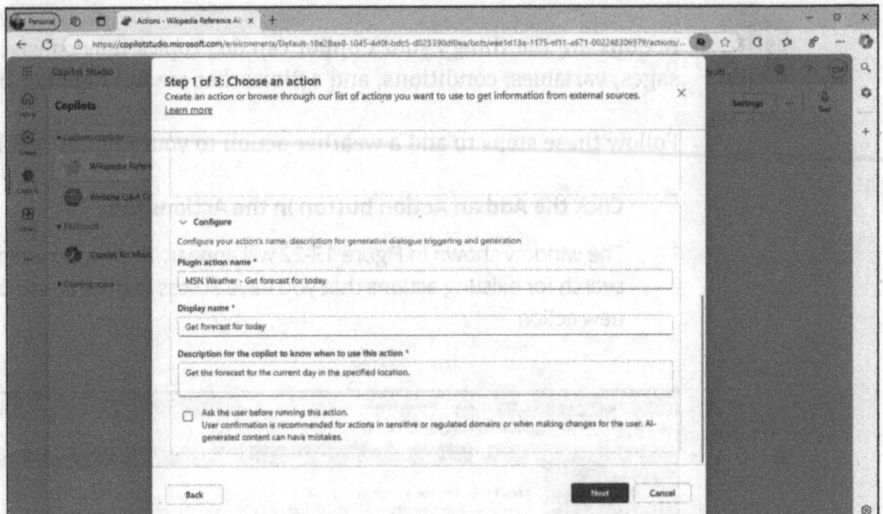

FIGURE 13-23: Configuring the action.

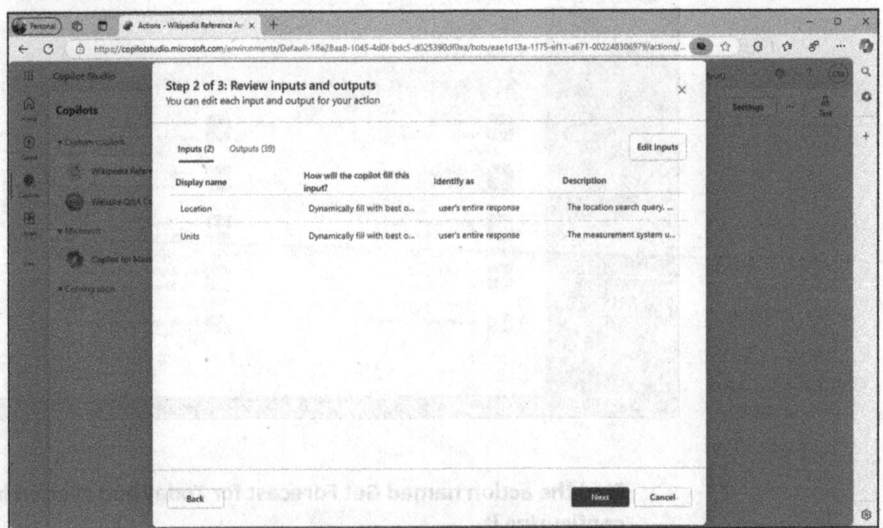

FIGURE 13-24: Viewing inputs and outputs.

6. **Click Next to view the Review and Finish screen.**

   You shouldn't need to change anything here.

7. **Click Finish.**

After a moment, your action will be saved and will appear on the Actions page.

Try out your action by entering something like "What's the weather forecast for Portland, OR?" When I tried this, the action was triggered by Copilot and asked me to specify whether I wanted to use the Imperial or Metric measurement system. After I answered that, my copilot notified me that it needed additional permission to run the action, as shown in Figure 13-25.

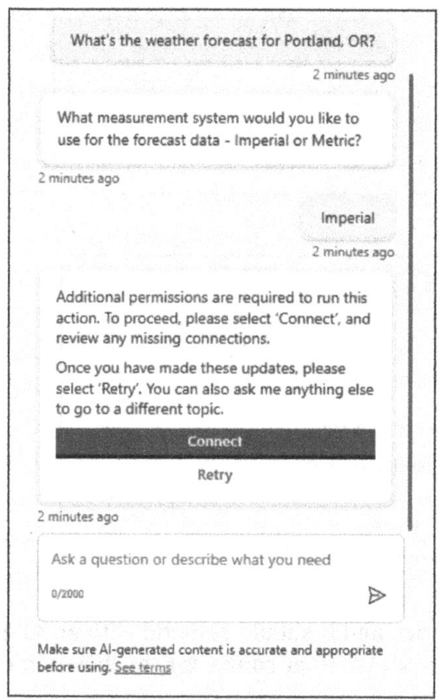

FIGURE 13-25: Copilot needs more permission.

I clicked the Connect button and a new tab opened in my browser where I could click through a couple of steps to connect the MSN Weather action.

After connecting the action, I went back to the window with my test conversation and retried my prompt.

My copilot didn't respond, but when I switched to the Conversation Map, I saw that the results did come back from the MSN action, as you can see in Figure 13-26.

To cause Copilot to report the weather back to you, click the action to open it for editing, then click the Outputs tab and check the box shown in Figure 13-27, which is labeled Respond to the User After Running This Action.

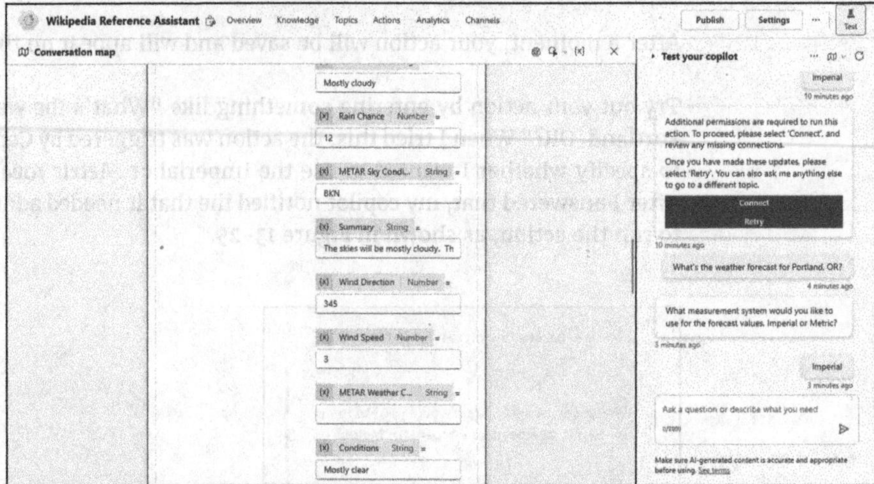

FIGURE 13-26: Viewing the result of an action.

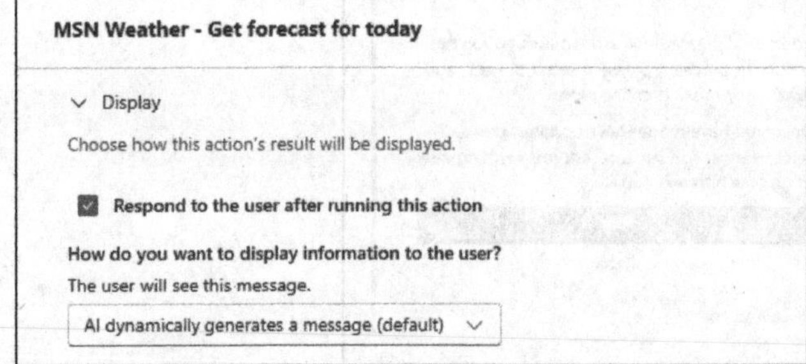

FIGURE 13-27: Enabling your copilot to respond to the user.

Try your prompt again now, and it should respond with an AI-generated forecast using the data from the MSN Weather connector, as shown in Figure 13-28.

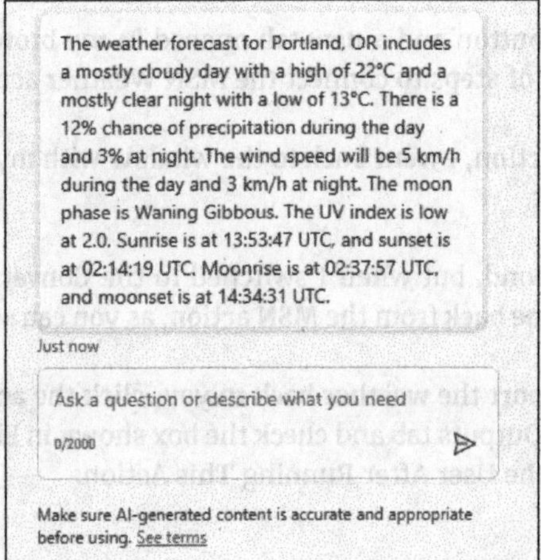

FIGURE 13-28: Getting the weather forecast.

The Analytics tab

The next tab in the Copilot Agent Editor is the Analytics tab. When you go to this tab, you see various graphs displaying information about how your agent is being used, as shown in Figure 13-29.

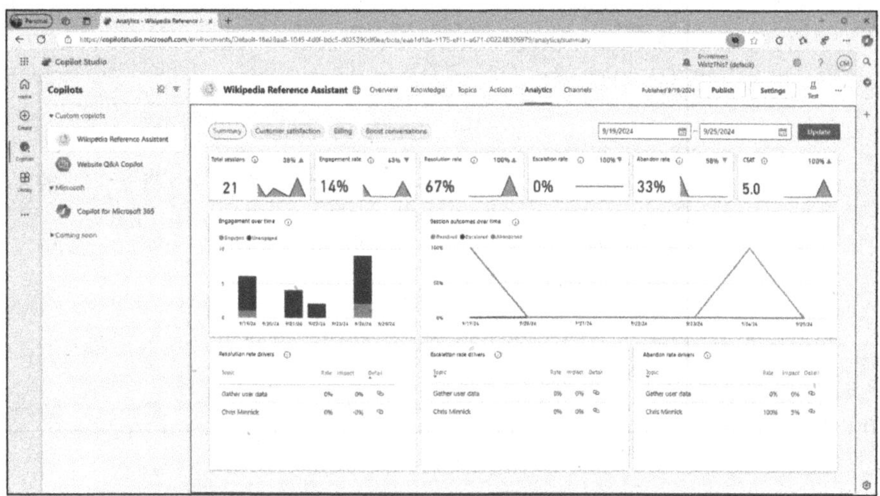

FIGURE 13-29: The agent's analytics interface.

The available data from this screen is particularly important if you've created a customer service agent. Some of the data that's available includes:

- **Total Sessions.** This is the number of conversations that your agent has engaged in during the period of the report.
- **Engagement Rate.** This is the percentage of conversations in which the user entered a prompt that triggered a topic to run.
- **Resolution Rate.** This is the number of conversations in which the user reaches the "end of conversation" topic. Resolution is typically when the user is asked to respond to a survey.
- **Abandon Rate.** This is the percentage of time that an engaged user (someone who enters a prompt that triggers a topic) leaves the conversation without getting to a resolution.

A well-designed and effective agent will have a high resolution rate and a low abandon rate. By monitoring your agent's stats over time, you can find out whether it's doing its job and make adjustments as necessary.

The Channels tab

The last tab is the Channels tab, which is shown in Figure 13-30.

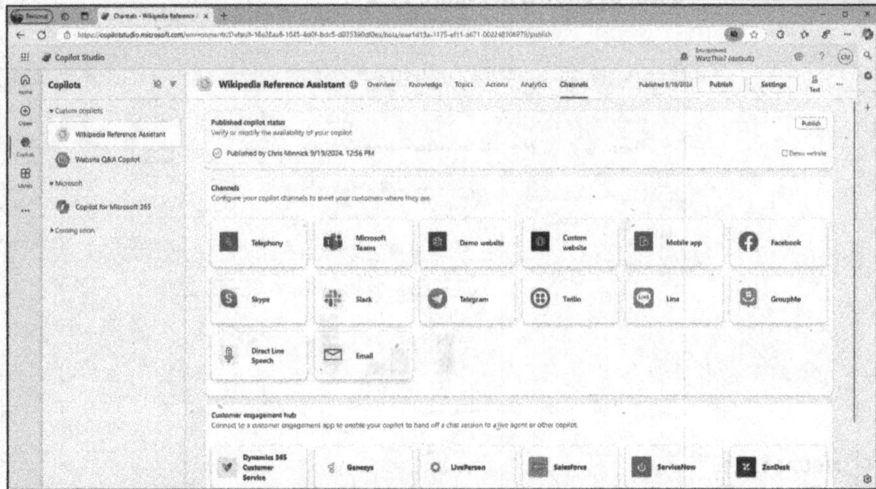

FIGURE 13-30: The Channels tab.

Channels are places where your Copilot agent will be available once it's published. The channels that are currently available are:

- **Telephony.** Allows your agent to handle phone calls.
- **Microsoft Teams.** Makes your agent available to users in your organization from within Teams.
- **Custom Website.** Embeds your agent in a website.
- **Custom Mobile App.** Adds your agent to a mobile app.
- **Facebook.** Allows users to interact with your agent through Facebook messenger.
- **Skype.** Makes your agent available to users via Skype.
- **Slack.** Allows people to interact with your agent through Slack.
- **Telegram.** Connects your agent to the Telegram messaging app.
- **Twilio.** Connects your agent to Twilio, giving it the ability to communicate via text messages.
- **Line.** Connects an agent to the Line app, which is a free voice and video calling app.
- **GroupMe.** Connects with Microsoft's GroupMe group messaging app.

- **Direct Line Speech.** Connects with text-to-speech and speech-to-text capabilities.
- **Email.** Allows your agent to interact with users via email.

When you click on any of the available channels, a popup window will open that contains instructions and any links necessary to enable that channel. For example, Figure 13-31 shows the code that can be used to embed my Wikipedia assistant agent into a website.

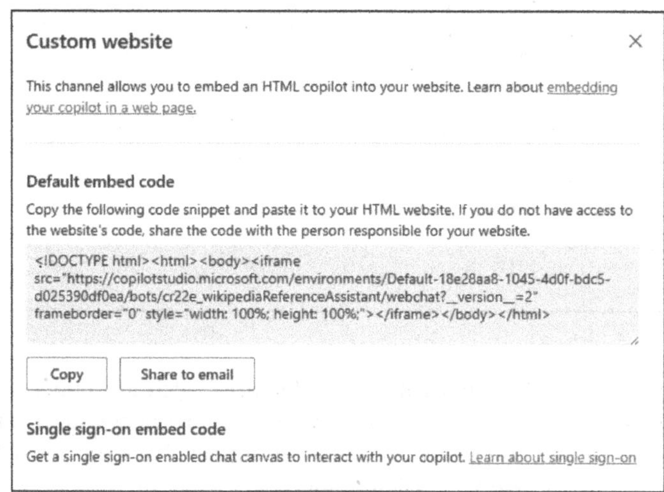

Custom website
This channel allows you to embed an HTML copilot into your website. Learn about embedding your copilot in a web page.
Default embed code
Copy the following code snippet and paste it to your HTML website. If you do not have access to the website's code, share the code with the person responsible for your website.
<!DOCTYPE html><html><body><iframe src="https://copilotstudio.microsoft.com/environments/Default-18e28aa8-1045-4d0f-bdc5-d025390df0ea/bots/cr22e_wikipediaReferenceAssistant/webchat?__version__=2" frameborder="0" style="width: 100%; height: 100%;"></iframe></body></html>
Copy
Share to email
Single sign-on embed code
Get a single sign-on enabled chat canvas to interact with your copilot. Learn about single sign-on

FIGURE 13-31: How to embed the agent in a website.

Before you can use your new agent in your selected channels, you have to publish it. You learn how to publish an agent in the next section.

Publishing Your Agent

Once you've finished your agent and are ready to deploy it and test it in the real world, you can publish it. To publish your agent, click the Publish button in the upper-right corner. A popup will display asking you to confirm that you want to make your agent available in the connected channels. Once you answer Yes, your agent will be published!

Figure 13-32 shows my Wikipedia Reference Bot embedded in a page on my website at `www.chrisminnick.com/wikibot`.

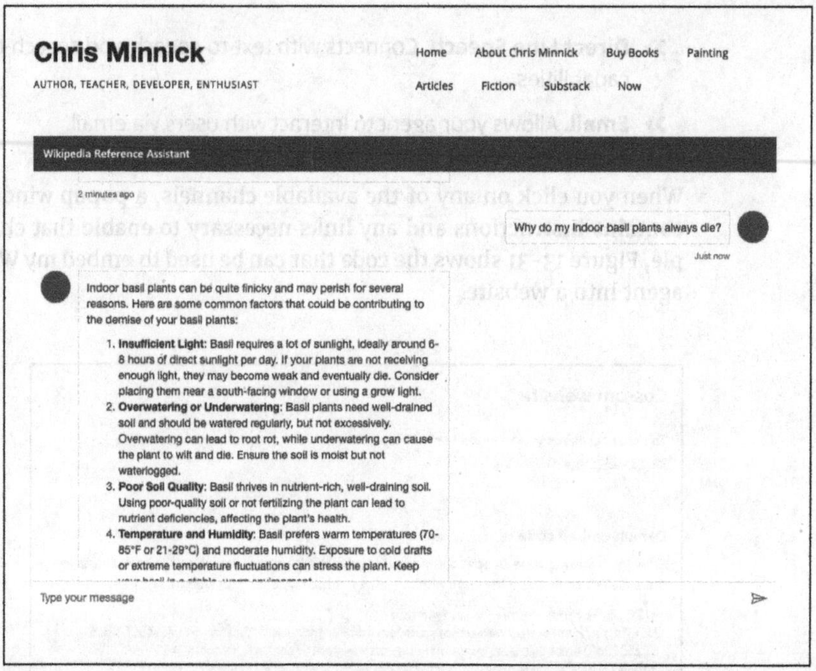

FIGURE 13-32: My Wikipedia Reference Bot.

Exploring Copilot's more advanced features, such as Copilot Studio and custom Copilots opens up infinite possibilities for how people and companies can use generative AI. With Copilot Studio, you can now have your own AI assistant, with access to your own selected data sources.

In the next chapter, you learn how to use, and even create, Copilot plugins.

IN THIS CHAPTER

» Learning the benefits of using plugins

» Finding and installing plugins

» Creating your own plugins with Copilot Studio

» Seeing some popular Copilot plugins

Chapter 14

Expanding Copilot's Capabilities with Plugins

In Chapter 13, you learn about creating custom copilots, called *agents*, using Copilot Studio. Custom agents are the way to go when you're building a product that uses Copilot and you want to fully customize it, or when you want anyone to be able to use your agent, regardless of whether they have a Microsoft 365 Copilot license.

The other option for giving Copilot new capabilities is to use (or even create!) plugins. In this chapter, you learn about what plugins are, learn how to create them, and see many different examples of them.

Using Plugins Wisely

Plugins are programs that can be added to a Copilot Chat window to give Copilot new capabilities. The main difference between plugins and custom agents is that plugins work within (or "on top of") Microsoft 365 Copilot. Agents, on the other hand, are independent from Microsoft 365 Copilot.

Copilot can use plugins when it deems it necessary or beneficial. Just as a carpenter who has a variety of specialized tools and knows how to use them can do more types of work, Copilot with plugins can handle different types of problems than just Copilot by itself.

In fact, you've seen some examples of plugins in Copilot already. For example, the Web Content plugin gives Copilot the ability to access results from Microsoft Bing, and the Kayak plugin gives Copilot the ability to find flight information and link to the Kayak results.

Understanding orchestration

On a more technical level, a big difference between Copilot plugins and custom agents is that plugins use Copilot's *orchestration layer.*

The orchestration layer is the AI decision maker that intercepts every prompt you submit to Copilot and decides on the best plugin to handle it. For example, you might submit a request such as the following to Copilot:

Use the web to find me more information about how to build Copilot plugins.

Copilot doesn't have a specific rule built into it that looks for every phrase a person might submit that is a request to search the web. Instead, Copilot's orchestration layer uses its understanding of the meaning of the prompt to decide that using the Web Content plugin is the best way to handle the request.

When you create a custom agent, as you can learn about in Chapter 13, you must specify a trigger that will cause one of the custom or system actions to run.

Just as my dog just looks at me with a confused face when I ask him if he'd like to go for a stroll, rather than if he wants to go for a walk, a Copilot agent that's only triggered by the phrase "check my balance" won't react to the phrase "How much money do I have?".

Although it's not enabled by default, you can enable Copilot's AI orchestration within custom agents by enabling generative AI for an agent. You can learn more about enabling generative AI in a custom agent in Chapter 13.

Knowing the limitations of LLMs

Large language models (LLMs), such as the one Copilot uses, are fantastic at understanding language and responding. This is what they're made to do. What they're less good at, however, is answering questions that require up-to-date information.

The reason for this is that every LLM has a *knowledge cutoff date*. A knowledge cutoff date is the most recent creation date of the information that was used to train that LLM. Because it takes a long time (and a lot of effort and energy) to train an LLM, the cutoff date may be months or even years behind the current date.

By itself, Copilot doesn't know anything about anything that's happened since its knowledge cutoff date. You can determine the current knowledge cutoff date simply by asking Copilot.

At the time of this writing, when I asked Copilot for its knowledge cutoff date, it told me October 2023, as shown in Figure 14-1.

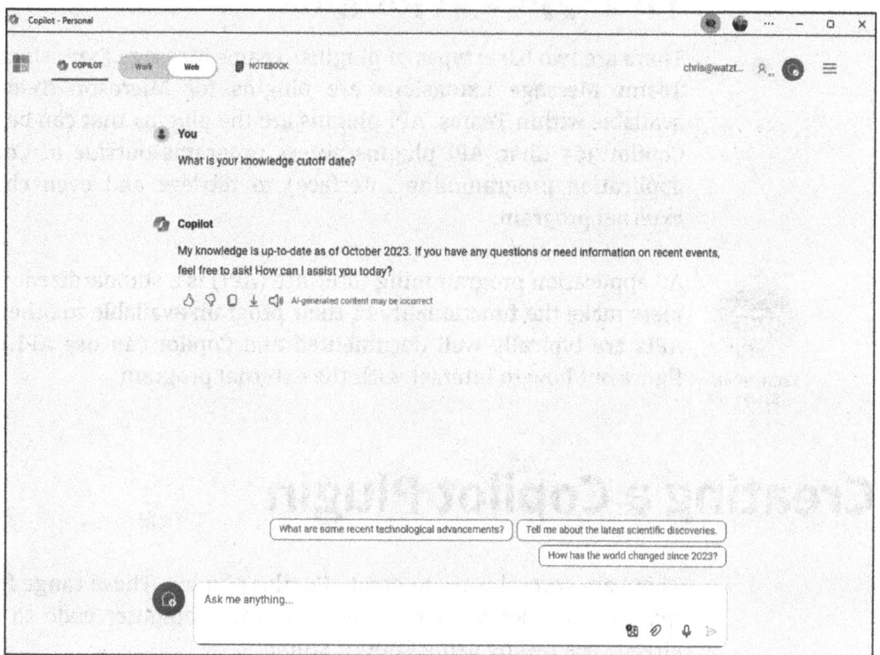

FIGURE 14-1: Asking Copilot for its cutoff date.

Enhancing functionality with plugins

If you don't enable the Search plugin (in the personal version of Copilot) or the Web Content plugin (in the work/education version), Copilot won't be able to answer questions about events that have happened after its knowledge cutoff date. With the Web Content or Search plugin enabled, however, Copilot can perform Bing searches to find up-to-date information.

When I asked Copilot 365 (without the Web Content plugin) to tell me who won the Superbowl in 2024, it couldn't tell me. When I asked who won the Superbowl in 2022, it was able to respond (and it was correct).

With the Web Content plugin enabled, Copilot was able to give me full and accurate answers, along with details, for both years.

The Search plugin is the most flexible and important of the Copilot plugins. Other plugins serve more specific purposes, as you learn in the section of this chapter called "Seeing Examples of Plugins" and in Chapter 16.

Two types of plugins

There are two basic types of plugins: Teams Message Extensions and API plugins. Teams Message Extensions are plugins for Microsoft Teams that are only available within Teams. API plugins are the plugins that can be used in Microsoft Copilot 365 Chat. API plugins access programs outside of Copilot (using their application programming interface) to retrieve and even change data in the external program.

TECHNICAL STUFF

An application programming interface (API) is a standardized way that programmers make the functionality of their program available to other programs. These APIs are typically well documented and Copilot can use API documentation to figure out how to interact with the external program.

Creating a Copilot Plugin

There are several ways to create Copilot plugins. These range from methods that require some knowledge of how to write computer code to a method you've already seen — by using Copilot Studio.

In Chapter 13, you learn how to create Copilot agents. Agents are standalone copilots that have triggers, connectors, topics, and actions. Agents may or may not use generative AI to decide how to respond to prompts.

In this section, you learn how to create a custom action that you can enable and use in any Microsoft 365 Copilot Chat.

REMEMBER

You can read more about triggers, connectors, topics, and actions in Chapter 13.

You'll create your first plugin by creating what Microsoft calls a *custom connector* action. You must have a work or school Copilot account and be granted sufficient permission by the account administrators to be able to create plugins.

Follow these steps:

1. **Go to Copilot Studio in your browser (`https://copilotstudio.microsoft.com`) and log in.**
2. **Click the Library icon on the left toolbar.**
3. **Click Add an Item on the Library screen.**
4. **Click New Action in the Extend Copilot for Microsoft 365 window.**

   The popup window shown in Figure 14-2 will appear.

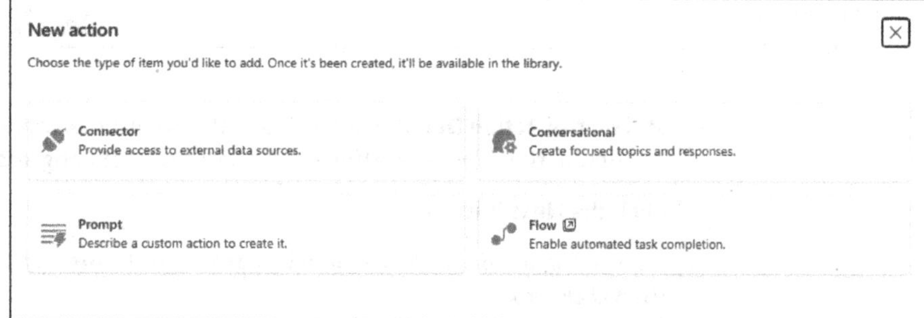

FIGURE 14-2: Select your action type.

5. **Click the Connector button in the popup window.**

   You'll see a long list of connectors. Take your time browsing through this list to see how many of the connectors are for websites and services you use. Many of the connectors require authentication and a lot of setup, but this exercise chooses one that you'll be able to use very quickly.

6. **Search for the Library of Congress connector and click on it.**

   The next screen, shown in Figure 14-3, shows a description of the custom connector and asks you to select a solution. A solution is a group of actions. For example, Copilot in Excel is a solution that includes actions for things like creating rows, deleting rows, summarizing data, and so forth.

7. **For the Action Name, enter** Search the LOC for Books. **You can leave the description as it is for now.**

   The Action Name and Description are what Copilot uses to decide whether to trigger the plugin, so you should pay extra attention to these. You may need to tweak them later, after you've tested your plugin.

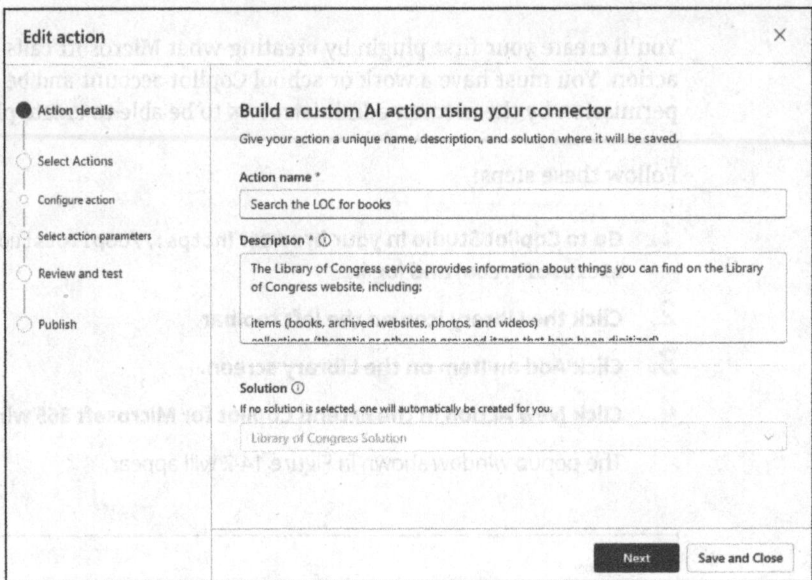

FIGURE 14-3: The connector's description.

8. **Still on the Action Details screen, leave the Solution blank, since this is the first action you're creating using the Library of Congress connector.**
9. **Click the Next button.**
10. **Choose the action named Search by Format for Items on the next screen, then click Next.**
11. **The next screen shows the inputs and outputs for the action. You don't need to change anything on this screen. Just click Next.**

    Your new custom action will be saved (which may take a minute or so), and you may need to click the Next button again once it finishes saving.

    If you now see the screen shown in Figure 14-4, you've successfully created a connector action! There are just a couple more steps before you publish it as a plugin.
12. **Click the New Connection link.**

    A connection will make the action available in Microsoft 365 Copilot.
13. **Click the Create button on the preview window that pops up.**
14. **Select the new connection you created from the drop-down menu then click the Test Action button.**

    Copilot Studio will get the plugin ready to be tested in Copilot. When it's ready, you'll see a link named Open to Test.

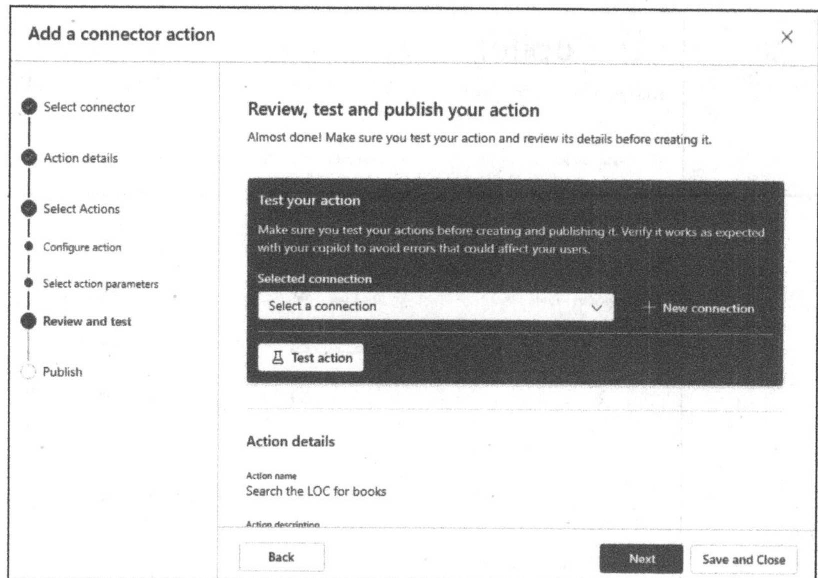

FIGURE 14-4: Your first action is saved and almost ready to test.

15. **Click the Open to Test link.**

    Copilot will launch Copilot.

16. **Click the Manage Copilot Extensions (or Plugins) in Copilot and look for your test plugin.**

    Its name will start with "Test," as shown in Figure 14-5.

17. **Make sure the test plugin is enabled, then test your custom plugin by entering something like** Search the Library of Congress for items about cheese.

TIP

In my experiments with this plugin, asking for "items" in the prompt seemed to work better than asking for "books." This may be due to the words that are used in the connector's description.

If everything works, you can return to Copilot Studio and click the Next button to publish your connector action.

TIP

Many factors influence whether a Copilot plugin works as you expect it to. If you don't get the results you're expecting, try changing the plugin's description, try out a different action from the same plugin to see if that one works, change the prompt you're testing with, or just wait an hour and try again to see if the problem is outside of your control.

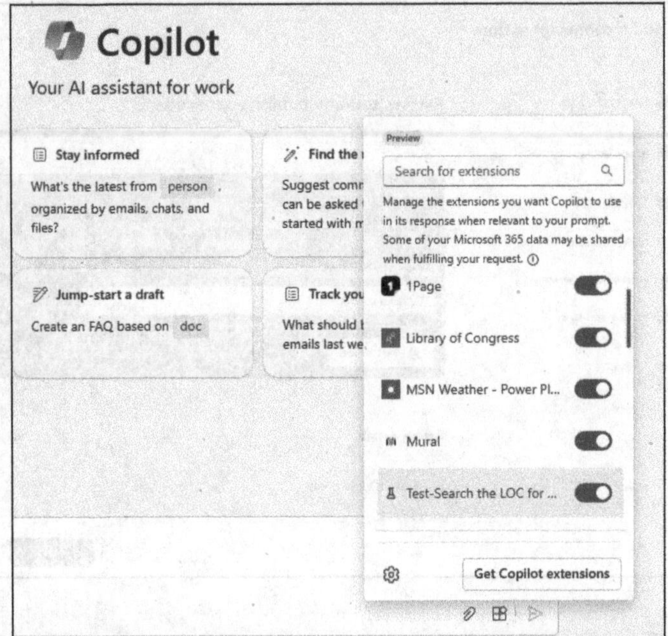

FIGURE 14-5: Your test plugin is now installed.

Once you enable the connector action, it will be available to you whenever you use Microsoft 365 Copilot in Teams. You can also share your plugin with other people in your organization.

TECHNICAL STUFF

Want to make your plugin available to anyone in the world? At the time of this writing, there isn't a process in Copilot Studio for doing that. However, it may be possible in the future. Because of the possibility of security or privacy concerns, publishing plugins for the world to find and install will likely require additional testing and approval.

Seeing Examples of Plugins

In the personal version of Microsoft Copilot 365, you can select up to three plugins to enable at a time from the list of plugins that appears when you open the Plugins sidebar, as shown in Figure 14-6.

In the work or educational version of Copilot, the account administrator can enable additional plugins using the Integrated Apps settings in the Microsoft 365 Admin Center, as shown in Figure 14-7, or you can create plugins for your own use, as you read about in this chapter.

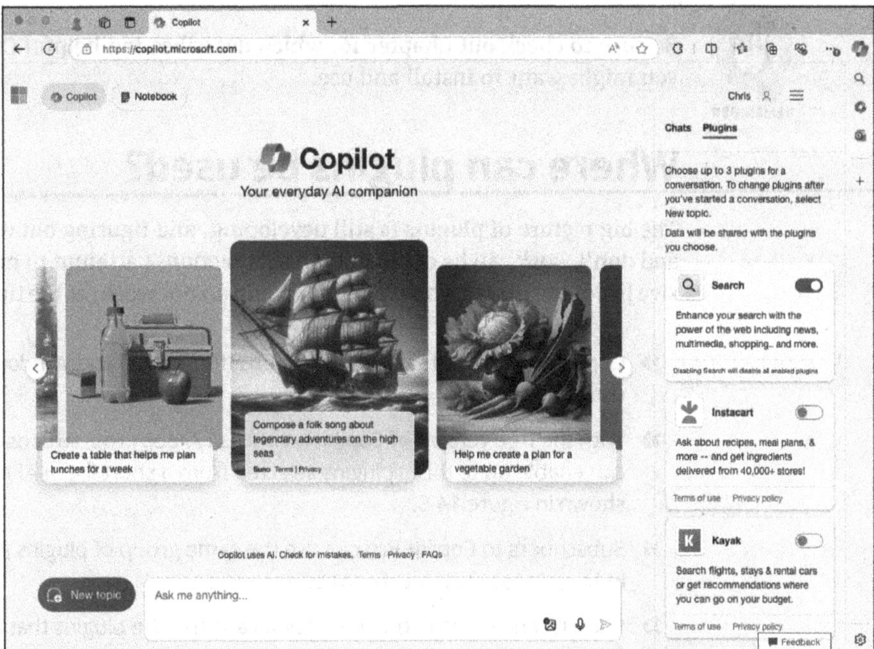

FIGURE 14-6: The Plugins sidebar.

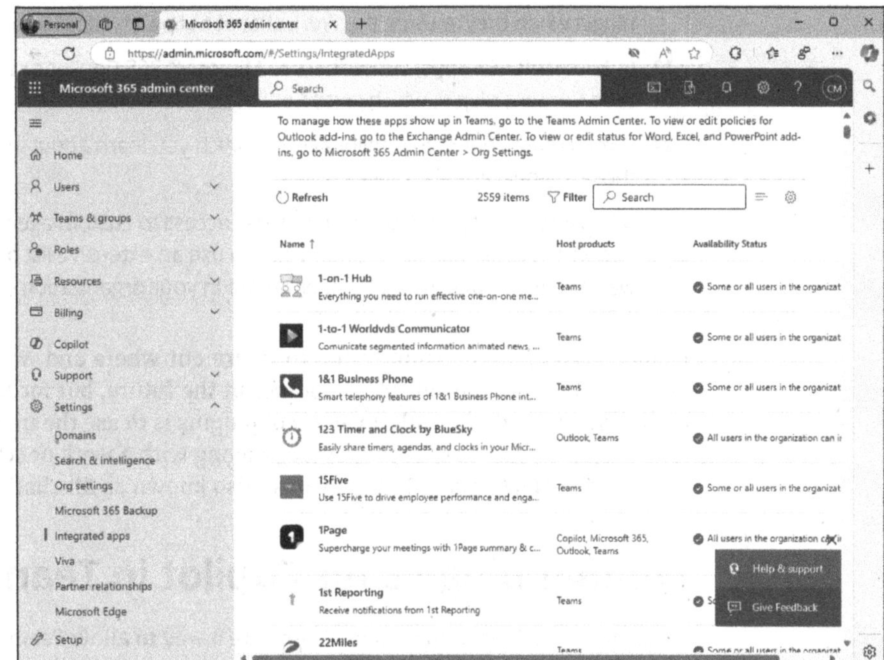

FIGURE 14-7: The Integrated Apps settings in Microsoft 365.

REMEMBER

Be sure to check out Chapter 16, which describes ten helpful Copilot plugins that you might want to install and use.

Where can plugins be used?

The big picture of plugins is still developing, and figuring out where plugins work and don't work can be confusing. In this section, I attempt to make a comprehensive list of the places where plugins do and do not work (at the time of this writing):

- Copilot in Microsoft Office applications (for macOS and Windows) can't use plugins.
- With the free version of Copilot (at `https://copilot.microsoft.com`) you can enable up to three plugins selected from a short list of API plugins, as shown in Figure 14-6.
- Subscribers to Copilot Pro can use the same group of plugins as free users at `https://copilot.microsoft.com`.
- Subscribers to Microsoft 365 Copilot can't use the plugins that are available to free users or Copilot Pro users.
- On Windows PCs, Microsoft 365 Copilot subscribers can enable the Web Content plugin when they're using the Work chat at `https://copilot.microsoft.com`.
- In Microsoft 365 apps, subscribers to Microsoft 365 Copilot can enable the Web Content plugin, which gives Copilot access to Bing.
- If you create your own Copilot agents, which you learn about in Chapter 13, those agents can't use plugins.
- Microsoft 365 Copilot Chat in Teams has access to custom agents created by people in your organization, and you can use an extensive list of extensions as well as custom plugins that you or others in your organization create.

Is your head spinning from trying to figure out where and when plugins work? Mine too. I expect this will get smoother in the future, but for now, the best way to experiment with the widest variety of plugins is to use the free version of Copilot at `https://copilot.microsoft.com` along with a work or school subscription to Microsoft 365 Copilot Chat in Teams (also known as BizChat).

Popular plugins for Copilot in Teams

Message extensions in Microsoft Teams are a way to allow Teams users to interact with other apps by clicking a button or typing in the Teams search bar. With a Microsoft 365 Copilot subscription, message extensions can be used as Copilot plugins.

When Copilot is enabled in Teams, not only can human users of Teams use these enabled message extensions, but Copilot can too!

The possibilities for things that can be done with this capability are enormous. In this section, you learn about some of the more popular Copilot extensions that you can enable in Teams. But, I only have space to touch on a few out of the hundreds of message extensions that have been created.

TIP

You can explore available Copilot extensions in Teams by clicking the Manage Extensions icon in the prompt input area of the Copilot Chat in Teams.

In the menu that opens when you click the Manage Extensions button, you'll see a button labeled Get Copilot Extensions, as shown in Figure 14-8.

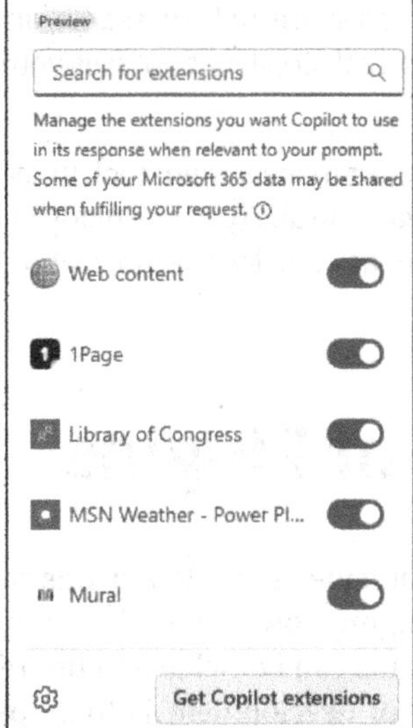

FIGURE 14-8: Get Copilot Extensions.

Clicking this button opens the Teams App Store, where you can explore all the available apps for Teams. Since we're only exploring Copilot Extensions at this point, I recommend you click the Filter link in the upper-right corner of the screen and narrow down the choices, as shown in Figure 14-9.

A few of the more popular Copilot Extensions in Teams include:

- **Mural.** Mural is a visual collaboration tool that allows teams to work together in a digital whiteboard environment. The Mural Copilot Extension allows you to ask Copilot questions about projects you're working on in Mural, ask for template recommendations, and search your projects.

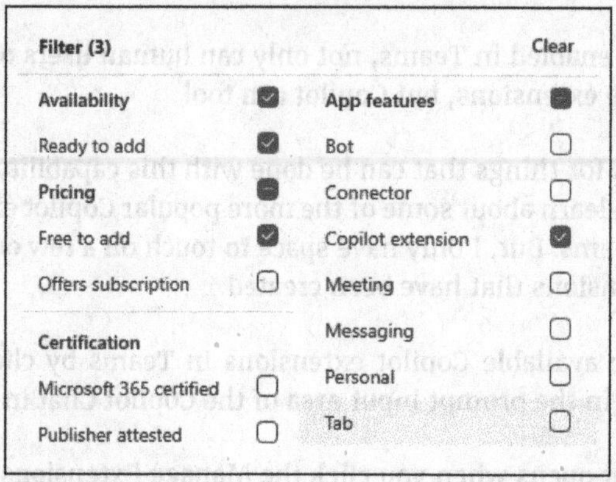

Filter (3) Clear

Availability
Ready to add
Pricing
Free to add
Offers subscription
Certification
Microsoft 365 certified
Publisher attested

App features
Bot
Connector
Copilot extension
Meeting
Messaging
Personal
Tab

FIGURE 14-9: Filtering the apps.

- **Dropbox.** Dropbox is a popular cloud file storage and sharing app. With the Dropbox extension enabled, you can share, upload, search, and preview files in Dropbox from within Teams and ask Copilot about files you've stored in Dropbox.
- **`Monday.com`.** `Monday.com` is a project management tool. When you install the `Monday.com` extension, you gain the ability to use many of `Monday.com`'s features from within Teams and to ask Copilot questions about your projects.

Considering the Future of Plugins

Plugins give Copilot access to data outside of the data it was trained on. The idea is simple, but the potential for changing how you work is impressive. Of course, there's always a downside, and plugins can be fickle and unpredictable. The keys to using plugins at this early stage of development is to be patient, understand what they can and can't do, and know when the job you want to do would be better accomplished using a traditional tool such as a search engine.

IN THIS CHAPTER

» Debugging configuration issues

» Navigating bad responses

» Understanding performance issues

» Getting involved in a community

» Getting help

Chapter 15 Troubleshooting Common Issues with Copilot

Copilot is still new technology. Although we've had chatbots for many years, it wasn't until the release of OpenAI's GPT-3 LLM and ChatGPT that they could do much of anything outside of giving preprogrammed responses to preselected questions.

Now that AI chatbots can convincingly communicate as fluently as humans, we've gained a lot in terms of capabilities, but we've also gained a lot of complexity when we're trying to figure out why they aren't doing what we want them to do.

In this chapter, you learn about some of the things that can go wrong with Copilot and some of the things you can try to fix them.

Troubleshooting Common Setup Issues

Setup and licensing issues are common with Copilot. Here are some of the things you can check to determine whether the problem you're having is a licensing issue. A licensing issue will sometimes prevent you from seeing the Copilot icon in an application, or it may cause an issue that looks like it might be Copilot's problem. This kind of issue is the most common reason for Copilot to not be working, so always make sure to check each of the items in this list.

Restarting your computer

This should be the first suggestion in any guide to fixing software-related problems, but it's often the last thing anyone tries. If something's not working the way it's supposed to, try saving your work and restarting your computer. I can't tell you how many times I've restarted my computer in a last ditch attempt to fix a problem and that's what it turned out to need.

Making sure you're signed in with the right account

It's common for a single person to have multiple Microsoft accounts. For example, I have a work account and a personal account. I also have several accounts that I've created as demonstrations for use in books.

To make sure you're logged in with the right account, click your profile picture in any Microsoft 365 application or in Copilot on the web. If you find out that you're signed in with the wrong account, you can use the Log Out button or the Switch Account feature, both of which can also be found (when available) by clicking on your profile picture.

TIP

You may also experience an issue where you're logged in to a work or school account and are unable to access the personal version of Copilot (at `https://copilot.microsoft.com`). If this happens to you, simply signing out may not be enough to fix it. In this case, clearing your browser's cookies will fix the issue.

Installing the latest updates

If you don't have the latest updates of Windows or any Microsoft Office app installed, this can sometimes be the cause of Copilot issues.

To make sure you have the latest version of Windows, use the Search box at the bottom of the screen to search for Windows Update and to check for updates.

TIP

Windows or macOS will usually nag you to install any available updates, but if you want to check for updates manually, you can also do that. You can check for updates in Microsoft Office applications on macOS by selecting Check For Updates from the Help menu of one of the applications. In Windows, choose File ➪ Account, click the Update Options button, and then click Update Now on the drop-down menu.

Checking that you're saving to OneDrive

Some Microsoft Office applications require that you save your files to Microsoft's OneDrive cloud storage in order for you to use Copilot. Make sure also that you're saving the file to the correct OneDrive account, which is the one associated with the Microsoft account attached to your Copilot license.

Turning on Autosave

Once you're saving to OneDrive, you also need to turn on Autosave in Microsoft Office applications by using the toggle button in the toolbar before Copilot will work with your document.

Updating your license

If you have a Copilot Pro or Microsoft 365 Copilot license and you're logged in with the correct Microsoft account, but none of the previous solutions for solving the issue are helping, updating your license can sometimes solve the problem.

Updating your license just means that you're reconfirming with Microsoft's server that your license is valid. The easiest way to update your license is to log out of your Microsoft account from any Office or Microsoft 365 app, then close any Office or Microsoft 365 apps that you have open. When you relaunch the application, you can log in again.

Working Through Bad Responses

If you're able to access Copilot, but a prompt isn't working the way you expect it to, here are some things you can try:

- **Modify your prompt slightly.** Remember, even changing one word can sometimes make all the difference.
- **Specify a role for Copilot.** For example, telling Copilot to act as a math genius might just get it to perform better when answering questions involving math.
- **Use prompt engineering.** You can learn more about prompt engineering techniques in Chapter 2.

» **Use the right trigger word.** For example, asking Copilot in PowerPoint to "write a slide" may not produce the same results as asking it to "add a slide."

» **Be more specific.** For example, if you want Copilot to look something up on the web, specifically telling it to search the web will increase the chances that it will.

If a prompt isn't working even after you try these techniques, it's likely that Copilot currently doesn't have the capability to handle your prompt. Microsoft has been known to remove capabilities from Copilot and add them back in without any notification. Check one of the sources listed at the end of this chapter (in the section titled "Seeking Help") to find out whether other people are having similar issues or to post a question to other users or to Microsoft.

Copilot Performance Tips

Generative AI tasks such as the ones done by Copilot require a large amount of computing power — much more than any desktop, laptop, or mobile device currently has. The fact that Copilot and other GenAI chatbots are so fast and reliable is due in part to a relatively recent advance in computing called *cloud computing*. Understanding the fundamentals of cloud computing can also help you understand why services such as Copilot sometimes slow down or become temporarily unavailable.

A high level look at the cloud

When you enter a prompt into Copilot, it's sent over the Internet to a gigantic building, called a data center, that's filled with specialized AI-processing computers. At the time of this writing, there are over 10,000 AI data centers spread around the world.

The average size of a data center is between 100,000 and 200,000 square feet (9,290 to 18,580 square meters). Packed into that space may be over 100,000 individual computers. Computers in a data center that handle requests from the Internet are also known as *servers*. Figure 15-1 shows the inside of a typical data center.

One of Microsoft's data centers, located in Boydton, Virginia, consists of 14 buildings that cumulatively add up to over 1 million square feet (92,900 square meters). To put that in the peculiar system of measurement that Americans love to employ, that's the size of 17 American football fields.

FIGURE 15-1: Inside a typical data center.

Connect world/Adobe Stock Photos

Your prompt will be routed to a data center that's relatively close to your location in order to reduce the time between when you submit your prompt and when you get an answer.

Not all of the servers in a data center are able to respond to Copilot prompts, however, so once your prompt is inside a data center, it must be routed to a specialized AI server for processing.

Even with thousands of these specialized servers, there are times when they (or the "tubes" carrying traffic in and out of the data center) get bogged down. During periods of particularly heavy Internet traffic or Copilot traffic, you may notice that your prompts don't get answered as quickly. You may even get a message telling you that Copilot isn't able to complete your request.

TECHNICAL STUFF

Each server in the Microsoft network runs its own software that gets upgraded with new versions from time to time. Included in these updates may be new Copilot features. Because Microsoft has so many servers, it takes time (perhaps months) to upgrade them all to the latest version. As servers are upgraded, users' accounts begin to see the latest version. Eventually, all users will get the latest version.

Improving Copilot performance

If you're using Copilot for something time-sensitive, or if you're just in the groove with working on a project, it can be frustrating to be told to try again later or to get slow responses. The following sections explain some of the things that you might be able to do about slowdowns.

Subscribe to a paid plan

If you're using the free version of Copilot and need better service, you can upgrade to a paid plan. Copilot Pro and Microsoft 365 Copilot users are given priority during peak times.

Check your Internet connection

If you're already on a paid plan and you're getting frequent messages telling you to try again later, the next thing to check is your own computer and Internet connection. If your computer or Internet connection is slow, it will have an impact on how quickly you receive responses from Copilot, especially when you're uploading large files or requesting images from Copilot. You can check your Internet connection speed at a site such as Speedtest (`https://speedtest.net`).

Change your schedule

If the problem isn't your computer, you'll likely just have to wait. But, how long do you have to wait?

I wasn't able to find data about when Microsoft Copilot sees the highest usage. However, when I asked Copilot, it cited a Copilot usage report written by Microsoft that found that the highest usage happens during standard business hours for your location.

Using Copilot during non-peak hours increases the chances that your prompts will be answered.

Seeking Help

There will come a time in your Copilot learning journey when you've tried every troubleshooting trick you know — maybe you even restarted your computer (remember: that should be your first step!). Fortunately, you're not alone. It's possible — likely even — that others have faced the same issue. In this section, you learn about some of the resources that are available for getting answers and support.

Official support channels

If you're a Microsoft 365 Copilot user, you can find an active discussion and community support forum at the Microsoft 365 Copilot community hub (`https://techcommunity.microsoft.com/t5/microsoft-365-copilot/ct-p/Microsoft365Copilot`), which is shown in Figure 15-2.

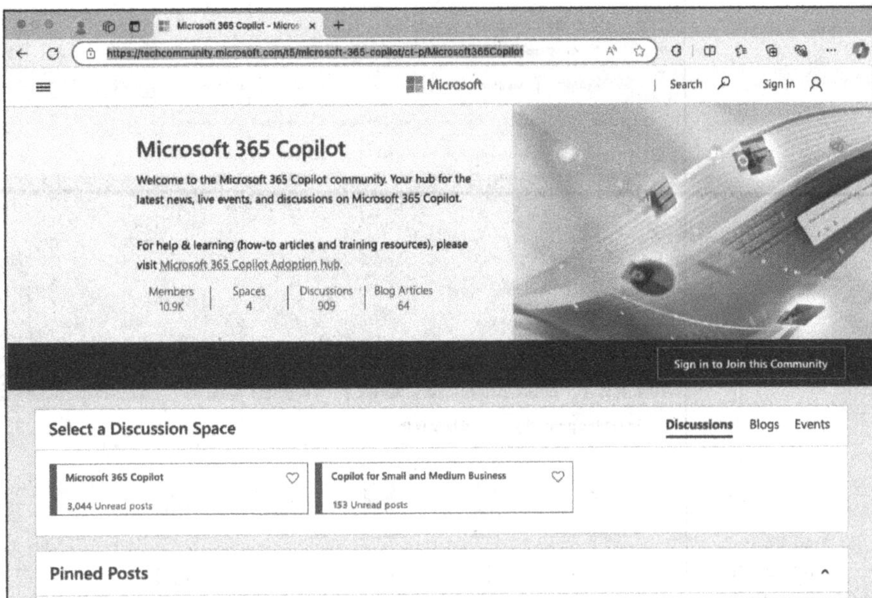

FIGURE 15-2: The Microsoft 365 Copilot community hub.

Here, you'll find posts about Microsoft 365 Copilot, announcements from Microsoft about Microsoft 365 Copilot, links to events, how-to articles, training, and blogs. If you're having a problem with Microsoft 365 Copilot and need support, this is the first place to check.

Unofficial support channels

You can find several unofficial forums where people are discussing (and sometimes ranting about) Copilot on the web. The largest such forums seem to be at `Reddit.com`. A good place to start is with the Copilot Pro subreddit (`www.reddit.com/r/CopilotPro/`). Since the web version of Copilot was previously known as Bing Chat, you'll also find posts about Copilot on the Bing subreddit (`www.reddit.com/r/bing/`). For more business-oriented discussions, check out the Microsoft 365 Copilot subreddit (`www.reddit.com/r/microsoft_365_copilot`).

Escalating issues to Microsoft

For official support from Microsoft, you can go to `https://support.microsoft.com/contactus`, which is shown in Figure 15-3.

On this site, you'll find links for getting support for various Microsoft products, including Copilot and Microsoft 365 Copilot. When you click on the Copilot logo, you'll have a choice between getting support as a home user or getting business support, as shown in Figure 15-4.

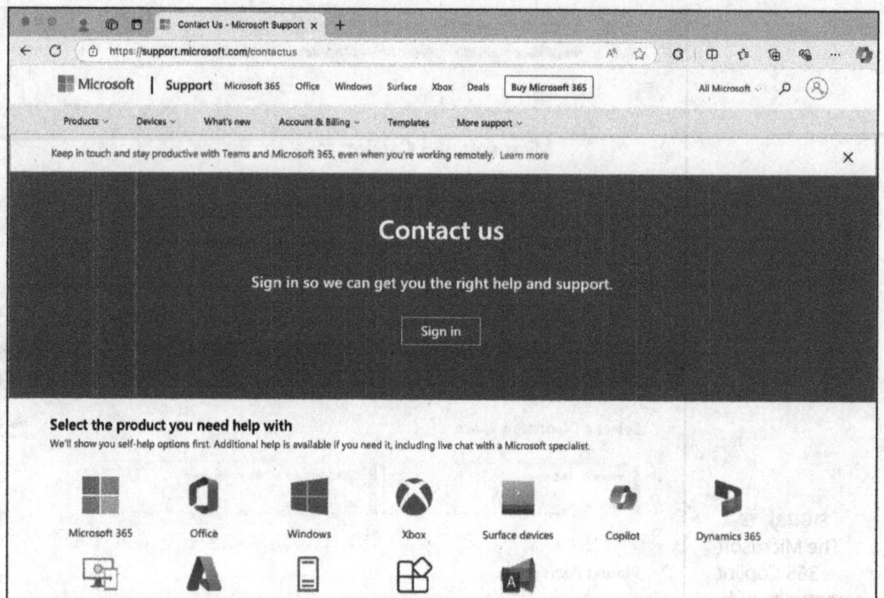

FIGURE 15-3: Microsoft's Contact Us page.

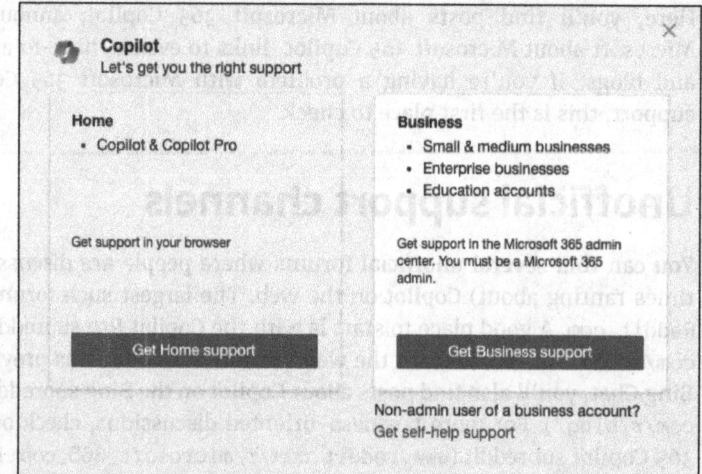

FIGURE 15-4: Choosing between Home and Business support.

REMEMBER

Keeping up to date with what's happening in the Copilot community and knowing where to go for support connects you with other power users and will expose you to new features and uses of Copilot that you may never have thought of. Especially with something that's changing as fast as generative AI, continuous learning is essential.

4 The Part of Tens

IN THIS PART . . .

Exploring the capabilities of Copilot's plugins

Learning about new and secret features of Copilot

IN THIS CHAPTER

» Cooking with AI

» Making travel plans and reservations

» Comparison shopping

» Generating music

» Collaborating visually

» Making your own plugin

Chapter 16 Ten Plugins for Copilot

Copilot plugins combine the creative and generative capabilities of Microsoft Copilot with traditional web applications and services to enable powerful new functionality. The most basic plugin is the Web Search plugin, which allows Copilot to search the web and use information that it finds when responding to you.

Interesting things happen when you get more specific with which websites Copilot can access and give it access to your account on that website.

WARNING

Understanding the potential privacy and security risks of using Copilot plugins is a big part of deciding whether to use them. Although I've installed and tried out every plugin I talk about in this chapter, I recommend that you always read the terms of use and privacy policies yourself before diving in. If the terms of use and privacy policies aren't acceptable to you (such as, for example, if they share your personal data with a company you don't want to share your personal data with), you can opt not to use that plugin.

REMEMBER

The list of plugins that are available to you will depend on whether you have a work/school Copilot account or a personal account. I've included some plugins from both categories, so there should be something for everyone here.

Search

The Search plugin is the most essential one. It enables Copilot to access the web and use search results from Microsoft Bing. Before you can use any of the other plugins for the personal version of Copilot, you must enable the Search plugin.

Instacart

The Instacart plugin gives Copilot access to the Instacart grocery delivery service website. When this plugin is enabled, Copilot will generally answer questions about cooking, food, or grocery shopping with information from `Instacart.com`.

For example, when I enabled the Instacart plugin and asked what I could make with kale, the results I got from Copilot included five recipes, with brief descriptions of each followed by the text "Here's the full recipe." For the first recipe in the list, this text was linked to the full recipe on `Instacart.com`. For the other ones, the text wasn't linked (which is obviously a bug, and hopefully it will be fixed soon).

If Copilot uses Instacart in generating its response, you'll see the Instacart logo at the beginning of the response. When you click on any links in the response, it will open the Instacart site where you can read the full recipe and order the ingredients for delivery, as shown in Figure 16-1.

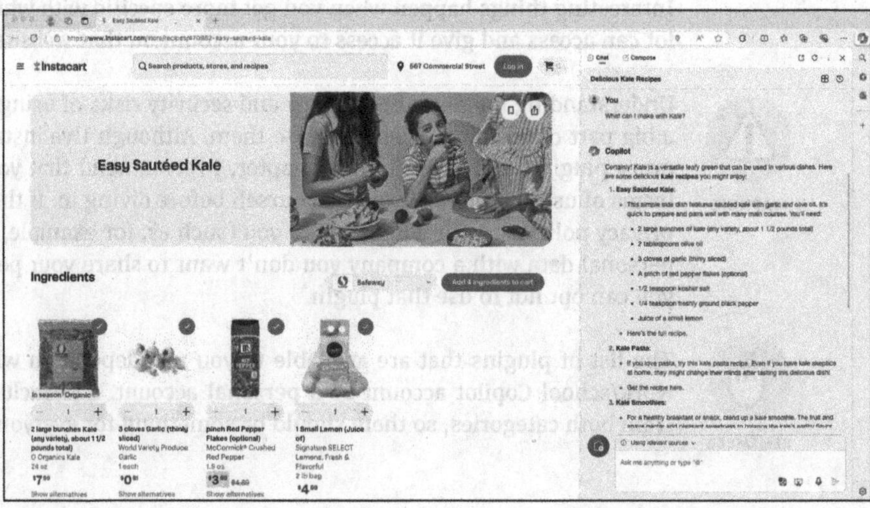

FIGURE 16-1: Using the Instacart plugin.

Kayak

With the Kayak plugin enabled, you can use Copilot to find flights, lodging, and car rentals. One particularly useful feature of the Kayak plugin is that if you ask for flight prices it will display a table of results. You can click on this table to open the results in your browser and further refine your search or book your travel.

TECHNICAL STUFF

Note that the results that the Kayak plugin finds are mostly links to results on Microsoft Bing Travel. This is because Bing and Kayak have a partnership where Bing's travel search results come from `Kayak.com`.

A typical response from Copilot while using the Kayak plugin is shown in Figure 16-2.

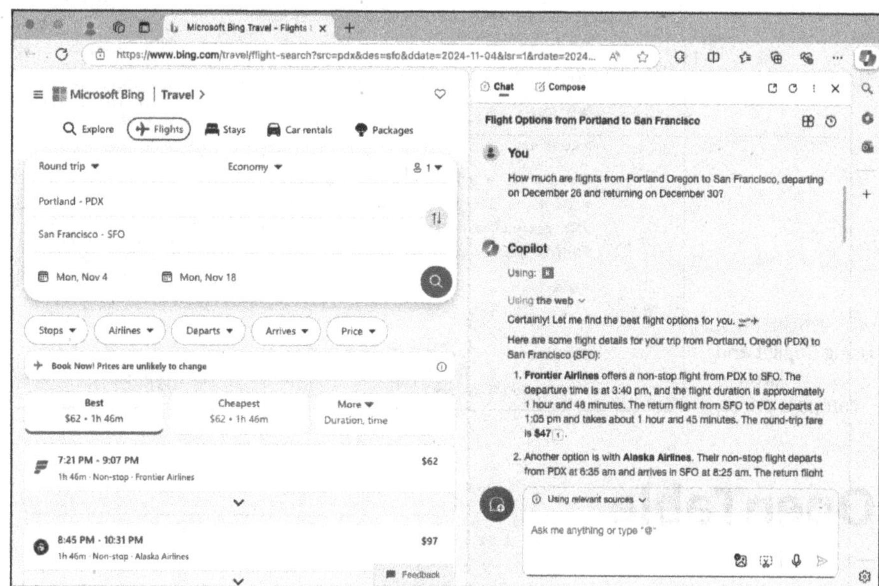

FIGURE 16-2: Using the Kayak plugin.

Klarna

When enabled, the Klarna plugin gives Copilot access to the `Klarna.com` comparison shopping site. In my experience with this plugin, it seems to work best when you specifically ask Copilot to use it and when you search for a specific product, by model number if possible.

For example, to compare prices for a printer, I used the following prompt:

Use Klarna to compare prices for Epson ET-2850.

Copilot's response is shown in Figure 16-3.

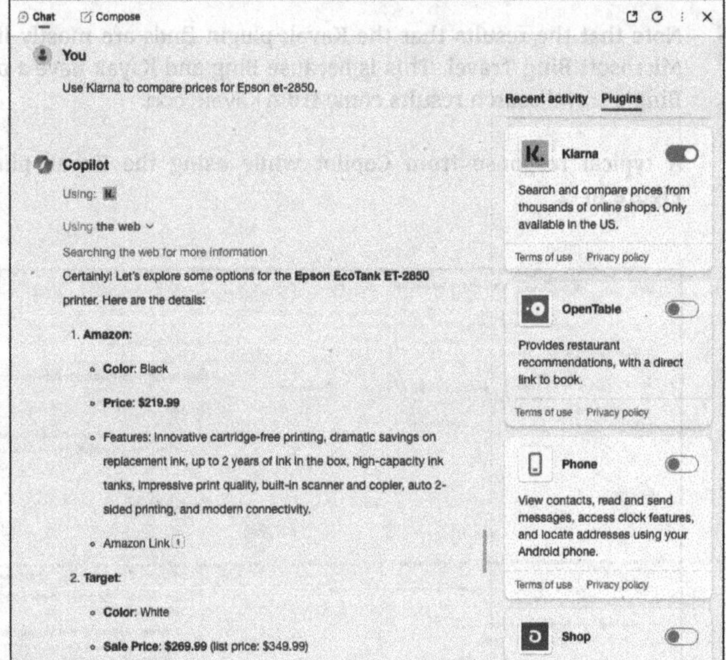

FIGURE 16-3: Using Copilot and Klarna to compare prices.

OpenTable

The OpenTable plugin lets Copilot retrieve information about restaurants from the `OpenTable.com` restaurant review and reservation app. When enabled, Copilot seems to reliably use this plugin when you ask for information about restaurants, even if you don't specifically mention that OpenTable should be used. Each restaurant is linked to the correct restaurant page on OpenTable, as shown in Figure 16-4.

However, if you're not specific about your location, the results may not be the most relevant. For example, I asked Copilot what the best restaurants near me are and it gave me a list of restaurants that are all 100 miles away, even though there are many good restaurants within one mile of my location.

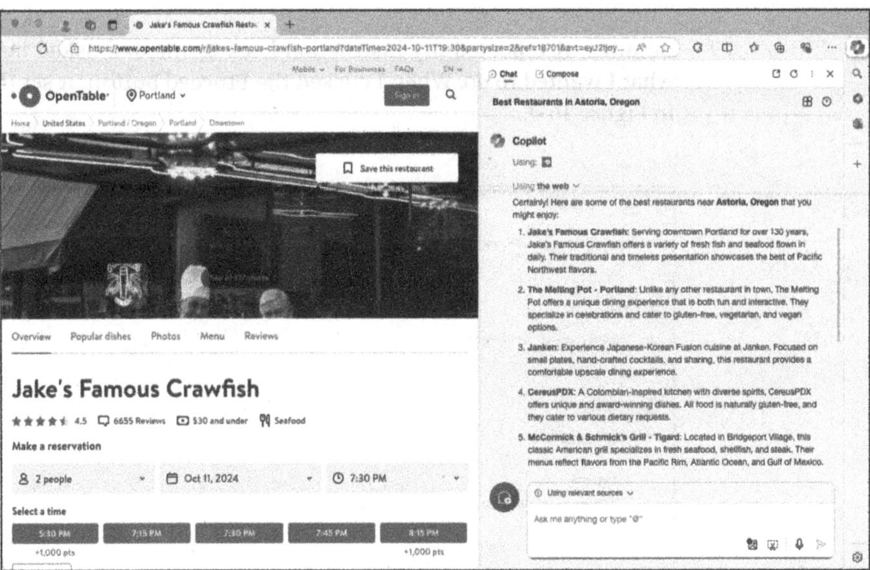

FIGURE 16-4: The OpenTable Copilot plugin.

WARNING

The results when asking for "the best" restaurants seemed to go strictly by the star ratings at OpenTable, rather than by which ones are actually the "best." This resulted in several so-so (in my opinion) chain restaurants being among the results.

When I was more specific about the location and the type of restaurant I was looking for, Copilot was more accurate with the location, but it sometimes struggled with showing results for a specific cuisine.

Phone

The Phone plugin, when enabled in the Microsoft Edge browser, allows you access certain features of your Android phone. You can use it to view contacts, read and send messages, access features of the clock (such as settings alarms), and locate addresses.

Figure 16-5 shows Copilot's response when I asked it to tell me about the features of the Phone plugin.

Before you can use the Phone plugin, you need to install the Link to Windows app on your phone and connect it to your Microsoft account.

Once you've connected Link to Windows with your account, you can ask Copilot to do things with your phone. I asked Copilot to set a timer on my phone for ten minutes. It repeated my instruction back to me and asked me to confirm that's what I wanted to do. When I clicked the Proceed button, it set the alarm, as shown in Figure 16-5.

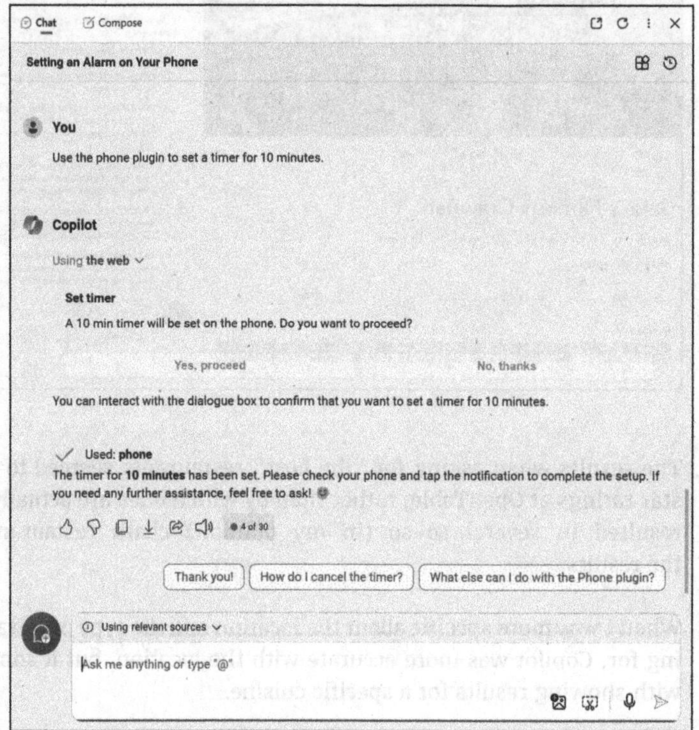

FIGURE 16-5: Learning to use the Phone plugin.

I also experimented with sending SMS messages and looking up contacts on my phone, which it was able to do.

Shop

The Shop plugin accesses results from Shop.com to answer questions about products and prices. Like many other plugins, this one doesn't reliably work unless you specifically tell Copilot to use it. Once I did that, however, it could find products, mention highlights from the products reviews, show prices, and link directly to the product on Shop.com.

Figure 16-6 shows the Shop plugin being used to find and link to a product.

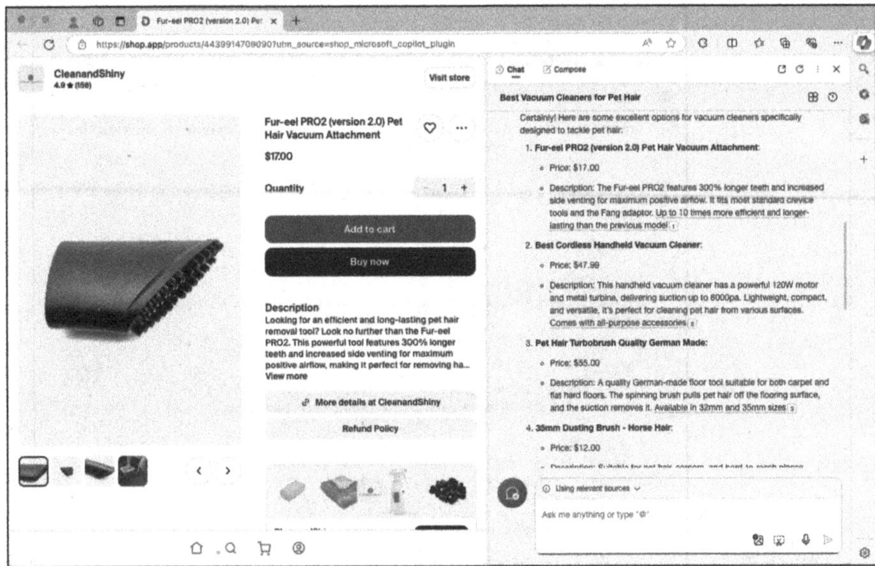

FIGURE 16-6: Using the Shop plugin.

Suno

Suno (`https://suno.com`) is an AI music-generation website. It allows you to enter a text prompt that it uses to generate a song.

WARNING

As you can imagine, AI song generation is controversial. Suno is currently involved in lawsuits with musical artists and music publishers who claim that the service violates their intellectual property. The nature of Suno and its availability when you're reading this will likely depend on the outcome of such lawsuits.

Once you enable the Suno plugin, you can ask Copilot to compose songs and it will respond with lyrics and music generated by Suno. You can generate up to five songs per day using the Copilot plugin. If you want to generate more songs than that, you can go directly to `Suno.com` and sign up for an account.

Once the plugin is enabled, the keywords to use to trigger Copilot to use it are "compose" and "song." For example, you might try using the following prompt:

Use the Suno plugin to compose a sad country song about tendonitis and how your wrist hurts when you pet your dog, but you're gonna do it anyway.

After I submitted this prompt, Copilot indicated that it was using the Suno plugin and said my song would be ready shortly. Copilot immediately displayed the lyrics and title of the song, then a progress bar displayed and took about a minute to finish. Figure 16-7 shows my prompt and the beginning of Copilot's response.

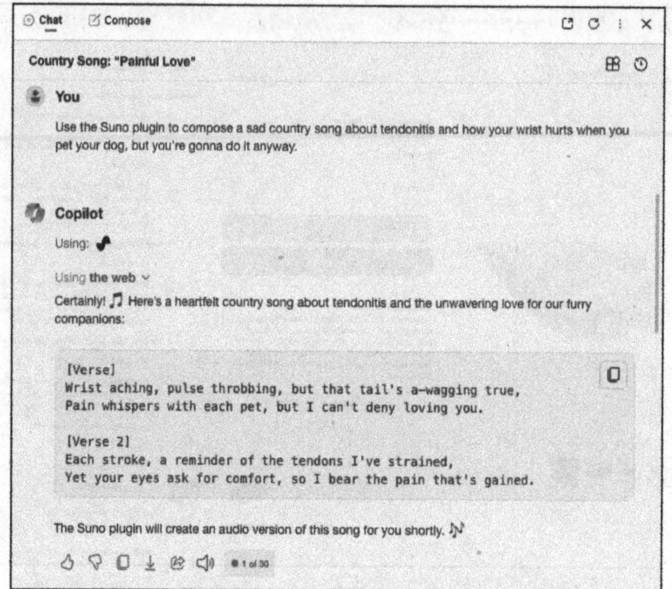

FIGURE 16-7: The Suno plugin.

When Suno finished generating, the resulting song was one minute long, and I could play it by clicking a play icon in the Copilot Chat. The song is absolutely going to be a hit. After the song finished generating, Copilot displayed several suggested next prompts, including "That's beautiful! Can you add another verse?" I submitted that prompt, and after another minute, a completely different one-minute song was ready for listening. So, it's not perfect, but Suno is my favorite plugin so far.

Mural

The Mural plugin for Microsoft 365 Copilot enables Copilot to work with and answer questions about collaborative spaces you create using Mural. Although many of the plugins for Microsoft 365 require a paid account with the creator of the plugin, Mural allows you to use a limited account for free.

When you install the Mural app in Microsoft Teams, you gain the ability to create Murals from within Teams. You can start with a blank whiteboard, or use one of the many available templates. Figure 16-8 shows a few of these templates.

The templates range from different kinds of calendars and planning tools to collaborative icebreakers that can be used in meetings. Figure 16-9 shows Copilot responding to a question about a collaborative icebreaker exercise.

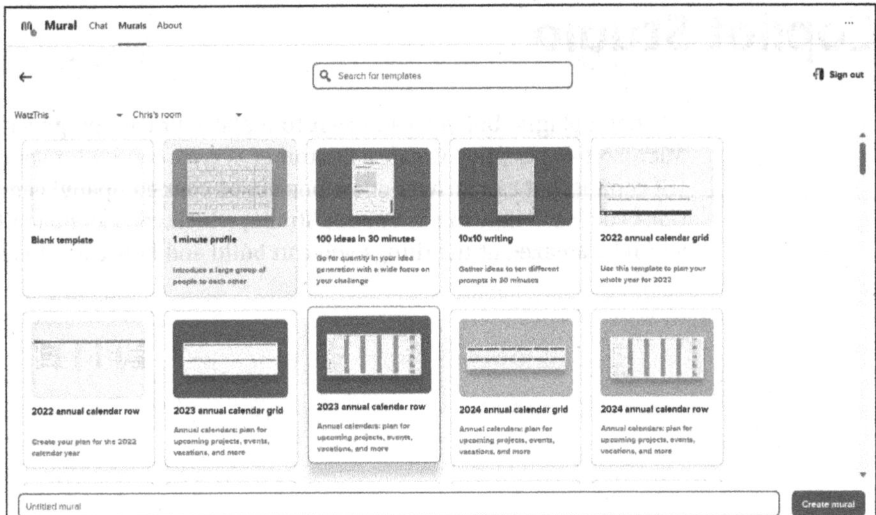

FIGURE 16-8: Mural templates in Teams.

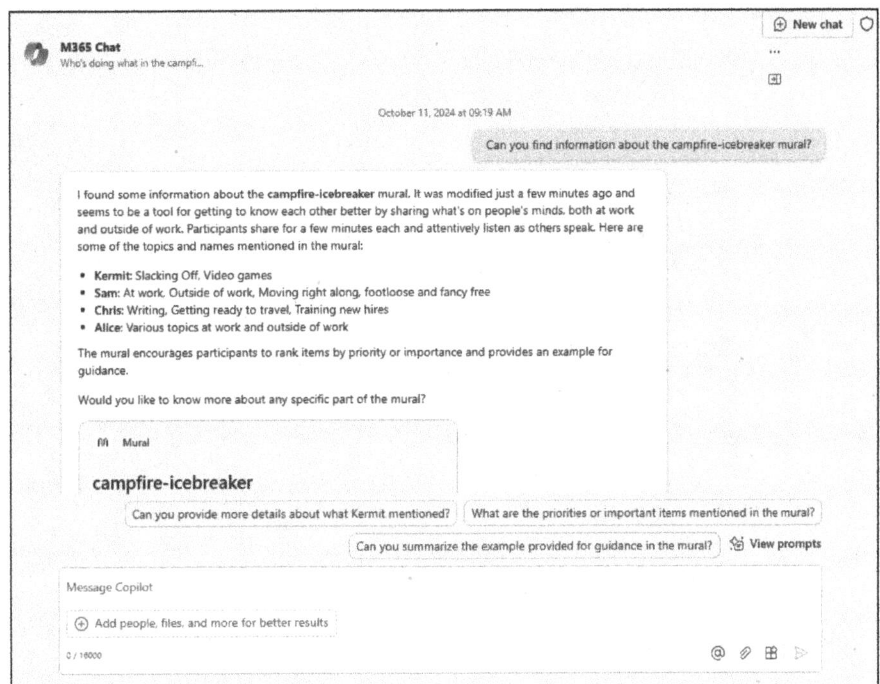

FIGURE 16-9: Asking Copilot about a Mural project.

Copilot Studio

It's not a plugin, but you can use it to make your own plugins that can be used in Microsoft 365 Copilot. Create a Customer Service copilot for your website! Build an HR copilot that can answer questions about your company's employee handbook! Once you learn how to use Copilot Studio, which you can do in Chapters 13 and 14, you'll be amazed at the things you can build and how easy it is to get started.

IN THIS CHAPTER

» Using Think Deeper

» Participating in the Windows Insider Program

» Customizing the Copilot key

» Using Voice Mode

» Scheduling prompts

» Drafting videos

Chapter 17

Ten Hidden Copilot Gems

Microsoft is constantly adding new features to Copilot. Some of these features are rolled out with a lot of fanfare, while others are quietly made available only to users who volunteer to serve as beta testers.

Even during the three months while I was writing this book, new features were added to Copilot (and some were removed) and I had to go back and update chapters.

In this chapter, you learn about some new features, unique uses, and tricks for using Copilot that may not be completely obvious at first. Some of these features were only available to beta users at the time of this writing and may not have made it into the final product yet. But, no matter what, you're sure to find at least a couple things here that are fun, interesting, or useful!

Think Deeper

Think Deeper is a feature that is currently available only to some Copilot Pro users, but it may become available to everyone in the future. With Think Deeper, you can get help with problems that require better reasoning capabilities, such as complex coding and math problems or working through a complex planning process.

I don't know the exact algorithm Microsoft uses to decide who has access to the latest Copilot features, but if you have access to Think Deeper, a Think Deeper button will appear in your prompt text entry area at `https://copilot.microsoft.com`, as shown in Figure 17-1.

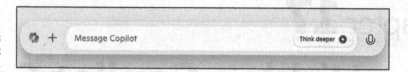

FIGURE 17-1: The Think Deeper button.

Clicking the Think Deeper button opens a description of the Think Deeper feature and presents some examples of things you might try, as shown in Figure 17-2.

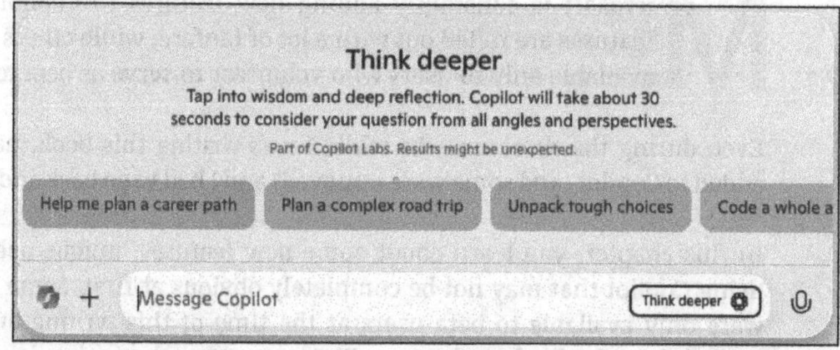

FIGURE 17-2: The Think Deeper suggestions.

One of the suggestions was to imagine an alternate reality. I chose this one and told it to imagine a world where the value of pi was changed and extrapolate what would happen over the next 20 years.

Copilot thought for a minute and then gave a lengthy, interesting, and in-depth response that included the flowchart shown in Figure 17-3.

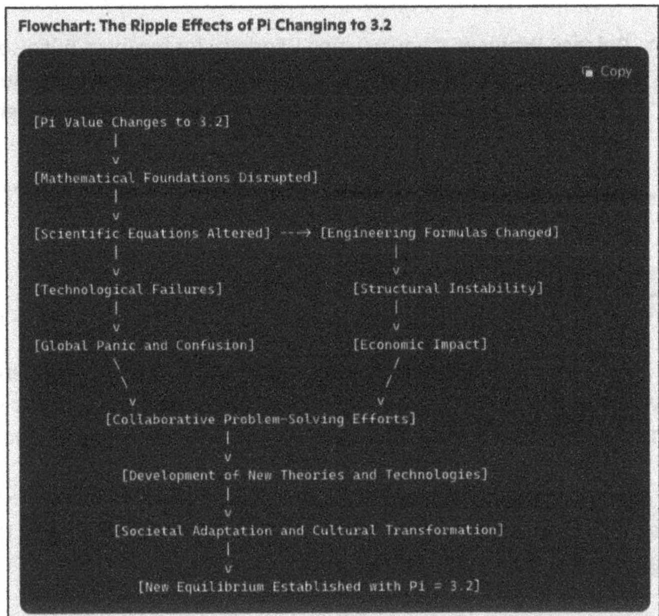

FIGURE 17-3: What if the value of pi were different?

Windows Insider Program

If you want to get new versions of Windows (and Copilot) before (almost) everyone else, you can sign up for the Windows Insider program. Versions of Windows that are received by Windows Insider users may have rough edges, or even things that don't work at all. However, they may also have new Copilot features that haven't yet been rolled out to the general public.

To sign up for Windows Insider, go to Settings ⇨ Windows Update. Scroll down on that page and you'll see a link where you can sign up for the Windows Insider program.

Once you're signed up, you'll have your choice of four different channels:

- **Canary.** This version is for highly technical users and risk takers. When I signed up for the Canary Channel and installed the latest version from it, I ended up with a computer that wouldn't start up again and the only way to fix it was by reinstalling Windows from scratch.
- **Dev.** This version is the one I'm currently using. It has some unfinished parts, but it also has a few features that haven't yet been integrated into more polished versions.
- **Beta.** The Beta channel is the recommended selection for most people who want a balance between getting features early and having a stable product.

» **Release Preview.** If you're using Windows for business but also want to get an early look at new features, this is the channel for you. It's the safest choice (other than the generally available version of Windows) and it gives you the option to see the next version of Windows before most people.

Customize the Copilot Key

On PCs with a Copilot key on the keyboard, the action triggered by the Copilot key can now be customized. As of late 2024, this ability was only available for Windows Insider users who choose to get early releases of Windows 11.

To customize the Copilot key, go to Settings ➪ Personalization ➪ Text Input. If you have a Copilot key and the ability to customize it, you'll see the option on this page, as shown in Figure 17-4.

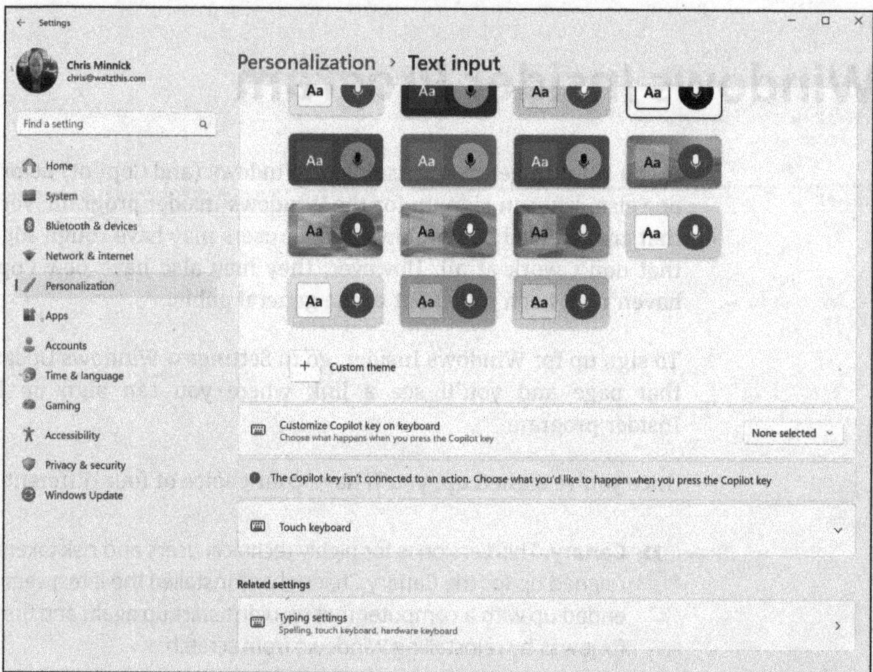

FIGURE 17-4: Viewing the Customize Copilot Key option.

In my testing, I was only able to select either Copilot or some of the apps and control panels that are built into Windows. I wasn't, for example, able to specify that Microsoft Word (my most used program) should open when I press the Copilot key. I like having the ability to open Copilot by pressing a single button on the keyboard, so I just set it up that way.

But if you decide that you'd rather have the Copilot key open, for example, the Camera or Windows Backup, you can now do that.

Copilot Daily

This isn't exactly a secret by now, but it is a brand new (at the time of this writing) feature in Copilot. Each day (or perhaps even more often), the personal version of Copilot (`https://copilot.microsoft.com`) has a new Copilot daily news summary on the homepage. Figure 17-5 shows an example.

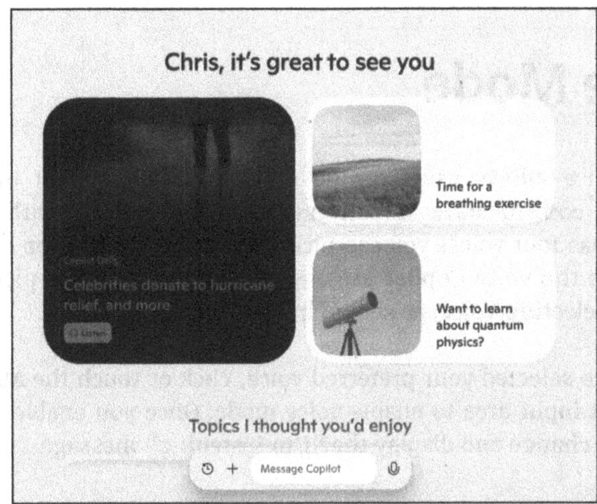

FIGURE 17-5: Copilot Daily.

Clicking Copilot Daily will cause Copilot to give you summaries of the latest news, along with generated images and pleasant music.

Each Copilot Daily is like a small newspaper, in that it contains a mix of current events, fun facts, business news, and science and technology news taken from various publications on the web.

Copilot Vision

Copilot Vision is currently only available to some Copilot Pro users. If you give Copilot Vision permission, it can view and interact with the webpage you're viewing.

If you have access to Copilot Vision, you'll see a Vision button in the Copilot Composer when using Copilot in Edge. Copilot in Edge has always had the ability to read the text of your currently open webpage. What Copilot Vision does differently is that it can also look at the pixels on the webpage and take action on the page.

I don't have access to this feature yet, but according to Microsoft's blog post (at `https://www.microsoft.com/en-us/microsoft-copilot/blog/2024/10/01/introducing-copilot-labs-and-copilot-vision`), Copilot with Copilot Vision can do things like suggest next steps by looking at the webpage you're viewing, answer questions about textual and graphical elements of a webpage, and help you navigate websites.

To help ensure the user's safety while using Copilot Vision, limits are placed on the types of websites Copilot Vision can interact with, and the list will be limited to a small list of popular websites at first.

Copilot Voice Mode

Copilot Voice allows users of the Copilot mobile app or `https://copilot.microsoft.com` to have a conversational interaction with Copilot. Copilot currently has four voices you can pick from. In either the app or on the web, you can change the voice Copilot uses by clicking your profile picture in the upper right and selecting Voice, as shown in Figure 17-6.

Once you've selected your preferred voice, click or touch the Microphone icon in the prompt input area to enable voice mode. Once you enable Copilot Voice, the screen will change and display the "I'm Listening" message.

When Copilot is listening, you can interact with it in a way that's similar to, but not quite like, talking to another person. Interrupting Copilot while it's talking causes Copilot to cut off abruptly, and if you pause or clear your throat while talking, Copilot will start answering what it thinks your question is before you finish talking.

TIP

Asking Copilot Voice to speak in unusual ways can sometimes result in discovering hidden gems or quirks. For example, I asked Copilot Voice to sing some songs, and it thought it was singing, but no sound was coming out. When I asked it to talk in an Irish accent (with the Grove voice enabled) it tried, but was unconvincing.

When you turn Copilot Voice off, you'll be returned to the normal chat mode, where you can continue the conversation using text prompts, as shown in Figure 17-7.

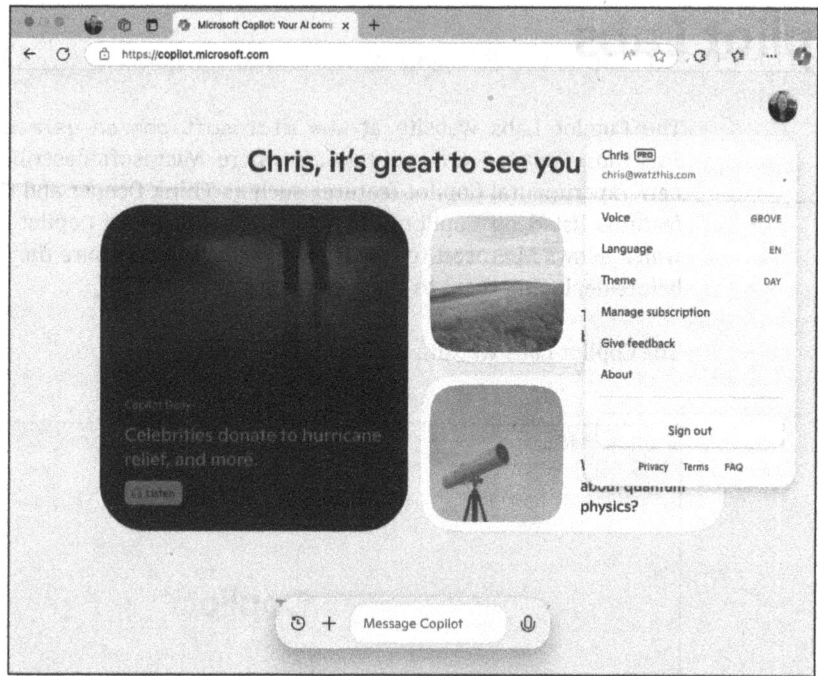

FIGURE 17-6: Accessing Copilot Voice settings.

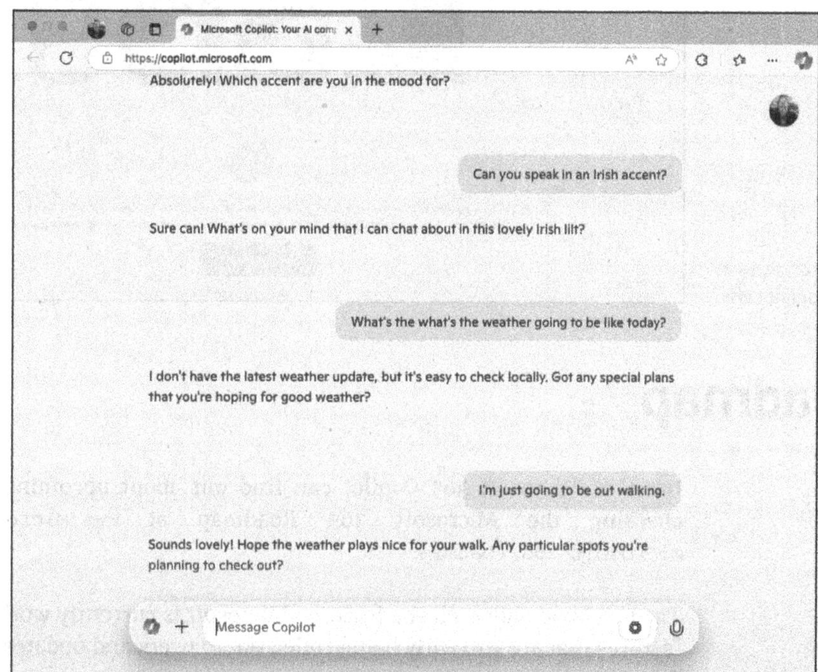

FIGURE 17-7: Returning to text mode.

Copilot Labs

The Copilot Labs website at www.microsoft.com/en-us/microsoft-copilot/for-individuals/copilot-labs is where Microsoft describes and announces new experimental Copilot features such as Think Deeper and Copilot Vision. The features listed on Copilot Labs are only available to Copilot Pro users at first, which allows Microsoft to test features out and make sure they work and are safe before deploying them to the general public.

The Copilot Labs website is shown in Figure 17-8.

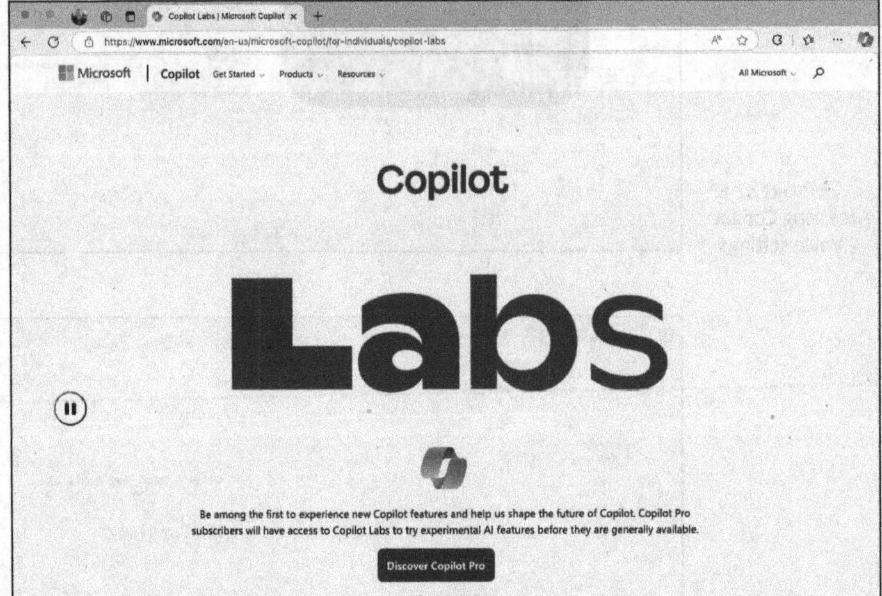

FIGURE 17-8: Copilot Labs.

Roadmap

Users of Microsoft 365 Copilot can find out about upcoming new features by checking the Microsoft 365 Roadmap at www.microsoft.com/en-us/microsoft-365/roadmap.

The Roadmap shows all the features Microsoft is currently working on, as well as features that are currently being rolled out to users and updates that have already been launched.

You can search the Roadmap site by keyword, product, and the phase of development or release they're in. Figure 17-9 shows a filtered list of the new Copilot 365 features that are in development.

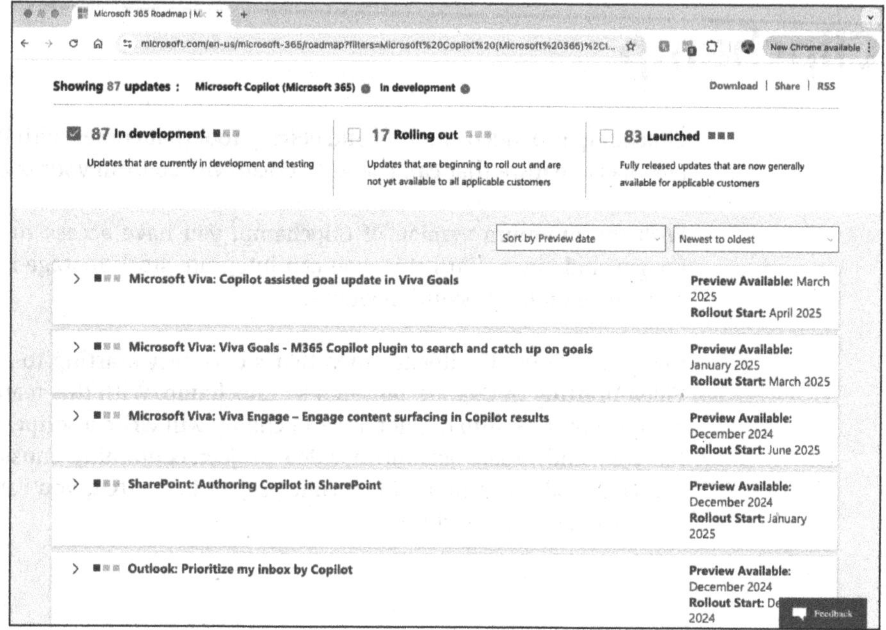

FIGURE 17-9: Viewing upcoming and new feature updates.

Schedule Prompts

The ability to schedule prompts is a new feature in Microsoft 365 Copilot that has only just started rolling out to users and that may only be available to a limited number of people at this time.

Scheduled prompts are prompts that you can write once, in Microsoft Teams or Outlook, and then tell Copilot to repeat on the schedule that you set.

Examples of things you'll be able to do with scheduled prompts include setting a prompt to give you a daily summary of your new email messages, or creating a prompt to list items on your to-do list each day.

Combined with plugins and existing integrations with Microsoft 365 applications, there will likely be many interesting ways to use scheduled prompts to enable you to delegate some of the tedious tasks you do on a daily basis to your AI assistant. When it becomes generally available, this promises to be one of the most exciting and interesting features in Microsoft 365 Copilot.

Clipchamp

Clipchamp is a video creation and editing tool that comes with Windows 11, and it now has a feature that can use AI to create videos from your own content.

With the premium version of Clipchamp, you have access to a library of stock images and video. With this, you can integrate stock footage into your creations and create higher resolution videos.

One of the latest Copilot features that's currently starting to roll out to users is Video Drafting in Copilot, powered by Clipchamp. With this feature, you'll be able to type a prompt into Copilot and Clipchamp will write a script, find stock footage for you, and create an entire video project containing music, voiceover, text overlays, and transitions. Once your project is created, you can open it in Clipchamp and continue editing it.

Index

A

B

C

D

E

F

G

R

S

T

U

V

W

Z

About the Author

Chris Minnick is a seasoned computer programmer, author, and technical instructor with over 25 years of experience. Specializing in AI education, Chris teaches professionals globally about generative AI, prompt engineering, and how to integrate AI into their work. In addition to AI, he also instructs on web and mobile computer programming. Chris has authored or co-authored more than 20 books, including notable titles such as *JavaScript All-in-One For Dummies* and *Coding with AI For Dummies.*

Dedication

Copilot, help me brainstorm ideas for the dedication of my book.

Sure thing! Here are a few ideas for your book's dedication:

*1. **To the Innovators:** "To the brilliant minds who continue to push the boundaries of technology, making the impossible possible."*

. . .

*14. **To the Problem Solvers:** "For the relentless problem solvers who see challenges as opportunities."*

Author's Acknowledgments

Thank you to everyone in the world who I like, but especially to Jill and the pets, who will be happy to have me back; Steve, Kezia, Guy, and everyone else at Wiley, who I've had the pleasure of working with on this and other books; Chris Penick, who is a real person who completely coincidentally has a similar name and who knows a lot of things about AI; my agent, Carole Jelen, who has had my back for 26 years; and my family and friends.

Most of all, thank you, the reader, for trusting me to be your navigator through the world of Microsoft Copilot.

Publisher's Acknowledgments

Acquisitions Editor: Steve Hayes

Senior Project/Copy Editor: Kezia Endsley

Technical Reviewer: Guy Hart-Davis

Proofreader: Penny Stuart

Production Editor: Tamilmani Varadharaj

Cover Image: © kelvn/Shutterstock